The Tuesday Club

Publisher's Note

Works published as part of the Maryland Paperback Bookshelf are, we like to think, books that are classics of a kind. While some social attitudes have changed and knowledge of our surroundings has increased, we believe that the value of these books as literature, as history, and as timeless perspectives on our region remains undiminished.

The Tuesday Club

 A Shorter Edition of
The History of the Ancient and Honorable Tuesday Club

by Dr. Alexander Hamilton

Edited by Robert Micklus

Published for the
Institute of Early American History and Culture
Williamsburg, Virginia
The Johns Hopkins University Press
Baltimore and London

© 1995 The Johns Hopkins University Press
All rights reserved. Published 1995
Design and composition by Wilsted & Taylor
Printed in the United States of America
04 03 02 01 00 99 98 97 96 95   5 4 3 2 1

The Johns Hopkins University Press
2715 North Charles Street
Baltimore, Maryland 21218-4319
The Johns Hopkins Press Ltd., London

This volume is abridged from Dr. Alexander Hamilton's *The History of the Ancient and Honorable Tuesday Club, In Three Volumes*, edited by Robert Micklus. Published for the Institute of Early American History and Culture, Williamsburg, Virginia. Copyright © 1990 by The University of North Carolina Press. The three-volume edition was published through the aid of a grant from a fund established by DeWitt Wallace, founder of *Reader's Digest*, and a grant from the National Endowment for the Humanities. This one-volume edition received indirect support from an unrestricted book publication grant awarded to the Institute by the L. J. Skaggs and Mary C. Skaggs Foundation of Oakland, California.

The Institute is sponsored jointly by the College of William and Mary and the Colonial Williamsburg Foundation. Alexander Hamilton's drawings are reproduced in this edition courtesy of the John Work Garrett Library of the Milton S. Eisenhower Library, Johns Hopkins University, Baltimore, Maryland.

The paper in this book meets the guidelines for permanence and durability of the Committee on Production Guidelines for Book Longevity of the Council on Library Resources.

ISBN 0-8018-4968-3
ISBN 0-8018-5008-8 (pbk.)

Library of Congress Cataloging-in-Publication Data
will be found at the end of this book.
A catalog record for this book is available from the British Library.

Contents

The Tuesday Club

Illustrations

Acknowledgments

Esp: thanks to G: Kelly, L:S:M: & G:G:, for years spent working on T:C: papers; to R: Vaughan, L:S:P:, for extraordin^y patience &c:; to F: Teute, L:S:P:, for commitm^t to pub: abr: ed:; to J: Hopkins, L:S: Pub^rs, for investing in A:H: & T:C:; & to L: Lemay, P:P:..

Introduction

Although Dr. Alexander Hamilton, alias Loquacious Scribble
in his comic narrative, *The History of the Ancient and Honorable
Tuesday Club*, once came close to losing his nose at the hands
of the club's president during a furious clubical skirmish, he
should not be confused with, nor was he related to, the Alexander Hamilton who lost his life at the hands of Aaron Burr.
To be sure, in *The Tuesday Club* (as presented here) Hamilton
relates the infamous duel that occurred in the streets of Annapolis on June 19, 1752, when Loquacious Scribble confronted
that arrogant fomenter of clubical mischief, Coney Pimp Frontinbrass, during the great clubical Battle of Farce-alia; but at
the approach of the formidable Frontinbrass, "mounted on a
lofty Chariot . . . drawn by two fiery Steeds" and armed with
"a whip of an Enormous Size . . . which he smacked as he
drove along," Scribble "did not stay to make him any answer,
but ran precipitately into [a] back alley and Immediatly betook
himself to flight, to save his bacon" (Book XI, Chapter 4). No
one was shot; no one was even injured. It was just another afternoon's entertainment in the life of the Tuesday Club.

This Alexander Hamilton was born in Edinburgh on September 26, 1712, fifth son of Mary Robertson Hamilton and
William Hamilton (professor of divinity and principal at the

University of Edinburgh), at a time when Edinburgh was rapidly becoming one of the intellectual centers of Europe. After receiving his medical degree from the University of Edinburgh in 1737, Hamilton followed the lead of his oldest brother, John, who had established a profitable medical practice in Maryland, and emigrated to Annapolis during the winter of 1738. He arrived in Maryland at the beginning of the period now commonly referred to as the golden age of Chesapeake culture (1740 to 1770), but had anyone called it that in 1738 he probably would have taken his pulse and checked his temperature. Hamilton was used to Edinburgh, and by comparison the majority of the people and the living conditions in Maryland were, he felt, crude. Five years after his arrival, when he referred to Maryland as a "Barbarous and desolate corner of the world," he was only half joking.[1] He learned to cope with the crude living conditions by laughing at them; more important, he helped to change those conditions so that by the time he died two decades later the idea of culture's existing in Maryland was no longer a laughing matter.

Like many colonial physicians, Hamilton worked double time as a physician and apothecary. Good physicians were scarce throughout the colonies, and those with Hamilton's training were much in demand. Most of the time he was too busy to be homesick, but during his leisure hours he keenly missed the society of his friends back home, especially his friends at the Whin-Bush Club in Edinburgh. A few months after his arrival he nostalgically invoked his brother Gavin to "be so good as Remember me to all the Members of the whin-bush Club, . . . Inform them that every friday, I fancy myself with them, drinking twopenny ale, and smoking tobacco, I Long to see those merry days again."[2] Letters from home and the companionship

[1]Alexander Hamilton (hereafter, AH) to Robert Hamilton, Sept. 29, 1743, Hamilton Letter Book, Dulany Papers, MS. 1265, Box 3, Maryland Historical Society (hereafter, MHS), Baltimore, Md.
[2]AH to Gavin Hamilton, June 13, 1739, Hamilton Letter Book.

of his brother John helped to alleviate Hamilton's homesickness, but what he needed most was a good club.

To help fill this void, Hamilton joined the Ugly Club of Annapolis in 1739. In *The Tuesday Club* he reports that, unlike the Ugly Club made famous by the *Spectator,* membership in the Annapolis Ugly Club was not determined by any physical deformity:

> It was Sufficient for [a member] Sincerely to profess and believe that he was not handsom, till he was declared to be a monstrous ugly fellow by the Ladies in public company. . . . A man was to show his Sincerity in this opinion of himself, by assuming a certain Slovenliness and peculiarity in his dress, by never throwing away his time at a looking Glass, and diligently evading all foppish and finical airs and affectation, . . . but, if he ever observed any oddity of Gesture, affected by another man, such as a wink, a cast of the Eye, a sudden toss of the head, . . . or wry twist of the mouth, . . . these he was Strictly to Imitate, . . . as being real deformities and deviations from nature in a much higher degree than bodily distortions and blemishes. (II, 7)

Shortly before the Ugly Club disbanded in 1744, Hamilton entered the contentious world of Maryland politics.[3] In 1743, "at the desire and Request of many of [his] fellow Citizens," he ran for the office of common councilman of Annapolis "in opposition to a certain creature of the Court."[4] Hamilton was not politically ambitious; he was, however, a gentleman, and

[3]The struggles between the proprietary and antiproprietary (court and country) parties in colonial Maryland have been enlarged upon in numerous works, but see especially Ronald Hoffman, *A Spirit of Dissension: Economics, Politics, and the Revolution in Maryland* (Baltimore, 1973), 44–59; David Curtis Skaggs, *Roots of Maryland Democracy, 1753–1776* (Westport, Conn., 1973), 84–109; Aubrey C. Land, *The Dulanys of Maryland: A Biographical Study of Daniel Dulany, the Elder (1685–1753) and Daniel Dulany, the Younger (1722–1797)* (Baltimore, 1955), 62–75.

[4]AH to Gavin Hamilton, Oct. 20, 1743, Hamilton Letter Book.

in his day "the quality that most nearly epitomized what was needed to make a gentleman was 'liberality,'" including "a certain disposition . . . to undertake important responsibilities in the community at large."[5] Hamilton met his obligations as a gentleman, but Maryland elections were far from gentlemanly. "There arose such tumults at giving of the votes in the Mayors Court," he wrote his brother Gavin, "that the majority of the Aldermen left the Bench in a passion. . . . In the afternoon the tumult was so high that the partizans went to Cudgelling and breaking of heads, . . . and they have been afraid ever since to proceed upon the Election." Eventually the election was decided in Hamilton's favor. "I doubt I shall stand again," he told Gavin, "for tho I be a Lover of Liberty, and abhor force or oppression of any kind, and especially when they are exercised by an Insolent Government party, yet I like better to be a peace maker, than an Instrument of disturbance in any Shape."[6] Gentleman that he was, he kept his seat as common councilman for the rest of his life.

Hamilton's greatest concern in 1743, however, was not the health of the body politic; it was his own health. He wrote to Gavin that he had contracted "an Incessant cough, which . . . makes me apprehensive that the consequence will be a confirmed Consumption."[7] To improve his health, Hamilton spent the following summer away from the muggy Maryland climate, touring the northern colonies. On May 30, 1744, he set out on horseback with his black slave Dromo on a four-month journey from Annapolis, Maryland, to York, Maine, and back, a trip totaling 1,624 miles. Upon his return to Annapolis, he compiled a narrative of his travels, the *Itinerarium*. First published in 1907, the *Itinerarium* has been called "the

[5]Rhys Isaac, *The Transformation of Virginia, 1740–1790* (Chapel Hill, N.C., 1982), 131.
[6]AH to Gavin Hamilton, Oct. 20, 1743, Hamilton Letter Book.
[7]Ibid.

best single portrait of men and manners . . . in colonial America."[8]

Shortly following his return to Annapolis, Hamilton helped to form the Tuesday Club, which met for the first time on May 14, 1745. Over the next eleven years almost everyone of some importance in the northern Chesapeake Bay area either joined or visited the Tuesday Club. In the beginning there were seven members besides Hamilton: John Bullen, captain of the Annapolis Independent Company and commissioner of the Paper Currency Office; William Cumming, Sr., arrested during the Jacobite rebellion of 1715 and transported to Maryland, where he became a lawyer and a member of the Lower House; the Reverend John Gordon, pastor of St. Anne's, Annapolis, and later of St. Michael's, Talbot County; Robert Gordon, Annapolis merchant, judge of the Provincial Court, and commissioner of the Loan Office; John Lomas, an Annapolis merchant; Witham Marshe, secretary to the Maryland Commissioners at the treaty of Lancaster in 1744 with the Six Indian Nations, and later secretary for Indian affairs; and William Rogers, chief clerk of the Prerogative Court. A varied bunch, but many of them Scots and all of them public servants in one capacity or another.

As the Tuesday Club grew, its lists expanded to include many of colonial Maryland's most distinguished residents and visitors, such as the Reverend Thomas Bacon, clergyman, musician, and one of colonial Maryland's most prolific authors; John Beale Bordley, judge, member of the Upper House, author, and member of the American Philosophical Society; the Rev-

[8]J. A. Leo Lemay, *Men of Letters in Colonial Maryland* (Knoxville, Tenn., 1972), 229. For further discussion of the *Itinerarium*, see Robert Micklus, "The Delightful Instruction of Dr. Alexander Hamilton's *Itinerarium*," *American Literature*, LX (1988), 359–384. For the *Itinerarium* itself, see Carl Bridenbaugh, ed., *Gentleman's Progress: The Itinerarium of Dr. Alexander Hamilton, 1744* (Chapel Hill, N.C., 1948; reprint, Pittsburgh, 1992).

erend Thomas Cradock, clergyman and author; Jonas Green, public printer of Maryland, poet, and publisher of the *Maryland Gazette;* the Reverend Alexander Malcolm, clergyman, author, and musician; and numerous other members and visitors, not the least of whom was Benjamin Franklin. All comers were welcome, and most men of any note who came to Annapolis visited the Tuesday Club.

The regular members—or the "longstanding members," as they liked to boast of themselves—were limited in number to fifteen. In *The Tuesday Club* they appear under pseudonyms typifying their characters and their roles in the club: John Beale Bordley (Quirpum Comic, Master of Ceremonies); Stephen Bordley (Huffman Snap); John Bullen (Bully Blunt, also Sir John Oldcastle, Club Champion); Charles Cole (Nasifer Jole, President); William Cumming, Sr. (Jealous Spyplot, Sr., Attorney General); William Cumming, Jr. (Jealous Spyplot, Jr.); Edward Dorsey (Drawlum Quaint, Speaker); Richard Dorsey (Tunbelly Bowzer); Walter Dulany (Slyboots Pleasant); Jonas Green (Jonathan Grog, P.P.P.P.P.—Purveyor, Punster, Punchmaker General, Printer, and Poet—and later P.L.M.C.—Poet Laureate and Master of Ceremonies); Thomas Jennings (Prim Timorous, Sergeant at Arms); John Lomas (Laconic Comas, Orator); Alexander Malcolm (Philo Dogmaticus, Chancellor); William Thornton (Solo Neverout, also Protomusicus, Chief Musician and Attorney General); and, of course, Hamilton himself (Loquacious Scribble, Secretary and Orator). Other longstanding members came and went, but these were the mainstays.

Every other Tuesday for the next eleven years, longstanding members, honorary members (those who could attend when they were in Annapolis without having to entertain the club), and visitors met, normally at the home of the high steward for the night, to share a side of bacon, some bread and cheese, a bowl of punch, but mainly each other's company and conversation. Hamilton establishes the formula for a boon club companion early in *The Tuesday Club*, maintaining that "none but your merry, droll, facetious, Jocose, good humored, risible companions, punsters, comical Story tellers, and *Conundrumifiers*, ought to be members of those nocturnal assemblies, called Clubs, for the Quintessence, marrow and main fulcrum of Clubs consists in gayiety, Jollity, pleasantry and Jocosity" (II, 1). On the other hand, he claims, "Those Solitary, moaping, morose, humdrum fellows, who evade, shun, run and fly, from all company, hate the Sight of men, as if they were Tygers, bears, Serpents, hobgoblins, Rhinoceroses and Panthers, . . . are mortal and Irreconcileable enimies to all Clubs, Jovial meetings, and humerous Conversations" (II, 1). The Tuesday Club was no place for such humdrum fellows.

The combined talents of the members of the Tuesday Club provided an almost limitless fund of entertainment. Those members familiar with law—and some not so familiar—entertained the club by conducting numerous mock trials; those with a flair for speechmaking—and some flaired better than others—entertained the club with their rhetorical effusions; and those gifted with musical talents—and some not so gifted—entertained the club by reciting popular songs and performing their own compositions. But the greatest source of entertainment in the club was the wit of its two principal comedians, Hamilton and Jonas Green—Loquacious Scribble and Jonathan Grog. As club orator, Loquacious Scribble took every possible occasion to impress the club with his erudition by haranguing them with numerous bombastic speeches, especially at each of the club's anniversaries, when he annually delivered a learned and lengthy speech commemorating the grandeur of the occasion. At those times his rhetorical talents were complemented by the literary talents of Jonathan Grog, who traditionally delivered his anniversary ode following Scribble's speech. Grog further entertained the club on many other nights with his humorous verses, practical jokes, puns, and conundrums. Together they jointly shared the distinguished post of club

"Conundrumificators," but Grog was the indisputable master and the more bawdy of the two. "Why is the king's prick," he asked the club one evening, "in marking down a Sheriff like an Elephant?"—to which Jealous Spyplot, Sr., rightly answered, "Because it *Stands*" (VII, 6). "I shall beg leave here to observe," Hamilton notes, "lest it should escape the observation of the Reader, that there seems to be an uncommon delicacy and Elegance in most of the Conundrums, composed by Jonathan Grog Esqr, as may be seen in the one Just now mentioned, Concerning *The king's prick*, which is not only a perfect Conundrum, but Contains also a delicate pun, as the word *Prick* may be Interpreted various ways" (VII, 6). Although it might be difficult to tell from a brief sampling of their elegant humor, Hamilton and Green are the best comic team in colonial literature.

While contributing essays to Green's paper, the *Maryland Gazette*, serving the Tuesday Club, recording and revising the club's minutes, and administering to his patients, Hamilton also found time, on May 29, 1747, to marry Margaret Dulany, daughter of Daniel Dulany the Elder. His marriage to the "vivacious" Miss Dulany was "the social event of the season,"[9] but was much lamented by Stephen Bordley, who had hoped that Hamilton would remain, like himself, one of the Tuesday Club's few surviving bachelors:

> Yet in vain was that hope, since I am now obliged to hold out alone against the numerous and powerful host we . . . formerly provoked by our united hostilities,—for poor Hamilton is gone!—not dead, but married, he was the day before yesterday obliged to surrender discretion to throw himself up to the money of Peggy Dulany, and is already become what you would from your knowledge of the lady now suppose him to be, a very grave sober fellow.[10]

[9]Land, *Dulanys of Maryland*, 191.
[10]Stephen Bordley to Witham Marshe, May 30, 1747, Bordley Letter Book, MHS.

As Bordley well knew, Hamilton's marriage to Margaret Dulany could only enhance his fortunes and lift his spirits. Hamilton was glad to be married, and although he and his wife had
no children—at least none that survived birth—they apparently enjoyed their life together.[11]

His marriage into the Dulany family produced several
changes in Hamilton's life, the first of which was a change in
religion from Presbyterianism to Anglicanism. It simply made
good sense socially to practice the Anglican faith in a predom-
inantly Anglican colony, and Hamilton was an eminently sensible man socially and religiously. Like his Latitudinarian
friend the Reverend Thomas Bacon, he believed in a rationally
ordered universe, one in which the "revealed Law of God" was
consistent with the "Law of Nature."[12] For Hamilton, as for
Bacon, God was a benevolent deity who "hath been pleased to
make all Men . . . dependent one upon the other, and by a mutual Exchange of Service and Assistance, to contribute to the
Comfort and Support of each in Particular, as well as the general Benefit of the Whole."[13] The Anglican church, which
stressed a similar brand of "rational piety,"[14] came close enough
to Hamilton's own beliefs that, even though he considered some
of the church's sacraments foolish, he was able to join in good
faith.

Hamilton's marriage also produced significant changes in his
financial and political status. Despite his whiggish sentiments

[11]Hamilton's mother wrote more than once that she had received letters from
him and his wife attesting to their happiness together (see Mary Hamilton
to AH, July 15, 1748, Feb. 15, 1749, and Oct. 25, 1749, Hamilton Letter
Book). Margaret Dulany remarried in 1757 after Hamilton's death. She and
her second husband, William Murdock, had two children, Rebecca and
Margaret.

[12]Thomas Bacon, *Four Sermons, upon the Great and Indispensable Duty of All
Christian Masters and Mistresses to Bring Up Their Negro Slaves in the Knowledge and Fear of God* (London, 1750), 1st sermon, p. 35.

[13]Ibid., 2d sermon, p. 56.

[14]Henry F. May, *The Enlightenment in America* (New York, 1976), 67.

(voiced in the letter to his brother Gavin cited earlier), his experience as an observer and as a participant in the tumultuous world of Maryland politics had caused him to lean increasingly toward moderation and stability, and consequently toward the proprietary camp. With the aid of the Dulanys, in 1753 Hamilton represented the court party in the election for the Lower House seat of his recently deceased club companion, Robert Gordon, who had been a faithful supporter of the proprietary camp. Once again, the election was contested, but Hamilton was officially sworn in on October 9, 1753. He served as a member of the Lower House until the Assembly adjourned on July 25, 1754, when he resigned, probably because of poor health.

Hamilton much preferred the convivial world of clubbing, and in 1749 he and several Tuesday Club members founded a Freemason's lodge in Annapolis. So much has been written about the nefarious rituals that Freemasons reputedly conducted behind closed doors that the least sensational but perhaps most essential fact about Freemasonry has often been overlooked: in an age when clubbing was the thing to do, being a Freemason was as much a part of the normal social fabric of eighteenth-century life as being a member of any other club. In his "Discourse Delivered from the Chair, in the Lodge-Room at *Annapolis*, by the Right Worshipful the Master, to the Brethren of the Ancient and Honourable Society of *Free and Accepted* Masons," Hamilton provided the framework by which not just all Freemasons but all enlightened men sought to structure their lives.[15] The "upright man," in control of his passions and guided by the "Lights of Reason" in his pursuit of liberty, was obliged, he concluded by saying, to perform works of *"Charity, benevolence, and Brotherly Love."* Freemasonry, Hamilton well

[15]Hamilton's speech appears at the end of the Reverend John Gordon's Masonic sermon *Brotherly Love Explain'd and Enforc'd* (Annapolis, Md., 1750).

understood, was not some mysterious, subversive organization but part of the eighteenth-century club of man.

Far more subversive for Hamilton was the consumption that had threatened his health since his first summer in Maryland. Although he managed to visit General Edward Braddock's battered army in the summer of 1755, his poor health made it increasingly difficult for him to attend the Tuesday Club with any regularity.[16] On February 11, 1756, he turned the business of recording the club's minutes over to his friend William Lux of Annapolis. But even though he was forced to abdicate his position as record keeper, Hamilton continued to work on *The History of the Ancient and Honorable Tuesday Club* right up until his death. Dr. Upton Scott, a club member who administered to him along with his brother John, wrote that Hamilton suffered from "excruciating pains" during his final months:

> A liberal Use of Opiates was requisite to make life bearable, & when relieved from pain he amused himself by writing this History, indeed the love of whimsicall drollery was so predominant in his constitution, that, a few days before his death, when I called upon him, I found him just finishing a Story that he had been employed in writing, which he read to me with as much Glee & delight as he was wont to do at the Club, laughing at the same time most heartily.[17]

As Scott states in his letter, Hamilton was the "Life & Soul" of the Tuesday Club. It met for the last time on February 10, 1756, even though Hamilton did not die until Tuesday, May

[16]Elaine G. Breslaw reproduces Hamilton's lengthy letter concerning Braddock's defeat by the French and evaluates his appraisal of the disaster in "A Dismal Tragedy: Drs. Alexander and John Hamilton Comment on Braddock's Defeat," *Maryland Historical Magazine* (hereafter, *MHM*), LXXV (1980), 118–144.

[17]Scott's letter (dated Aug. 28, 1809), which attests to Hamilton's "strict honour & integrity" and calls him "the most eminent Physician in Annapolis," is in the Howard Family Papers, MS. 469, MHS.

11, 1756, which would have been the club's eleventh anniversary. In the *Maryland Gazette* for May 13, 1756, Hamilton's good friend Jonas Green lamented the passing of the man they had all come to love:

> On Tuesday last in the Morning, Died . . . ALEXANDER HAMILTON, M.D. Aged 44 Years. The Death of this valuable and worthy Gentleman is universally and justly lamented: His medical Abilities, various Knowledge, strictness of Integrity, simplicity of Manners, and extensive Benevolence, having deservedly gained him the Respect and Esteem of all Ranks of Men.—No Man, in his Sphere, has left fewer Enemies, or more Friends.

Since Hamilton did not live to complete *The History of the Ancient and Honorable Tuesday Club,* one can only conjecture about the influence that it might have had on colonial literature had it been published in his lifetime. Its influence might well have been great, for it is a book that is both rooted in its time and well ahead of its time. It is particularly rooted in its time as a political satire of the proprietary struggles in colonial Maryland,[18] in its rich allusiveness to contemporary political, literary, and scientific developments, and in its humorous treatment of the outcry against luxury, probably "the greatest single social issue" during the 1750s.[19] But above all, the *History* is a splen-

[18]For further discussion of the political implications of the *History*, see Elaine G. Breslaw, "Wit, Whimsy, and Politics: The Uses of Satire by the Tuesday Club of Annapolis, 1744–1756," *William and Mary Quarterly* (hereafter *WMQ*), 3d ser., XXXII (1975), 295–306; and Breslaw, "The Chronicle as Satire: Dr. Hamilton's 'History of the Tuesday Club,'" *MHM*, LXX (1975), 129–148.

[19]John Sekora, *Luxury: The Concept in Western Thought, Eden to Smollett* (Baltimore, 1977), 75, 66. In Hamilton's day *luxury* meant extravagance in one's domestic and political behavior; it therefore implied not only drunkenness, gluttony, lust, avarice, ceremony, vanity, effeminacy, and affectation, but also ambition, pride, enervation, corruption, and subjection. The first set of vices, many feared, inevitably led to the second set. In a humorous

did gauge of eighteenth-century wit, loaded with pseudo-learned essays and digressions, surprising metaphors and allusions, raillery and repartee, bombastic letters and speeches, doggerel verses and mock trials, brain-teasing riddles and conundrums, delicate and often indelicate puns, even nonsensical hieroglyphics and missing passages—and, of course, a generous dose of scatological humor and "polite smutt."[20] Hamilton's wit runs the gamut of eighteenth-century comedy—from satire to humor to irony to farce—creating a comedic extravaganza matched, perhaps, but unsurpassed in eighteenth-century literature.

But *The History of the Ancient and Honorable Tuesday Club* is more than just a comic microcosm of its times; it is a unique and innovative narrative. It is, to use one of Hamilton's favorite words, a "puzzlementationful" book. Hamilton employs and burlesques so many literary and nonliterary forms that one hardly knows what to call the *History*. In each of its fourteen books, he typically treats the reader to an opening essay on some grand or trivial subject, and then continues his narrative of the club's misadventures, introducing letters, speeches, trials, indictments, commissions, set dramatic pieces, poetry, drawings, and music—anything he can use to embellish his narrative. It is an extraordinary attempt to merge various literary, rhetorical, and artistic modes into one narrative—but what, finally, *is* it?

Today we would call it a comic novel. Written between the publication dates of the two great comic novels of the eighteenth century—Henry Fielding's *Tom Jones* (which Hamilton read and admired) and Laurence Sterne's *Tristram Shandy* (which was published after Hamilton's death)—it in many ways resembles both. Two of its most prominent features—the introduc-

---

way, that is precisely what happens in the *History*. (For further development of this thesis, see Robert Micklus, "'The History of the Tuesday Club': A Mock-Jeremiad of the Colonial South," *WMQ*, 3d ser., XL [1983], 42–61.)

[20]Bridenbaugh, ed., *Gentleman's Progress*, 177.

tory essays to each of its fourteen books and the dominant voice of its witty, self-dramatizing narrator—owe much to the example Fielding set in *Joseph Andrews* and *Tom Jones*. But Hamilton's narrative is, by design, far more experimental and discursive than the "architectonic" *Tom Jones*.[21] More often than not, the *History*'s loose plot—concerning the rise of the Ancient and Honorable Tuesday Club to its peak of clubific felicity, and its fall as the insidious forces of luxury, ambition, and pride infest its members—is lost behind a maze of digressions. In the end, the plot hardly matters; structurally and thematically, digression is everything. In its intrinsic structural and thematic discursiveness and in the variety of verbal high jinks Hamilton incorporates into his narrative, the *History* anticipates *Tristram Shandy* as much as it imitates *Tom Jones*.

Like *Tristram Shandy*, *The History of the Ancient and Honorable Tuesday Club* is a comic novel that borrows heavily from the "anatomy," a genre particularly popular during the eighteenth century.[22] As Northrop Frye has argued, the "anatomist"—Swift, for instance, in *Gulliver's Travels*, or Voltaire in *Candide*—is primarily concerned with "intellectual themes and attitudes" and with "piling up an enormous mass of erudition about his theme or . . . overwhelming his pedantic targets with an avalanche of their own jargon." The novel and the anatomy are not, however, mutually exclusive; indeed, particularly during the eighteenth century they frequently converged in the same work. "It was Sterne," Frye says, "who combined them with greatest success. *Tristram Shandy* may be . . . a novel, but the digressing narrative, the catalogues, the stylizing of character along 'humor' lines, . . . the symposium discussions, and the constant ridicule of philosophers and pedantic critics are all

[21]The symmetrical structure of *Tom Jones* is the focus of Robert Alter's chapter "The Architectonic Novel" in his *Fielding and the Nature of the Novel* (Cambridge, Mass., 1968).

[22]Throughout this paragraph I use *anatomy* as Northrop Frye defines it in *Anatomy of Criticism: Four Essays* (Princeton, N.J., 1957), 308–314.

features that belong to the anatomy."[23] Much the same can be said of Hamilton's *History*. It is a comic novel whose narrative centers around the social behavior of a humorous cast of characters, but at the same time one whose narrator provides a comic anatomy of eighteenth-century society and ideas.

Hamilton himself, of course, did everything possible to disassociate himself from the common herd of writers of "novels." Like Fielding and other eighteenth-century novelists, he chose to call his narrative a "history," and he would not have been flattered had anyone in his day called *The History of the Ancient and Honorable Tuesday Club* a novel, any more than Fielding would have been flattered had anyone called *The History of Tom Jones* a novel. At the time they were writing their novels, *novel* and *romance* were virtually synonymous and equally pejorative terms: both were perceived as being overly concerned with the past, with impossible situations, and with idealized characters. During an age that valued factual observation and expected writers to focus their narratives on daily life, authors such as Hamilton and Fielding turned not toward the "novel" or "romance" in defining their works but toward "history," the most respected prose genre in the eighteenth century. Like Fielding in *Joseph Andrews*, Hamilton defines his narrative as a "true history."[24] By doing so he meant not only to indicate that his narrative was rooted in fact but also, like Fielding, to distinguish between "a naively empiricist and a more 'imaginative' species of belief."[25] Some historians, Hamilton felt, were "too strictly attached to what they call truth and demonstration," and others were "only dry drivelling narraters of Incidents and facts" (I, 1).

---

[23]Ibid., 311, 312.

[24]Hamilton's conception of "true history" and the distinctions he draws between history and romance are very similar to Fielding's remarks in *Joseph Andrews*, bk. 3, chap. 1, and bk. 9, chap. 1; and in *Tom Jones*, bk. 4, chap. 1.

[25]Michael McKeon, *The Origins of the English Novel, 1660–1740* (Baltimore, 1987), 404.

For Hamilton, as for Fielding, the "true historian" sought not simply to present facts accurately but also to frame those facts with "the proper and decent seasoning of apposite remarks and observations" (I, 1); to create characters who were more than one-dimensional; and most of all to copy Nature in all its fullness (I, 1). What both authors were attempting to define as "true histories" we now call novels.

In his opening chapter, "Of History and Historians," Hamilton, much like Fielding in his "Bill of Fare to the Feast" in *Tom Jones*, invites the judicious reader to partake of his historical feast and to keep in mind the distinction between his learned labors and the more dubious labors of romance writers or novelists. "Histories founded upon truth, and wrote in a plain, easie and natural Stile," he says,

> are Sirloins of beef plainly dressed, wholesome, hearty and nourishing to a robust and healthy Stomach, but those erected upon fiction, and stuffed with Bombast and fustian phrazes, are vapid, windy, unwholsom and adulterated with your damn'd sauces and pickles, fitted only for crazy and luxurious apetites, which require a Spur to excite them to a proper pitch, and are apt to breed worms, maggots and monstruous Crudities, in the brains and Intelects of such students as feed upon them. Such are Romances, novels, fairy tales, Love adventures, . . . and other such verbose trumpery, with which the french Artists have crouded our Libraries, as their Cooks have confounded our kitchens and loaded our tables, with Devilish Ragoos, fricassies, anduilles, amulets, Solomongundies, and the like. The first kind of Cookery breeds as many crudities in the Intellect of the readers, as the other does in the Stomachs and habits of the eaters. (I, 1)

"The History which I am now about to present to [the reader]," Hamilton asserts, "is none of your vamped up Frenchified pieces of Cookery, it is a Solid and Serious performance, plain and homely, and withal true, every article thereof, being copied exactly from nature and the life" (I, 1).

Hamilton's declaration of intent is in part a serious attempt to distinguish his narrative from previous narratives and in part an ironic pose designed to fool no one. For all of his high seriousness, he loves nothing better than to deflate the customary grandeur of any topic or occasion by bombastically inflating it beyond recognition or digressively whittling it away to nothing. Some critics, he is aware, will deplore his trifling methods and his trifling preoccupation with club history:

> [They] will either be mightily astonished, or pretend to be so, that any Mortal Wight, could waste, as they Call it, so much precious time, besides paper and ink, in compiling and Collecting, the History of, (as it may seem to them) a Ridiculous Club, whose chief pastime (they'll say) appears from the face of the History it self, and from the Grotesque Stile of its Idle Author, to have been the carrying on, a Silly, Stupid and unmeaning farce. Very well, my good friends, what if I should grant you all this, . . . the Subject of this History is a farce, and a very Silly one too, since you will needs have it so, I will not Indeed so easily grant you that it is an unmeaning one, since it bears an exact resemblance to many other farces in human life, esteemed (tho they are not really so) of a more Serious nature. (Preface)

According to Hamilton, life is a comedy full of trifles—great and small, to be sure, but, regardless of the size, still trifles—and the most trifling figure of all is the critic who cannot enjoy the human comedy. *The Tuesday Club* is not designed for, nor can it hope to reform, these "Incorrigible Anticlubarians" (V, 1); it is designed for those who, like Hamilton's favorite authority, Democritus, know how to laugh good-humoredly at human folly. Who can observe "this medley of absurdity," Hamilton wonders, "without Laughing Immoderatly, either with Democritus, or any other Gelastic Philosopher; and who can blame the members of the . . . Tuesday Club, for Laughing at all the world, as well as at themselves, and furnishing a fund of Laughter to all those who have a turn for the Gelastic humor" (XIII, 4). *The Tuesday Club* will appeal to many readers of many different interests, but most of all to those interested in exercising and improving their gelastic faculties. I want to welcome those readers to the world of the Tuesday Club. "Begin in the middle of the Book & read backwards" if you like, "then forwards & skip about; I think now & then you will find something that will set you a roaring."[26]

Editorial Note on the Shorter Edition

The complete edition of *The History of the Ancient and Honorable Tuesday Club*, published for the Institute of Early American History and Culture by the University of North Carolina Press, in three volumes with critical apparatus, spans some fourteen hundred pages in print. In its entirety, the *History* presents a text rich in literary and historical interest but formidable in length and expense to most readers. In this shorter edition the Institute, the Johns Hopkins University Press, and I have therefore sought to provide at a more affordable price and in a portable size a healthy selection (while avoiding snippets) of the feast of literary and historical delights that constitute the *History*. We hope that a wider range of readers will come to enjoy one of colonial America's foremost wits, and that many will be enticed to follow up by taking Hamilton in full measure.

A complete discussion of the editorial decisions involved in transcribing, editing, and presenting *The History of the Ancient and Honorable Tuesday Club* appears in the three-volume edition. The shorter edition presented here follows those decisions with two exceptions: the marginal page numbers keyed to

[26]In a letter dated May 4, 1824, James Carroll addressed these remarks to a member of the Baltimore Library Company upon presenting him with his copy of the "Record of the Tuesday Club." Carroll's remarks, like the rest of his delightful letter, apply equally well to *The Tuesday Club*. The entire letter appears in Elaine G. Breslaw, ed., *Records of the Tuesday Club of Annapolis, 1745–56* (Urbana, Ill., 1988), xxxiv.

Hamilton's manuscript in the complete edition are here eliminated, along with the vertical bars indicating page breaks; and words divided there to signify the end of a manuscript page are here closed up.

The objective in this edition has been to signal faithfully all omissions or deviations from the complete edition while preserving an aesthetically satisfying text. Omission of a whole chapter can be inferred from the chapter numbers. Omission of a whole paragraph or more is noted by a decoration. Omission of a whole sentence or more is signaled by four ellipsis points; omission of less than a full sentence, by three points. Ellipsis in verse or dialogue is usually signaled by a row of points. Brackets signify the addition or substitution of wording or punctuation necessary for transition, continuity, or sense; the content alone will readily distinguish those interpolations from Hamilton's own bracketed remarks. In instances of ellipsis and interpolation, the initial word of the new or of the original sentence is silently capped or lowered as appropriate. Numbered footnotes are mine, and lettered ones are Hamilton's; Hamilton's footnotes of cross-reference are dropped. A title was invented for Book XIII, where the manuscript was silent; the table of contents identifies the untitled Book XIV by the title of the chapter excerpted; and book and chapter titles are truncated appropriately to describe the contents of this edition.

Although scholars are encouraged to follow the full, three-volume edition, they are here assured that exact quotations from this edition will replicate the larger edition and follow the practices of the American academic publishing community.

The Tuesday Club

The Preface

Nothing more Common in every man's mouth than That time is precious, and therefore ought to be well husbanded, and yet, precious as this time is, we meet with but few, who are nigh so careful about saving it, as about saving their money, since we see it often squandered away, in foolish, vapid, tasteless, foppish and Impertinent conversation, and, that even among such people, as have the Assurance to call themselves men of taste, we find it also lavished, in Silly unimproving and Childish diversions and amusements.—How many for Instance, sleep one half of their time and dream the other half? how many follow Chimerical and Romantic pursuits, and gallop full Speed after a Shifting Cloud, how many plod and plod on from day to day, and do nothing but build Castles in the Air, how many are Entertained with a tooth pick, a Shuttle cock and battle door,[1] . . . a bagpipe, a french horn, a ring of bells and a pack of Cards, for much the greatest part of their time, and triffle thro' a triffling life, in a promiscous multitude and medley of triffles,—But 'tis well we have these toys to amuse the great Babies of the Age, and keep them out of mischief, to which it is the nature of children to be prone,—These serve to keep our

[1] A *battledore* is the racket used in badminton.

3

human puppies and kittens in play, for, were it not for these curious Inventions, very properly called time killers, they would, after running alittle round and Round in pursuit of their own tails, or perhaps the tails of others, drop asleep, for want of a proper Stock of Consistent Ideas, to employ the mind, which being a very busy and active principle, cannot be a moment without some Subject to work upon, . . . it was therefore highly expedient, that many bawbles and chip in porridge[2] amusements, should be Invented and Introduced, to keep at least three fourths, of what we presume to call the rational world awake, and the Remaining fourth out of mischief.

Some people, who may find time enough to throw away in reading of this, will undoubtedly exclaim, Well! and what the Deuce is the meaning of these grave observations? I'll tell them In short what they mean; Many, I am satisfied, will either be mightily astonished, or pretend to be so, that any Mortal Wight, could waste, as they Call it, so much precious time, besides paper and ink, in compiling and Collecting, the History of, (as it may seem to them) a Ridiculous Club, whose chief pastime (they'll say) appears from the face of the History it self, and from the Grotesque Stile of its Idle Author, to have been the carrying on, a Silly, Stupid and unmeaning farce. Very well, my good friends, what if I should grant you all this, since you are pleased to assert it, the Subject of this History is a farce, and a very Silly one too, since you will needs have it so, I will not Indeed so easily grant you that it is an unmeaning one, since it bears an exact resemblance to many other farces in human life, esteemed (tho they are not really so) of a more Serious nature, I will grant you too, that I the Compiler, am more Silly if possible in collecting the history of this arrant farce, than any of the members of that ridiculous and foolish Club, (as you esteem it,) in acting of it, and I have squandered a deal of precious time, Ink and paper, besides fire and Candle, in the Compiling

[2]A *chip in porridge* is a matter of no importance; here, trivial amusements.

of it. . . . Now, when all this is granted, Let us examine how I, the Compiler, of this here farcical history, differ from other men, with regard to the Importance and utility of my painful Labors to others and myself, and, how this, as a history, differs from other Histories, with regard to its Subject and Contents.

If I have laid out much time in writing of these triffles, as you call them, pray, have not you and many others as wise as either you or I, that is, in their own Conceit, laid out an equivalent of time, upon equivalent, if not greater triffles, only with this difference, that this triffling Scribble of mine, required some thought and application, and your triffling Occupations require no thought at all, at least none worthy of a rational being, for the very pursuit of them is directly repugnant to thought and reflection, and proceeds originally from a privation of both. Have I not been poring reading studying and turning over Ancient Authors, and modern wits, in the composition of this History, to the great Solace and Improvement of my Rational, Intellectual and Gelastic[3] faculties, when you, and twenty other such Loggerheads as you, who pretend to call me to account for it, have been exercising the keenest acumen of your obtuse thoughts upon a game at whist, piquet, [or] Cribbage, . . . while you have been gazing and gaping at a Sign post, bawling at a boxing match or Cock pit, sotting in an alehouse or Tavern, over trite Sophisticated and Stupifying Conversation, and more Sophisticated and Stupifying liquor, . . . or, if you Employ any thought at all about these, your paltry amusements and pastimes, 'tis perhaps how to dress and deck out your mortal Clay, to entrap the Ladies, how to ensnare the virtue and Innocence of some Simple girl, how to erect a character upon the ruins of your neighbour's, . . . or in short any other Idle or vicious occupation, which requires a deal of low Cunning, but little thought. Now, I would Seriously ask you, which of us have been employed to the best purpose, you, in

[3]*Gelastic,* meaning "risible," stems from the Greek "to laugh."

these triffling pastimes, and wicked and pernicious Schemes, which, upon a Strict examination, you'll find, Consume much the greatest part of your time, or I, in writing this (as you call it) Silly history; I believe upon a due Scrutiny I shall have the advantage of you, as my employment has been in it Self at least Indifferent and harmless, whereas yours must turn out to be prejudicial both to yourselves and others.

As to this History, it needs no apology, . . . if it cannot plead its own Cause, it deserves no advocate, every trevat ought to stand upon its own legs, and every tub upon its own bottom, if this History has no bottom or legs to stand upon, e'en let it tumble down a gods name.

Histories are no farther Instructive, than as they display to us human nature in a true picture, & as a picture is not compleat, without the Coloring and Shading, to fill up the design or outlines, so history is not compleat, without proper observations remarks and reflections, Interspersed or Interlarded with the bare Narration of facts, . . . the more then of these observations and remarks are disseminated in a historical piece, the more Instructing it becomes to the understanding of the reader, and Indeed, as to the bare narration of facts and occurrences, there is really but a triffling difference between the histories of the smallest Clubs, and those of the greatest Empires and kingdoms, we find in the latter, a parcel of mortals, denominated Emperors, kings, potentates and princes, contending and scrambling about little parcels and portions of this terrestrial ball, . . . we find grand and grave councils and Senats in deep Consultation, about things that are as plain and Self evident, as that two and two make four, and In fine we find the whole world in an uproar, about certain matters in themselves, abstractedly of a very mean Consideration, and of a perishing transitory Nature, can any thing worse be said of these trivial Transactions, that are to be met with in Clubs, whose members being men, (tho esteemed in a Lower rank in life) have the very same affections and passions, with those mortals called the great, and go upon pursuits and Schemes of a parallel and like Insignificant and ridiculous Nature, for the bringing about purposes equally vain and transitory, tho under a different Class and denomination.

If Histories of Nations and kingdoms then, are only capable to Instruct, in so far as they Justly point out the passions Incident to human Nature, and their effects, and exhibit a general Character of Mankind, and, in so far as they are Salted and Seasoned, with useful Remarks and observations, I hope the same may be allowed to the Histories of Clubs, which are composed of men, as well as greater Societies, I have done my utmost, to Season the following history with such apposite observations and remarks, upon such Incidents, as were worth observing and remarking upon, so, that I hope, my Readers, if any there be, may Gather some Instructions from them, if so, my reward is Sufficient, but if none will be at the pains to read these historical Collections, which may be the case for aught I. know, I am satisfied, and quite easy about the matter, they may, and will do, Just as they please, nay, even should they apply these Labored papers, to wipe a part wch decency forbids me to name, I shall not Care one single farthing, and nevertheless, shall sleep as Sound as usual, Remembering that golden Maxim of Epictetus, never to make myself, over Solicitous or uneasy, about matters that are Intirely in the power of another, and altogether out of my own reach or command.[4]

[4]See Epictetus, *Moral Discourses*, bk. 1, chap. 1, "Of the Things Which Are, and of Those Which Are Not, in Our Power."

BOOK I

From the earliest ages, to the
Transmigration of the Club to
America, and the foundation
of the Red-house Club,
of Annapolis in Maryland.

Chapter 1 ❧ *Of History and Historians.*

❋❋

Various are the Subjects of History, The transactions of Empires, kingdoms, Republics and *Clubs*, yield an Inexhaustible
fund of matter, not to mention the atchievments of great men
and Presidents, a Sort of History Called Biography, in which
many incidents relative to the public are Interwoven.

Yet notwithstanding this great variety of Subjects, and redundancy of matter, which the various Scenes around us afford
for History, we find that good Historians are very thinly sown;
which I cannot account for in a more plausible manner, than
that the talents necessary to produce a good Historian, are so
many and so great, that it is a rare thing to find one man possessed of them all, or even a moderate portion of them. Some
wanting Judgement and Invention of their own, copy too Slav-
ishly from others & are not masters of a proper stile and expression, some confide too much in common rumor, others are too
strictly attached to what they call truth and deomonstration,
some are only dry drivelling narraters of Incidents and facts,
and like Slovenly cooks neglect the proper and decent seasoning
of apposite remarks and observations, others Indulge too great
a Luxuriance of Stile, and stepping out of their rank, turn
poets, some will be too Superstitious and credulous, others too

Sceptical, and in fine the far greatest part, if not the whole herd, will have a wicked or rather Senseless byass to a party.

※※

Histories founded upon truth, and wrote in a plain, easie and natural Stile, are Sirloins of beef plainly dressed, wholesome, hearty and nourishing to a robust and healthy Stomach, but those erected upon fiction, and stuffed with Bombast and fustian phrazes, are vapid, windy, unwholsom and adulterated with your damn'd sauces and pickles, fitted only for crazy and luxurious apetites, which require a Spur to excite them to a proper pitch, and are apt to breed worms, maggots and monstrous Crudities, in the brains and Intelects of such students as feed upon them. Such are Romances, novels, fairy tales, Love adventures, private, or Secret memoirs of Courts, and persons of Quality of both Sexes, and other such verbose trumpery, with which the french Artists have crouded our Libraries, as their Cooks have confounded our kitchens and loaded our tables, with Devilish Ragoos, fricassies, anduilles, amulets, Solomongundies, and the like. The first kind of Cookery breeds as many crudities in the Intellect of the readers, as the other does in the Stomachs and habits of the eaters.

The History which I am now about to present to your worships, is none of your vamped up Frenchified pieces of Cookery, it is a Solid and Serious performance, plain and homely, and withal true, every article thereof, being copied exactly from nature and the life, and yet, Simple and true as it is, I shall be bold to affirm, that it contains as great a variety, and as many Surprizing and unaccountable events, as any true history that ever yet appeared, and, the Characters of the eminent persons therein concerned, are so nicely touched, as to strike at first view, and excite in the mind of the Reader, the Idea of a well executed piece of painting, in it self so highly picturesque, as to force the attention and admiration of all that view it.

While I am penning these prologomena, to this most excellent history, my genius and parts, are not alittle furbished up, sharpened and exalted, by the delightful prospect, of procuring to myself thereby Immortal fame, and a lasting Character, to be transmitted to future ages, and Indeed it gives me no small pleasure to reflect, that a thousand years hence, I shall share the same rank of honor, with Herodotus, . . . Tacitus, Salust and Livy, as also I shall stand in the same degree with Homer, Hesiod, Pindar, Æschylus, Virgil and other ancient poets, there being in this work, abundance of poetical flowers, and noble flights, which by the bye, I must honestly own, to be Sprouts of the Luxuriant Genius of Jonathan Grog Esqr, poet Laureat to that ancient and honorable Club, of which I now Collect the History. These great, these Invaluable advantages, I shall Enjoy, as being Historiographer, to the most Honorable Mr President Jole, some degrees I hope, above those celebrated authors, who have penned the Histories of *Tom Thumb, Jack and the Gyants* & *the wise men of Gotham*,[1] and a hundred degrees above our moderen french Romance compilers, . . . to whom not (to say) only the Tobacconists and spice Shops, but even the Houses of office, have been of late years so Infinitely Indebted, who, had they not been supplied from these vast piles of waste paper, would have been at a Sad loss how to wrap up their grocery and haberdashery, and besides, many honest well meaning Christians, must have run the risque of befowling their fingers, in using the tender leaves of vegetables, which are not of so tough a nature, as that same other Historical Stuff is, besides the risque they must have run, of getting that most grievous distemper called the piles, by means of the Corrosive down that often abounds upon the leaves of the said vegetables, which like so

[1]Hamilton is referring to the famous nursery tales "Tom Thumb" and "Jack the Giant-Killer." By "the wise men of Gotham" he probably means the *Merrie Tales of the Mad Men of Gotam by A. B.* (possibly Andrew Boorde [ca. 1490–1549], a physician). This collection of tales concerns Gotham, a village in Nottinghamshire, whose inhabitants acquired a reputation for folly, perhaps as a result of an actual incident in which they feigned idiocy to prevent King John's displeasure.

much low Itch, would vellicate in a dreadful manner, the Tender plicæ of the Rectum, where it terminates in the anus; and here I shall terminate this Chapter, lest I vellicate the ears of my reader by talking too much in my own praise.

[handwritten marginalia: + not w/ bodily humor ?]

Chapter 3 ※ Of Clubs in general, and their Antiquity.

By *Clubs* I mean those societies, which generally meet of an evening, either at some tavern or private house, to converse, or look at one another, smoke a pipe, drink a toast, be politic or dull, lively or frolicksome, to philosophize or triffle, argue or debate, talk over Religion, News, Scandal or bawdy, or spend the time in any other Sort of Clubical amusement. Out of this definition I expressly exclude, all your card matches and meetings, those properly belonging to the celebrated moderen assemblies called Routs and Drums,[1] which are many degrees Inferior to Clubs, as being less ancient.

It has been observed by some ancient philosophers, particularly one Sir Isaac Newton, that there exists a certain affection or fellow feeling, between all bodies in nature, by which they have a strong tendency, to approach, one towards another, to Join, and even to Incorporate, and that a perfect antipathy is never, a partial one seldom to be met with;[2] This has been called

[1] *Routs* and *drums* were fashionable gatherings much in vogue in the 18th century.

[2] The analogy between the attractive power of gravitation, which governs the behavior of physical bodies, and the attractive power of love and sociability, which governs human conduct, was frequently drawn in the 18th century (see, e.g., George Berkeley's essay in the *Guardian*, no. 126, Aug. 5, 1713). The roots of the idea antedate Isaac Newton's discovery of the laws of universal gravitation, but certainly Newtonianism underlay much of the 18th-century commentary on the subject. If Hamilton is indeed making a specific reference to Newton, he could be recalling the passage that concludes New-

by these Philosophers, the power of attraction, which we find prevails and governs very much, among men and other Animals, and occasions that great propensity in human nature, to unite and form into Clubs.

In these Clubs, formed thus, by one Individual attracting another, we find that the several members are apt to communicate to each other, their own faculties and dispositions, their own sentiments and particular turn of thought, whether this is done by the perpetual flying off of thin Surfaces from one member to another, as the old philosophers used to account for vision,[3] before the discovery of optics, or, by the communication of some Imperceptible Sympathetic qualities, . . . I cannot take upon me to resolve, this being a more Intricate and difficult enquiry than perhaps most men may Imagine; I am only certain that the fact is so, that there is a particular Sympathetic Social quality in Mankind, that makes them fond of Clubbing, whether they be adapted for conversation or not; this may be undenyably proved, from the example of many moderen Clubs, which have consisted of members, who had little or no turn or talent for that Sort of conversation, that is carried on by Language or speech, or, at least, if they used Speech, it was to no better purpose, than one that says *Bo to a goose*, their whole dialogue consisting in, you've baulk'd your glass—you drink kelty[4]—put about the bowl—fill tother pipe—here's to you—pledge you—and such like short Sentences.

Is it not probable then, that the whole and Sole pleasure of

ton's *Principia* (1687), where Newton remarks that there is "a certain most subtle spirit which pervades . . . all gross bodies; by the force and action of which spirit the particles of bodies attract one another . . . and cohere" (*Sir Isaac Newton's Mathematical Principles,* trans. Florian Cajori [Berkeley, Calif., 1946], 547).

[3]The "old philosophers" are Democritus and all the Atomists. The prevailing Scholastic view before the 18th century had been that visual perception occurred as a result of the transmission of minute bodies from the object to the eye.

[4]A term denoting the complete draining of a glass of liquor.

such humdrum Clubs, consists in barely looking at one another, in successively kissing the Glass or bowl, or benevolently Intermixing the Smoke of one pipe, with that of another, to account for this Strange, tho' true Circumstance, let us suppose, that there is some very Subtile Effluvium, or Aura, that goes from one member to another, and Communicates a titulation or pleasure to the nerves, by setting the animal Spirits in a sort of undulatory motion, which has puzzled our Physiologists so much to account for; If any body should object to this my hypothesis, let them consider, that here I follow the example of the learned and Ingenious Doctor Cheyne, in his Elaborate treatise of health and long life,[5]—it is to be hoped tho' that the late Ingenious experiments on electricity, will give some light into this dark phênomenon, and confirm this my new hypothesis.[6]

※※

Of these Societies called Clubs, there are numberless kinds, which I shall not pretend to treat of particularly, other Authors having done that before me, to much better purpose, than I, with all my Clubical learning can pretend to, and therefore, I shall directly proceed to say alittle, concerning the great antiquity of these Societies.

I have heard of a certain author, who took abundance of pains to prove the antiquity of music, and very learnedly traced it from Jubal,[7] its reputed Inventor, . . . in order to establish

[5]George Cheyne (1671–1743) was a Scottish physician and mathematician whose works include An Essay of Health and Long Life (London, 1724; 9th ed. 1745).

[6]A good contemporary account of the experiments of Jean Antoine Nollet, Benjamin Franklin, and others appears in Histoire de l'Académie Royale des Sciences (Paris, 1753), 6–39. Hamilton may also be referring to the medical applications of electricity proposed by Ebenezer Kinnersley, a club visitor (see J. A. Leo Lemay, Ebenezer Kinnersley: Franklin's Friend [Philadelphia, 1964], 72).

[7]Hamilton is referring to his friend Alexander Malcolm's A Treatise of Musick, Speculative, Practical, and Historical (Edinburgh, 1721). In chap. 14,

this learned authors assertion for an undenyable truth, it will be necessary to suppose, that neither men, birds nor beasts, had throats, or vocal organs before Jubal's time, nor had they the power of framing Sounds, either articulate or Inarticulate, emitted upwards thro' the throat, or downwards thro' the anus, since some nice ears have discovered a kind of music even in the fundamental eructations, as may be seen in a learned treatise concerning the practice and theory of farting, by that Ingenious Philosopher, Don Fartinhando puffendorst. . . .[8]

Were I to trace the origin of these Societies called Clubs, in the same manner, as this Ingenious Author, has done that of music, I should bring myself under the same dilemma, for example, should I affirm, that Cain, by building a City in the land of Nod, was the first erector of Clubs, because, it is in towns and Cities, that those Societies are commonly held, I might in the opinion of many Superficial Critics, talk very plausibly, but to cut the matter short, and clear away all Rubs, Stumbling blocks and cavils, I will venture to say that Clubs and Clubbing, began as soon as the first men were created, and therefore are certainly as ancient as mankind & very nigh as ancient as the Globe it self. . . .

And thus having settled this great and Important point, I proceed to the next Chapter.

is true a mocking of the historical project here

"Of the Ancient Musick," Malcolm traces instrumental music back to Jubal, but, he writes, "we have sufficient Reason to believe that *Musick* was an Art long before [Jubal's] Time; since it is rational to think that *vocal Musick* was known long before *Instrumental*" (pp. 463–464). Hamilton is being intentionally obtuse in interpreting his friend's argument.

[8]*The Benefit of Farting . . . Explained by Don Fartinando Puff-indorst* (London, 1722) is attributed to Jonathan Swift.

Chapter 5 ❧ *The more Immediate origin and rise of the Ancient and honorable Tuesday Club, of Annapolis in Maryland.*

It has been the misfortune of most Historians, while they grope, fumble and blunder in the dark, among the Rubbish of Antiquity, and vainly try to tack together fragments, and broken hints of history, to produce a Chimêra, or monstruous birth, which seems to every Judicious Reader, altogether Inconsistent in it self, ridiculous, and Indeed Incredible, hence we have, what are called the fabulous accounts of the Poets, the Stages and periods of the Golden, Silver, Brazen & Iron ages, which, in themselves, duely perpended & considered, contain as much of the Legend, as the famous books of knight Errantry, or the accounts of the Miracles, done by the Saints of holy Catholic Church.

That I may evade splitting upon this dangerous rock, I shall lay aside all disquisitions and Dissertations, concerning ancient times, enveloped In obscurity, and at once making a skip, shall trace in a direct line, our ancient and honorable Tuesday Club of Annapolis, from a Celebrated Club, called the ancient and venerable Tuesday (or whin bush) Club of Laneric, in the ancient kingdom of Scotland.[1]

❀❀

This venerable Club was under a total eclipse, during the Cromwellian usurpation, in the presidentship of the venerable Zachary Auchmoutie the great, and part of the time of the Venerable Jeremiah Majoribanks, for Oliver Imagining that they were a Cabal a plotting against the common wealth, seized their

---

[1] Although exaggerated, much of what Hamilton says about the Whin-Bush Club in the following pages is probably based upon fact. For verification of Hamilton's membership in the Whin-Bush Club, see his letter to his brother Gavin (June 13, 1739, Dulany Papers, MS. 1265, Maryland Historical Society, Baltimore).

[handwritten margin note: history (undifferentiable) from lit)]

Records, and dispers'd them, but, upon these being examined, by a learned Committee of the *Rump*, there appeared nothing of politics or State matters in them, but only Simple facts, relating to fines and forfeitures, and drinking of toasts in bumpers &ct:

Politics

But, in the Presidentship of the venerable Rowland Macpherson, on the happy restoration of the Steuart family, who, to be sure, had an Indefeasible hereditary right to the British crown, derived in a curve line, direct, Indirect and collateral, from William the Bastard of Normandy, . . . those valuable records were again restored, to this venerable club, when most of the other national records were lost, a lucky Incident, and what at this day will give us great Insight into the history of the ancient and honorable Tuesday Club of Annapolis.

❊❊

Chapter 6 🐌 *A Succinct account of the Ancient and Venerable Tuesday (or whin bush) Club of Lanneric, in the kingdom of Scotland.*

The ancient and venerable Tuesday (or whin bush) Club of Lanneric, was time out of mind governed by a president, who, once he had attained the Chair, continued *durante vita,* or *quam diæ bene se Gesserit,*[1] for we have an Instance of one being deposed, vizt: the Venerable Luke Tomlinson, who was degraded in 1502 for heresy, and eating roast beef on Good fridays. This place was neither elective nor hereditary, but was possessed by seniority, the oldest member of the Club, always holding it, but in case there was a parity of age, that person who was the member of the longest Standing, took that place of honor, from

[1]"During his lifetime," or "so long as he behaved himself well."

OED

whence we derive the title of *Longstanding member*, in the ancient
and honorable Tuesday Club of Annapolis, the members of that
Club, taking to themselves that title, from a certain noble emulation and ambition, sometime or other to ascend the chair,
each in his turn, and not from any Waggish Entendre, as some
Imagine was Intended by Jealous Spyplot Esqr, when he Revived that Significant term, in the ancient and honorable Tuesday Club. In case two or three members, were of equal age, and
of equal *Long standing* (I desire none may misinterpret my
words in the manner that some evil minded females, have done
the mysteries of the Free Masons) then, and then only, the Chair
was elective and the Club determined the affair by a majority of
voices. . . .

As to the Laws of this venerable Club, they were few and
Simple, one Law was, that the Club should meet once a week
upon Tuesday Evening, at the Hour of Six, Summer and winter, and not to exceed eleven o clock at night, and, by the very
old records we find, that this venerable Club, went by the name
of the Tuesday Club of Lanneric, but, in the Presidentship of
the venerable Mr President Majoribanks, the day of meeting
of this Club was changed into Friday, for what Reasons is not
known, unless it was upon account of the Turbulent times of
persecution, which broke out sometime after the happy restoration, when so much countenance and favor was shown to pa-
pists and high Church Caviliers, that Sober discrete moderate
whigs could not sleep in a Sound Skin. It is thought, that then,
the members of this venerable Club, being all true blue whigs,
and many of them concerned in the battle of Bothwell Bridge,[2]
. . . were obliged to abscond and skulk, and met under the shel-
ter of the whin or furz bushes . . . , [and] being constrained
to assume the Sham name of true Catholics, for their own
Safety, they absconded on fridays, pretending to be fasting and

[2]In this battle fought on June 22, 1679, the rebel Covenanters of southwest
Scotland were defeated by 10,000 men under the duke of Monmouth. Of
about 4,000 rebels perhaps 200 to 400 were killed, and 1,200 captured.

praying, while all the time they were soaking their noses in two-penny ale, smoking tobacco, and devouring bread & cheese, this food they were particularly fond of, and one of their Bay-lies, vizt: Anthony Dottle, choaked, while he was voraciously swallowing a great mouthful of Cheese in Club, in the year 1650; This custom they continued for some time, lurking in the fields among the furz and broom, 'till the times began to relax in their Severity, then they betook themselves to a taveren, which hung out for a Sign a whin bush, (hence their moderen name of whin bush Club) in honor of this club; their day of meeting still continued to be friday, and their meetings were very private (this was in the presidentship of the venerable Praise-god Maccartie) 'till the happy revolution, at the coming over of King William of Glorious memory, . . . then they sung whig Songs with all the Jollity and freedom Imaginable, mounting a large table, clapping each his wig under his right foot, holding a pipe of tobacco in one hand and a bumper of punch in the other. . . .

Having but Just now mentioned bread & cheese, It will be proper to take notice in this place, that this ancient and vener-able Club, had a Standing law, that nothing was to be admitted of eatables but this, which was only to give a relish to their Li-quor, formal Suppers taking up too much time, and occasion-ing too much Ceremony and Confusion in the Club, this Law, the ancient and Honorable Tuesday Club of Annapolis at first adopted, in Laudable Imitation of their patrons of the whin bush, but Luxury by degrees crept in among them, and they now Indulge themselves In sumptuous Suppers, which some have attributed to the custom established by that Club, of Cele-brating their anniversary, at which time, the honorable Mr President Jole, out of the overflowings of his generosity and re-spect to the club, always provides them in a most elegant en-tertainment, and the longstanding members, (as it is natural for the Inferior class of mankind to ape those above them) in Im-itation of his honor, try who shall outdo one another, in pomp and elegance of Club Suppers, and this is not alittle promoted, by the ambition and Emulation of the females, related to the Club, to shine & be remarkable in this particular.

This circumstance will admitt of a few grave reflexions; all allow, that Luxury is a destructive thing, and sooner or later fatal to every society or Community that once admits of it; as having a tendency to Introduce abject Slavery, by means of its being a promoter of bribery and Corruption, yet, we have Instances of the wisest Societies, that have, sometime or other fallen into her traps; Did not the Greeks, a wise and warlike Nation, after having for several ages, mantained their honor and dignity, in arts and arms, and Integrity of Morals, sink by degrees into Softness and effeminacy, by which, the persians overcame them, after they had subdued the persians by their arms and warlike prowess; and what are they now? how degenerated from their ancient honor and bravery, are they any better than a parcell of Quacking, pedling, rope dancing Juggling knaves, and withal, abandoned Slaves to the Law and government of Mahomet; what now are the Romans? once a wise honorable and warlike people, who ruled the world, and grasped the Globe at a handful, are they any wise like the Ancient Romans, or do they Resemble them in the least feature? No. They are a parcel of Singers, dancers, fidlers, pipers, effeminate catamites, Silly eunuchs and Idle Sauntering priests. . . . We may thence see & beware of the danger of admitting luxury into any Society, and, tho wise Societies and nations, have embraced this Cockatrice, yet that does not at all prove, that there is any good to be had of her, and tho' the ancient and honorable Tuesday Club, of Annapolis, be one of the wisest Clubs that ever yet appeared, yet she may see the time, when her constitution will feel the Smart of admitting Luxury to gain ground among her longstanding members, when she may receive such a Shake, as she may never be able to recover.

BOOK II

*From the transmigration
of the Club to America,
To the first Sederunt of the
Ancient and honorable Tuesday Club
of Annapolis in Maryland.*

Chapter 1 ❧ *A learned Dissertation, in the Stile and manner of the Ingenious Mr Robert Burton.*[1]

Those Solitary, moaping, morose, humdrum fellows, who evade, shun, run and fly, from all company, hate the Sight of men, as if they were Tygers, bears, Serpents, hobgoblins, Rhinoceroses and Panthers, and of the fair Sex, as if they were no better than Basilisks, cocatrices, harpies and Crocadiles, *Lemures Nocturni, mentulæque tersores,*[2] are mortal and Irreconcileable enimies to all Clubs, Jovial meetings, and humerous Conversations.

When I see a fellow of this Stamp, with his Clouded brows, and Lowring countenance, *monstrum deforme Ingens,*[3] I Imagine

---

[1]Famous author of *The Anatomy of Melancholy* (Oxford, 1621). The influence of Burton's *Anatomy* appears throughout Hamilton's narrative. He frequently parodies Burton's inflated rhetoric and pilfers passages from the *Anatomy*, clearly intending to set forth an anatomy of humor at Burton's expense.

[2]"Night demons and penis purgers" (similar to Horace, *Epistulae* 2.2.109).

[3]"Unnatural, deformed monster" (similar to Vergil's description of Polyphemus, *Aeneid* 3.658).

I behold a black cloud, rising from the dirty blustering South
east, saturated with hollow murmuring Smouldering blasts,
sending before it grumbling, tumbling, Jumbling thunder,
and Infectious puffs of pestilential Steams, darkening the face
of the fair day with polluted murky and Stiffling vapors, ex-
halations and damps, saturated, loaded, Impregnated and over-
charged, with morbific Sulphureous atoms, bursting from the
mouth of Tartarus it self. . . .

Your Insipid, havy dull drivelling moralizers, Criticisers
and Censors on the times, I do veryly think, also, are not at all
fitted to be members of free, frolicksome, gay and Gamesome
Clubs, those who will draw a moral Conclusion, out of a decayd
turnip, or rotten Cheese, and gravely infer from thence, that
all flesh is grass; make a bad omen of two Straws accross, a Salt
Seller overset, a Jacket buttoned awry, or a Coffin, as they call
it, in the candle, . . . are as little fit to make Companions of,
and therefore, I would have all such fellows banished from our
Clubical, as Plato banished Poets and musicians from his Philosophical Commonwealth, for they are fit for nothing but to be
shut up in Solitary desolate caves or celles, and there to become
mouldy, musty and worm eaten, with a pack of Lazy, loitering
Idle monks, Hermits and Anchorites, and, to pass thro' the
world silently, without leaving any the least trace or tract or path
behind them, as a Ship in the wide ocean, or a bird in the air.

❉❊

Having excluded these, and many others, whom it is needless
to enlarge upon, such as your eternal wranglers, disputers, con-
tradictors, falsifiers, Sceptical Doubters &ct: from our Clubical Commonwealth, I will now assert and mantain, that none
but your merry, droll, facetious, Jocose, good humored, risible
companions, punsters, comical Story tellers, and *Conundrumifiers*, ought to be members of those nocturnal assemblies, called
Clubs, for the Quintessence, marrow and main fulcrum of
Clubs consists in gayiety, Jollity, pleasantry and Jocosity.

What shall I then say, to every true Clubical genius but this. . . .

Live merry my friends, void of care, perplexity, anguish, grief, live merrily, *lætitiæ Cœlum vos creavit*,[4] again, and again I request you to be merry, if any thing trowbles your head, or frets your guts, neglect it, let it pass, and this I enjoin you, not only as a Philosopher, but as a Physician, for, without this mirth, which is a Clearer of the head, (for laughing is preferable to Sneezing) and enlivener of the fancy, there is no Science, no wisdom . . . ; medicine and whatever is applied to prolong the life of man, without this, is dull and dead, and of no force, *dum fata sinunt vivite læti*, says Seneca the Philosopher, ὁ βιοσ βραχους, says Hippocrates the Physician,[5] and I say, be merry, be merry.

Would you shun Charon the ferryman,
Consult Doctor Diet, Doctor Quiet and Doctor Merriman.

❋❊

Chapter 2 ❧ *The History and Character of Mr George Neilson, and the Cause of his coming to America.*

It is the Indispensable duty of all Historiographers, and Biographers, to collect and compile, in the most Impartial, Candid, and unprejudiced manner, the Glorious actions atchieved by great men, and faithfully to transmitt them to posterity.

The lives of great princes, Generals, poets, Philosophers, orators, and founders of Clubs, hold the first Rank in Biography, and shine like the Stars of the first magnitude among those of

[4]"Heaven made you for joy."
[5]"While the fates permit, live happily"; "Life is short."

Physicians, Logicians, magitians, arithmeticians, musicians, Lawyers, Divines, mechanics and Almanac makers, which may be Compared to the fainter constellations.

Micat Inter Ignes
Luna minores. Horat:[1]

The Illustrious person, of whose life I am now going to give some account, as being the founder of a Club, Immediatly derived from, and established upon the constitution, and police of the Ancient and venerable Tuesday (or whin bush) Club of Lanneric, stands therefore in the foremost rank of such worthies as have decorated Biography.

As the public is generally curious, to know the Stature, dimension, features, dress and air of Great and Illustrious men, I shall here present my readers with the portraiture of our Hero, and finish it off as well as I can.

Master George Neilson then, was a man of a small Stature, about four feet eight Inches high, of which he Cared not to lose one quarter of an Inch, for he strutted in his walk, and stood bolt upright like a pike, he was of a slender make, long visage, nose Inclinable to the aqueline, his chin alittle peaked, his eyes lively and full of motion, he was neither bandy legg'd nor battle Ham'd, nor Spla footed, as it is said most Scotsmen are, but he had, I know not what Sort of peculiarity about his legs, which I cannot otherwise describe, but that it did not resemble that of any other person, but, we often find, that great and Illustrious men, have had Certain peculiarities in their make, Thus, Alexander the great had a wry neck, . . . The Duke of Luxemburg was Hump backed,[2] and Alexander Pope Esqr had a crump Shoulder.

❋❊

[1]"The moon shines out among the lesser fires" (Horace, *Carmina* 1.12.46).
[2]François Henri de Montmorency-Bouteville, duc de Luxembourg (1628–1695), was a French soldier who served in wars against Spain and Holland and was created marshal of France in 1675.

Mr Neilson was in principle a Jacobite, having Imbibed in his tender years, before the maturity of his Judgement, (as indeed most Jacobites do) the heroic tenets and maxims of that Illustrious party. He firmly believed that kings were *Jure Divino*, and God's vicegerents upon Earth, and therefore, their actions of what nature soever were not to be enquired into or Canvassed; That they had an Indefeasible hereditary right to their Dominions, provided they were true kings, and not usurpers, and Creatures of popular formation; That they were accountable to no earthly power; That the Steuart family had the only Indefeasible and Indisputable title and Right to the Crown of Great Brittain France and Ireland, and were the only True Defenders of the faith; and that all and every person or persons, who secluded them from that Claim and right, were *Ipso facto*, Usurpers, traitors and Rebels, If any one contradicted him in these tenets, . . . he would either answer them by drawing his Sword, and bidding them encounter cold Iron, or presenting his pistols, and daring them to smell powder. . . .

As to Mr Neilsons Religion, I can say but very little, he having never been very communicative on this point, Some however, have Imagined he was a nonjuror, others, a high flown Episcopalian, others a Roman Catholic, and there have not been wanting some, who have maliciously asserted that he was a Presbyterian, an Anabaptist, Seventh Day man, Quaker, and even a muggletonian,[3] nay some have suspected him for a Jew, and of the Seed of Abraham, because forsooth he did not love pork, and was thought to be circumcised, but, as for the first, it is a food, which many Scots men detest, and yet are no Jews, and as for the other, we all know, that their are some Circumstances, a man may be under, that may oblige him to part with a Slice of his foreskin, and when that is the case, there is so small a

---

[3]A member of a sect founded in 1651 by Lodowicke Muggleton (1609–1698) and John Reeve (1608–1658), who claimed to be the "two witnesses" of Rev. 11:3–6; Muggleton, a journeyman tailor, was imprisoned and fined for blasphemy.

difference between the Scar, made by the priests knife and the Surgeons, that they cannot easily be distinguished, but, as this affair is at best uncertain, I shall leave it where I found it.

※※

Mr Neilson was a man of very warm passions and stood much upon points of honor, very apt to be highly provoked at Slight affronts, and upon all occasions of this Sort, out flew the Spado, or pistol. . . . These excursions or flights passed upon many simple people, and they submitted to the prowess of his Invincible Arm, but Mr Neilson sometimes met with undaunted heroes, who were not to be Intimidated by these methods, and once in particular, a Gygantic Champion, clapped him in a hamper, with his tie wig, Sword, and other warlike Accoutrements about him, and throwing him headlong into the river, he narrowly escaped a drowning, and after he was draggd out of the water, he Remained as mute as a fish, and made no more words of the matter.

※※

The Case then with Mr Neilson was this, being a Loyal and hearty espouser of the cause of the Steward family, in the year —15, he took the field, with many other valiant and hardy Champions, who then made a bold attempt, to set James VIII, as they called him, upon the British Throne, and after many Skirmishes, and one decisive battle at Sherrifmuir,[4] where much blood was spilt, and many bones broke to no purpose, our heroe fled, among the rest of the vanquished Rout, and being unluckily taken, luckily escaped a hanging, and was sent over Seas to America, to plot out the remainder of his life, with others of that Loyal party, to retale rum & punch & to found Clubs.

[4]An engagement during the Fifteen rebellion (Nov. 13, 1715), between 10,000 Jacobite rebels under the earl of Mar and 3,300 loyalist Scots under the duke of Argyll. After an indecisive confrontation, Mar retreated and his uprising collapsed.

Chapter 4 🐦 *The first Institution and foundation of the Red-house Club of Annapolis, by Mr George Neilson and other Illustrious personages.*

Mr George Neilson, after his arrival in Annapolis, Took some time to look about him, and having maturely considered, the wretched and Confused condition, that the Clubical constitutions were under in that City, he set himself Strenuously about working a Reformation in these Clubs, and, having an ample Commission in his pocket, under the Privy Seal of the Venerable Mr Neal Gilpin, Impowering him to erect Clubs in any of his majestie's plantations in America, he made the best use of the power conveyd to him by that commission.

His first business was, like all other wise and long headed politicians, to hear all and say nothing, for which Reason, he, in the beginning, attended these Clubs like a Pythagorean Philosopher, resolving with himself to keep a Strict Silence, till such time as he should discover the bent and Genius of these Clubs and the humours of the members, at the same time, he constantly had his Scouts out, to make observation, and bring him due Intelligence, these were some Ingenious persons, his own countrymen, who perhaps may make, some of them, a conspicuous figure in this history; they frequented these Clubs themselves, drank with them, roard with them, laughd with them, fought and squabbled with them, and were Crowned kings with them; but they carried their policy farther in making cunning enquiries into the particular private Characters of the members, by frequently visiting the matrons and old women of the City, where Certain Gossoping Clubs of females, Informed themselves carefully of every private occurrence in families, and as carefully divulged them again, sometimes by way of Secret, and sometimes with openness and frankness free of all reserve.

Upon account of this silent, reserved, and politic behavior, Mr Neilson passed among these people, for either a bashful Sheepish fellow, or a morose Sullen companion, and some Imagined he was melancholly mad, others, that he was in love, and, if he had not constantly drank his bumper in his turn, and tossed off the Bowl, and suffered himself to be crowned king by the Club, without saying a word, they would have expelld him from their Clubs as an useless member.

Mr Neilson, by this behaviour, put a very great constraint upon himself, for he was naturally of an airy and volatile disposition, much adicted to talking and fond of displaying his Learning and parts, besides, being of a hasty and passionate temper, it Cost him many a hard Struggle to contain himself, when any of these Club wits passed their Jokes upon him, and made him the but of the company, which they were very apt to do, upon the account of the oddity of his appearance, vizt: his oblong Sharp visage, his peaked Chin, his Snuff besmeard countenance, his large wig and his long Sword, Sometimes his passion would so ferment and fret within his breast, that his color, would come and go in his face, now turning pale as chalk, and then as red as a turkey Cock, and, it is said, he was once screwd up to such a pitch, by their running their rig, and making their game and fun of him, that he was seen to lay his hand on the hilt of his Sword, but, his Philosophy, overcoming his passion, he quickly retracted it again, and composed his countenance.

It is Inconceivable what hardships, abuses, and Scurrilous usage, this great personage suffered and went thro' to bring about this laudable Scheme, for clubical liberty. They would call him a hundred abusive names in half an hour, such as lousy scabby scot, poor rascally pedlar, Itchified Son of a bitch, Scoundrel, knave, fool, ass, Goose, blockhead, ugly beetle browd, squint eyed, Lenteren Jaw'd, Jacobitish, Skip kennel

Mr Neilsons anger restrained by Philosophy

Scrub, nasty, blewbellied, blanket ars'd, hip-shotten, maggot
eaten, round about, Snuff besmeard, flyblown Son of a whore,
and conclude all, with the epithet of bloodthirsty traitor and
 Rebel and No-nation Spawn of Vexation. This, for some time,
Mr Neilson bore with christian like patience, notwithstanding
the natural heat and Impetuosity of his temper, but at last, an
Accident happened, which brought about the great end, that he
and his asociates had been for a long time plotting, and it was
thus.

One Evening, Mr Neilson being at one of these Royalist
Clubs, upon a dispute arising concerning Clubical Government, The king called him a Gallows fac'd Rebel; Mr Neilson, who was alittle warmed with liquor, and not brooking this
harsh apellation, hastily drew upon his majesty, and in a trice
overset him and his throne, Immediatly all was in an uproar,
decanters, Glasses, and Tobacco pipes flew about like hail, his
majesties guards at last seized upon Mr Neilson, tore his tye
wig and neckcloth, stuffed his mouth full of tallow and Candle
wick, wrung his nose, broke his Sword, and tossed his whole
box or mull of Snuff in his Eyes, and taking him by the legs
and arms, carried him out of doors, and threw him headlong
into a puddle, so that he was the most woefull Spectacle ever
was beheld by the eyes of any Christian, and leaving him
there, in a most miserable nasty pickle, his Scouts soon had Intelligence of it, and, coming to his asistance, they beset, begirt
and besieged the Club house; but it was too late, the enimy had
secured the Doors, and fortified the place, so strongly, that
they found the fort Impregnable, and resolved to turn the
Siege into a blockade; but being much annoyed with Stink-
pots from the besieged, they were obliged to raise the Siege
and march off.

Immediatly after this tumult, the Club Royalists, who found
that several of their members had a warm Side towards Mr
Neilson, and his party, in order to put a stop to this Scism and

division, raised a hot persecution against the Neilsonists, the most cruel punishments were Invented, for those, whose consciences would not allow them, to toss off the bowl to be made king, the whole quantum of punch was poured upon their heads, which made them look like drowned rats, they were condemned to be pica-fousted, and Scabarabused,[1] and had the most unmerciful thumps on the back, and blows on the breech bestowed upon them, and withall, had their Crowns most miserably Clapperclaw'd, so that when they came abroad they seemed most pitiful Spectacles, being all over bumps, bruises and Scratches. This Inhuman persecution, naturally raised pity and Compassion, in the breasts of many, and being daily Joined by fresh numbers, they unanimously pitched upon Mr Neilson for their leader, upon this, an Intire Separation was made from the Royalists, and Mr Neilson Conveen'd his adherents in a house in Market Street, which was painted red, where having harangued them in a very Learned manner, he proposed, that they should Erect themselves into a Club, under different regulations from the Royalist Clubs, which Regulations he should propose to them, then pulling some papers from his pocket, among which was his Commission under the Venerable Mr Neal Gilpin's hand and privy Seal, and a Scheme or plan of a Club, he read both with a Clear and audible voice, and they unanimously agreed to form themselves into a Society, under the name of the *Red house Club.* . . .

[1] *Pica-fousted* seems to be Hamilton's invention, deriving from the Spanish *picar* ("to pierce") and the obsolete *foutch* ("sword"); *scabarabused*, another invention, obviously means "abused by striking with a scabbard," or "scabbarded."

Chapter 6 ❧ *The translation of the Seat of Government in the Red house Club, the Cause of its dissolution, and the place of meeting converted to a Nunnery.*

This Club was for some considerable time governed by a Rotation of (presidents) and, we do not find, that there were any Subaltern officers in the Club, excepting only the taster, it does not appear that they had even a Secretary or kept Records, or, if there were any Records they are lost, for, what is here delivered, is collected only from oral tradition, for the Greatest part of which we have been obliged to Mr Prim Timorous, a member of that Club, and since Serjeant at Arms to the honorable Nasifer Jole Esqr, president of the ancient and honorable Tuesday Club.

But, as there is a Constant fluctuation among Sublunary things, and nothing, not even Clubs, tho well Constituted, are exempt from this mutability, the Seat of Government, or place of meeting in this club was Changed in the year 1732, which happened thus.

The house where they met was struck with Lightning, and was thereby shattered in such a woeful manner, that it became unhabitable, all that were In it at that time were stunned or knocked down, excepting one old woman, who happened to be in the Cellar making candles, who was not hurt, which lucky escape, has since been ascribed by many, to the tallow with which she was besmeared all over, from head to foot, and tallow, wax, rozin and such like, being non electrics, the elementary fire only Glanced upon the Surface of the old womans Skin and Cloaths, but did not penetrate her body, . . . if this should be true, it would be prudent for those who are afraid of Lightning, to have a Slush bucket always at hand, to besmear themselves with, which I think would be an easier preservative against it,

not kings

and less expensive, than fixing iron rods and wires upon houses, for, this Method will preserve people from it out of doors, as well as within, and, perhaps this may be the reason, why the native Indians of America, (a quarter of the world very subject to violent thunder gusts) smear their bodies all over with bears grease.

❈❈

This Club then, changed its place of meeting to a large house near Bloomsbery Square, where were many Spacious apartments, but one of these they pitched upon, in particular, for the Club to sit in, where, for a considerable time, in great peace and tranquillity, they smoked their pipes, took their Snuff, drank their punch, eat their gammon and bread and Cheese, and carried on a Clubical conversation, concerning various Subjects.

In this happy State were they, when the death of Mr George Neilson, put an end to all their Glory by putting an end to their peace and quiet, which is a lesson to men in prosperity and easy circumstances not to be too vain or secure, for adversity and distress may suddenly come upon them, e're they are aware; In short, after the Death of their founder and leader, they split into factions and parties, every one aspiring to the management of affairs, and showing a desire to rule the roast, but none being of capacity or wisdom equal, or even nigh to their Illustrious founder, they bilged upon this Sandbank, and like a mouldering wreck, gradually separated one from another, till at last from a numerous Club, they became nothing, and from their ruins Immediatly after, there sprung up another Club, which we shall describe in it's proper place.

❈❈

After the breaking up of this Club, the house was converted to a nunnery, several females fixing their habitation in it, who afterwards were dignified with the name of nuns. . . .

These nuns It is said, resembled the Roman vestals in one thing, that they fed and kept up a perpetual fire, and were visited every night, by many of the priests and votaries of Venus, who seldom went away from them, without carrying some of that same Sacred fire, or rather *Ignis fatuus*,[1] concealed in their Breeches, these priests payd divine honors to these Nuns or vestals, and worshiped them with great devotion, for, they seldom or never went In their presence, but they fell down upon their knees, and seemed moved and agitated with great extasies, fetching deep Sighs, and earnest groans, but we shall leave these nuns and priests, to carry on their pious frauds, and proceed with our Clubical History.

Chapter 7 ❧ *The Rise of the Ugly Club, from the Ruins of the Red house Club.*

As Empires, kingdoms and States may be compared to the Hydra, new ones springing up continually from the Downfal of the old, so it is the same with Clubs, for no sooner is one of these nocturnal assemblies dissolved, or dissipated, but Immediatly another Rises up in its place, as is plainly exemplified here in our History, for scarce was the Red-house Club, a branch of the ancient and venerable Tuesday (or whin bush) Club of Lanneric, at a period, but Immediatly sprung up from it's remains, like the Phoenix from its own ashes, a Club Called the *Ugly Club*, a description of which we are now to give.

❀❀

My Readers are not here to Imagin, that they assumed that appellation, upon account of ugliness of feature, or deformity of body in the members, like another Club of that name described

[1] As Hamilton was aware, *ignis fatuus* literally means "foolish fire" (a flame-like phosphorescence produced over marshes by the spontaneous combustion of decayed vegetable matter, which eludes those who attempt to follow it).

by the *Spectator*,[1] it was not at all necessary, that a man should
be hard favored, crooked, or hunch backed, to qualify him to
be a member of this Club, it was Sufficient for him Sincerely
to profess and believe that he was not handsom, till he was declared to be a monstrous ugly fellow by the Ladies in public
company. . . . A man was to show his Sincerity in this opinion
of himself, by assuming a certain Slovenliness and peculiarity
in his dress, by never throwing away his time at a looking Glass,
and diligently evading all foppish and finical airs and affectation
either in his gesture of body, Speaking or gait in walking, but,
if he ever observed any oddity of Gesture, affected by another
man, such as a wink, a cast of the Eye, a sudden toss of the head,
to one Side or other, or wry twist of the mouth, . . . these he
was Strictly to Imitate, and perfect himself in, as being real de-
formities and deviations from nature in a much higher degree
than bodily distortions and blemishes, which the members of
this Club, did not think Carried in them so much deformity, as
to entitle their possessors to a Seat in their Society.

❋❋

Thus was it Solely upon account of the Slovenliness of the members (who looked when met like a parcel of ragged philosophers) their affectation of odd gestures, and the dirtiness and
unseemliness of the Club room, that this Society had the name
of the Ugly Club; and not from any bodily deformity in the
members themselves, for, in that respect, some of them were
proper enough men, and tollerably well made.

❋❋

[1]The Ugly Club is mentioned in nos. 17, 48, 52, 78, 87, and 553 of the
Spectator, but the most extended account of the club—and the one to which
Hamilton is probably referring—appears in no. 32.

Chapter 8 ❧ *The first Scheme for erecting the Ancient & Honorable Tuesday Club of Annapolis in Maryland.*

❧❧

After the Decease of this Club, which Indeed could not be of long Continuance, having no such able Genius as Mr Neilson's to support it, out of its remains sprung a Club, which since has made the most Shining figure of any that have yet appeared in America, vizt: the ancient and Honorable Tuesday Club of Annapolis, in the frame and Constitution of which, In process of time, arose the real likeness and Image, of the Ancient and Venerable Tuesday (or whin bush) Club of Lanneric, . . . the effecting of this, was what the Great Mr Neilson aimed at, with all his might, but the Inexorable Destinies, cut the thread of his life, before he had half accomplished his Laudable design, however, he had the honor to lay the foundation of this great Superstructure, tho he enjoyed not the pleasure of seeing it perfected.

This happy lot fell upon persons much less conspicuous than he, viz: Prattle Motely Esqr, and Loquacious Scribble M:D: who were the only two members of the Late Ugly Club that stuck together and Strenuously operated to keep alive the taste for Clubbing in Annapolis, for which purpose they called to their asistance two very able politicians, vizt: Jealous Spyplot Esqr, Serjeant at Law, and the Revd Mr Smoothum Sly parson of the parish, the first had been a companion of the Great Mr Neilson in his trowbles, came to America with him, and was also of his privy council in the Red house Club, he was a Gentleman of great discernment, and could see into men's breasts and fortell Events at a distance, as well as any Conjurer of the Age. The latter was a Gentleman very well adapted for Clubs, being of a free airy disposition, full of compliment and panegyric to all, and of a Jocose turn, much given to quaint Repartee, dowble Entendre, & withal a hearty & loud laugher, these four gentlemen having procured four more to be of their party, whom we shall afterwards mention, laid the first foundation of that famous Club, whose History I now write. . . .

BOOK III

From the first Sederunt
of the Ancient and
honorable Tuesday Club,
to the Cathedration of
the Honorable Nasifer
Jole Esqr President.

Chapter 2 🦟 *The first Sederunt of the Ancient and honorable Tuesday Club, and the wise Laws then framed.*

Such of my readers, as have perused the last chapter of the preceeding book, if their memory be not very short, will Remember, that Messiurs Prattle Motely and Loquacious Scribble
M:D: the residue of the Ugly Club, called to their asistance
Jealous Spyplot Esqr, Serjeant at Law, and the Reverend Mr
Smoothum Sly, parson of the parish, in order to form a new
Club, and fix it upon a better and more lasting foundation, than
any of the Clubs hitherto erected, They presently got four more
to Join them, vizt: Captn: Seemly Spruce, a Jolly boon companion, and no early Starter, being one who usually wore his
Sitting breeches at a nights compotation, Captn: Serious Social,
of the same kidney, and noted for Singing of old Club Catches,
Mr Laconic Comus, a Jolly old cock, of Surly aspect and few
words, but gifted with an excellent musical voice, and a Sincere
lover of the Bowl and tobacco pipe, these had formerly been
members of the Red house Club; and Captn: Bully Blunt, a person of a very happy turn to the Burlesque, which made him an
exceeding good Clubs man.

These Gentlemen then, meeting upon Tuesday the 14th day

of May, in the Year 1745, the same month and day on which the Red house Club met, under Mr George Neilson Sixteen years before, formed and erected themselves into a club, which they called by the name of the *Tuesday Club;* they met first at the Lodging of Doctor Loquacious Scribble, who first exercised the office of Steward, and Chairman to the Club; and the Candles being lit, the punch made, and the pipes fairly set a going, after two or three rounds of the punch bowl, they applied themselves to make and pass some wholesome Laws, for the good government and regulation of the Society, In which, they did not trust so much to their own Judgement, and Invention, as some vain people are apt to do, but took for a pattern, the regulations and laws of other Clubs, particularly those of the ancient and venerable Tuesday, (or whin bush) Club of Lanneric, of which, they reckoned themselves a direct continuation, on the same line, and, upon this position they assumed the name of the *Ancient and honorable Tuesday Club, of Annapolis in Maryland,* and thus having fixed their ancient and honorable title, they, at their first Sederunt established the following Laws.

> *Law I.* That the meeting of the Club be weekly, at the members houses, by turns, thro' out the year, upon Tuesday evening.
>
> *Law II.* The Steward for the time being, shall provide a gammon of bacon, or any other one dish of dressed vittles and no more.
>
> *Law III.* No Liquor shall be made, prepared or produced after eleven o clock at night, and every Member shall be at liberty to retire at pleasure.
>
> *Law IV.* No members shall be admitted without the concurring consent, of the whole Club, and after such admission, the member shall serve as Steward next meeting.

Happy, O happy had it been for this ancient and honorable Club, had they always kept to this golden mean of frugality and temperance, but the mode soon changed, and Luxury crept in by degrees, as we shall find in the Sequel.

※※

Chapter 3 ❧ *The Introduction of the Batchellor's Cheese into the Club, the passing The Gelastic law, and other matters of Importance.*

We shall meet with some Histories, where there is nothing but a dry relation of facts, without any useful reflections, or observations interspersed, which are Indeed the Salt of History, and afford it a Savor which makes it agreeable to the palat of every Judicious reader, without this, it would look like the York-shire Squire's Story of himself and his friend, which consisted chiefly of—and so quoth he, and so quoth I, and so we agreed on this, and so we differed on that, and so I went there, and so he came here, and so—and so—and so &ct:

Whoever reads this history, must not expect to find any such trumpery in it's structure and composition; I never Intended it for the entertainment of nurses children and Shallow wits by a winters fire, but have adapted it to the taste of the learned & Ingenious, by Interlarding the narration of facts In several places, with proper and apposite observations and remarks, and these, my readers are to expect to meet with, wherever the nature of the Subject will permit, and, if any Slender wits happen to be among my readers, I advise them, for their own ease, to pass over these learned Remarks, as being above their capacity

he imagines to
history to have a
learned and unlearned
learned audience.

From the first Sederunt · 41

and understanding, but, I hope all my learned Readers will esteem them the very marrow and Cream of this history, and
therefore read them over with attention and Carefully store
them up in their Intellectual warehouses and magazines, which,
as the learned Descartes says, is in the middle Ventricle of the
brain, near the pineal Gland, where memory keeps her court.[1]

This virtuous and frugal Club, Imagining that they were still
too lavish in allowing a Gammon of bacon, or one dish of
dress'd vittles for Supper, passed at Sederunt 5th June 11, the
following Law, viz:

> *Law VI.* That such as are batchelor members of the
> Club may have a Cheese upon one Side board, instead
> of dress'd vittles.

This not only exhibited, a Singular Instance of frugality and
moderation, but also, a high degree of Indulgence to those
batchelor members, who, not always having cooks at home, and
for the most part, little or nothing for Cooks to lick their fingers
upon, must be at abundance more trowble in providing, than
such of the members as were matirmonized. . . .

Happy then was it with the members of this ancient and honorable Club, for, without Interruption, let or molestation, they
could sit with their legs across, loll upon the table or an Elbow
chair, smoke their pipes, kiss the Glass or bowl, in their turns,
converse upon Clubical matters, either grave or facetious, drink
toasts either loyal or amorous, crack Jokes, frame puns or conundrums, and, should their Stomachs call for a whet, without
Ceremony or trowble to themselves or fellow members, they
might rise up, go to the Side board, and after having taken their
Slice of cheese or Sliver of Gammon standing, return again to

[1]Hamilton is recalling Descartes's 1664 *Essay on Man* (*Traité de l'homme*),
in which he explains that memory is located in the pineal gland (see *Oeuvres
de Descartes*, ed. Charles Adam and Paul Tannery [Paris, 1897–1910], XI,
177–178).

their compotation, Jocosity, and Clubical conversation, how
charming, how regular, and how much like the Simple frugality of the Golden age was this, and how different from that luxury and profuseness that prevails in most of our moderen
Clubs.

❀❀

. I come now to relate a transaction, which shows in a very conspicuous Light, the wisdom of this ancient and honorable Club;
It is a truth not to be disputed, that the greatest pest of Clubs,
and the most common disturber of the peace of those Societies,
is that violent propensity in human nature to dispute, every one
thinking himself the wisest and most learned person in company, and therefore not obliged to yield one ace to the opinion
or Judgement of another. This has been the cause of the dissolution of many Clubs, and, where disputes have arisen about
such Important matters, as what is the right, and what the
wrong end of a black pudding, at what end one shall break an
egg, . . . which is the most amicable, or familiar way of Sa-
luting a friend, to shake him by the hand, or clap him on the
Shoulder, what is to be reckoned among men of nice honor, the
greatest affront, a twitch o' the nose, or a kick o' the breech, the
consequences of these learned disputes, have been fatal to those
Clubs, where they have been fomented or encouraged, have en-
tirely broke them up, and rendered those who were before,
good Club Companions and friends, bitter enimies to one another, to the great hurt and Dammage, of that Social Clubical
disposition, which nature has been so careful to Implant in
mankind.

This sage Club therefore, considering how dreadfully fatal
the consequences might be, if such Subtile disputes were suffered to take place in their Society, thought of a method to prevent this mischief, and fell upon the most effectual remedy,
which shows their deep Judgement and Sagacity; they pitched
upon ridicule, as the most effectual way to Cure it, and Indeed,
we find it to be true, that men are much sooner laughed out of

their follies and faults, than cured of them by grave admonition and advice, they therefore at Sederunt 6th, June 18, passed the following law.

> *Law VII.* That if any Subject of what nature soever, be discussed, that levels at party matters, or the administration of the Government of this Province, or be disagreeable to the Club, no answer shall be given thereto, but after such discourse is ended, the Society shall laugh at the member offending, in order to divert the discourse.

This Law was called the *gelastic Law,* and, in its Substance and Structure, shows the wisdom and Sagacity of the Long-standing members, of this ancient and honorable Club, as much as any Law framed by them, either before or since, and, we shall find in the Sequel, this Law put in execution, against several offending members, sometimes with effect, and sometimes with none at all, which shows us, how difficult a task it is, for even the utmost Strech of human wisdom, to frame a Law or Laws, that cannot be evaded.

Chapter 4 ❧ *The private Character of Nasifer Jole Esqr, and other prodigious matters.*

I am now entering upon a chapter in this History, in which I shall have occasion for the asistance of all the muses, which Inhabit Parnassus, from its top to its bottom, from the highest of the Sublime, to the lowest of the bathos; from Virgil to Bavius, from Milton to Pryn and Wythers, from Cervantes and his fol-

lower Henry Fielding Esqr, to the Reverend Mr Gazeteer Eachard & the Celebrated Mr John Bunyian.[1]

Upon the celebrated 2d of July, O:S: in the year 1745, a day
ever to be remembered by the ancient and honorable Tuesday
Club, at Sederunt 8, Mr Secretary Motely being Steward, were
admitted to the Club several members, vizt: Messieurs Nasifer
Jole, Dumpling Gundiguts, Drawlum Quaint, Slyboots Pleasant, and Joggle Hasty; The first of these Gentlemen is the Subject of this dignified and distinguished Chapter, and Indeed,
will be the Chief heroe of our Succeeding History, as for the
others, we shall mention them only occasionally as we go along,
according to the Station they hold, and figure they make in the
Club.

Mr Nasifer Jole, otherwise Carlo Nasifer Jole, was a native
of old England, and the County of Kent claims the honor of his
birth, he often Justly values himself on his being born an Englishman, and is not alittle fond of letting it be known, that he
is a man of Kent, sprung of a race of ancient heroes and true
british blood, not a kentish man,[2] who is only the mungerell
Issue of the Roman, Saxon, Norman, Dane, Scot, pict, and a
hundred other mixed foreign Nations, that gained footing in
England but of late.

He was educated in the mercantile way, and made such progress in the Science of traffic and trucking, that he could tell at

[1]Bavius (fl. first century B.C.), a Roman poetaster, was rescued from oblivion only by Vergil's contempt. William Prynne (1600–1669), a Puritan
pamphleteer, wrote against Arminianism and endeavored to reform the
manners of the age, for which he was confined to the Tower of London.
George Wither (1588–1667), an English author, was noted for his satires
(*Abuses Stript and Whipt* [London, 1613]). John Eachard (ca. 1636–1697)
was an English divine and satirical writer whose works include two dialogues
ridiculing Hobbes's philosophy (1672, 1673).

[2]A man of Kent is one born east of the Medway; these men went out with
green boughs to meet William the Conqueror and consequently obtained a
confirmation of their ancient privileges from the new king. A Kentish man
is a resident of the western part of the county.

The Honorable Carlo Nasifer Sole Esqr. President of the
Ancient & Honorable Tuesday Club

Prandum flos, alta infixus ecce Cathedra
Consortii nostri et decus, et gloria.
Cedito, o Hugo, tu Cognominate Maccarty
Vestrum nam caput, nostra tiara timnit.

Behold of Presidents the prime prick'd up in lofty Chair
Who of our Club the Glory is, and ornament Right fair
Yeild then to us, O haughty Hugh, who Sirnam'd art Maccarty
Since that your Cap is by our head, held in Contempt right hearty.
[Hamilton's translation on back of drawing]

his fingers ends, all the noble Ingredients that Compound the Character of a reputable merchant, or storekeeper, & could distinguish such from a Scots pedlar at a miles distance without the help of a perspective glass, his chief Characteristic of a merchant, was one that bought very Cheap, and sold at a living price, as he called it, which golden rule he followed himself, as much as in him lay, and his distinguishing mark of a pedlar, was a fellow, that presumed to vend his wares at a low, or what some call a reasonable rate, (whatever price he purchased them at) to the prejudice of the Reputable merchant, he would prove very clearly, by unanswerable arguments, that 300 per cent, tended more to the public good, (vizt: the good of the merchants or Storekeepers, who were of public Service) than 50 per cent, because, said he, 300 per cent, is a living price, and enables the merchant to carry on trade and commerce, with vigor and life, whereas, any thing under that is a pitiful peddling price, and occasions trade, (vizt: Storekeeping) to languish and decay, . . . but, I never heard that he made any proselytes to this way of thinking, not only because this doctrine was *gratis dictum*,[3] as the Logicians term it, but because the Sordid Love of money is so generally prevalent, that people would still buy where they could at the Cheapest rate. . . .

Mr Jole had a great part of his education on board a man of war, where he had learned many useful arts, particularly that of Cookery, and he was such a proficient in that noble Science, that he understood as well as any notable husiff, how to stew a frecassée, or ragout, mix, compound, boil or bake a pudding, or raise a pasty, and he knew his own Skill in these Important operations so well, that with reason he picqued himself upon it, and people approved of, and acquiesced in his Judgement herein so far, that they often eat of his dishes with high relish and pleasure, Indeed, his fondness for these niceities, and desire

[3]"Freely asserted."

of applause on that Score, might Justly be called his weak side; for, tho' he was a person pritty tenacious of his property, yet, he would spare no expence in making a Show with such delicacies, and dainties, and any hungry fellow or abandon'd Epicure, might get a good meal out of him, as often as he pleased, by only praising his Cookery, and saying that it put one in mind of *Old England.* . . .

Carlo Jole had a very elegant taste, in most things relative to houshold affairs, which he acquired by long and painful experience and application, during the many years that he spent in a Single life; he understood perfectly well how to set out a mantle piece or bofett, with plate, Glass and China, in the neatest and most Showy order; how, and in what places to dispose of flowers in the season, how to paper candlesticks and adorn glass Sconces, how to hang pictures, filigrams and pettipoints, and such like ornaments in a room, how to cut papers for decoying the flies from the hangings and Valence of beds, and how in the most charming and elegant taste to dress up a nosegay, . . . and at all times, when he went to Church, he wore one in his buttonhole, so beautifully decked, that it attracted the eyes of all the Congregation, particularly those of the Ladies, while he kept twirling a Charming pink Iris, Jonquille, or Ænemonie betwixt his finger and thumb.

❈❈

Even in his Dress Nasifer showed a peculiar elegance of taste, he always went clean, and neat, tho never tawdry, he wore a large full flaxen wig, sometimes too a laced hat, his favorite color was red, for he often wore a Scarlet Coat, edged round with gold galloon, and ornamented with gold buttons and button holes, but this was properly his military dress, he being Leutenant General of the Independent foot Company of Annapolis, and had formerly been ensign thereof, but was promoted, in reward of his brave behaviour in the Dangerous expedition of that warlike Corps, against the Nanticock Indians,

whom they took prisoners to the number of about 30, out of a
boat at Wapping dock at Annapolis, and Conducted them safe
to the City prison, without stricking one blow, or sheding one
drop of Christian blood.[4]

❄❄

Our heroes person, which in general was genteel and well
made, sett off his dress, rather more than his dress his person,
he is of a fair complexion, long and Sharp visage; somewhat
Inclinable to a Square countenance, his nose aqueline, his chin
of a Considerable length and prominent, in short, he is what
many call in their vulgar Stile somewhat hatchet faced; his body
is thick and well built, of a middle Stature and every way pro-
portional except a little (tho' not disagreeable) *prominentia chī-
nium,* resembling somewhat the description of Rob Morris in
the old Scots Song,[5] who is described in the following distich
thus.

> Auld Rob Morris, I ken him fou well,
> His arse it sticks out like ony peet creel.[6]

His presence is grand and majestic, especially when he ascends
the Club Chair, and sits erect in it, his walk is stately and upright, tho' alittle on the hobble, which is not natural but from

[4]In 1742 the Nanticokes briefly participated in a revolt against the English
settlers on the Eastern Shore of Maryland. While the Nanticokes and other
tribes on the Eastern Shore were engaged in a war dance, a Choptank Indian
exposed the plot and the revolt came to an abrupt end. The Nanticokes were
severely reprimanded by the Maryland Assembly for their part in the uprising, and by 1744 they removed themselves from the province to live
among the Six Nations.

[5]"Auld Rob Morris" appears in Allan Ramsay's *Tea-table Miscellany* (1724–
1732), I, 59–60. The comparison between Jole and Rob Morris is none too
flattering. In the song, a girl's parents try to coerce her into marrying Morris, and she swears she would rather die than marry such a poor excuse for
a man.

[6]Peat basket.

a gouty weakness in his feet, but he has contracted a habit of Seesawing often when he sits, especially if he be telling of a Story, at which he has a particular genius or knack, and tho' he be somewhat circumstantial or prolix, yet, he seldom fails to fix the attention of his hearers, and affords them abundance of Instruction and agreeable amusement.

※※

His knowledge in music, he has merely by the force of Genius, having never been taught, and his talent this way lies in vocal execution, he having a number of old Songs by him, to the words of which, he affirms, he never is at a loss to find a tune, and Indeed, give him words at any time, and he'll Immediatly clap a tune to them, with so Sweet and small a voice, and so delicate a trill, that some people have doubted whether or not he has in his youth been Italianized, but, be that as it will, (tho it may be said of him, as it was of *Aurelius Philippus Paracelsus Theophrastus Bombastus de Hohenheim, Testimonium virilitatis prebet rigida barba*)[7] he has a most exquisite pipe, and, were he not obliged sometimes to wear his Spectacles, to read the words of the Song, . . . his voice would be quite clear, and without asperity, but this nasal machine, will sometimes in the high notes, occasion a Snuffling, which a nice ear will easily excuse, . . . among many other favorite Songs, which shall afterwards be mentioned, Mr Jole had one of the amorous kind, entituled, *Whilst I gaze on Cloe trembling*,[8] which Song in the printed editions, wants about twelve or 15 Stanzas, . . . this Induced some

[7]Full name of Paracelsus (1493–1541), a famous Swiss physician, alchemist, and astrologer. The quotation about him—the source of which is uncertain—means "A stiff beard bears witness of virility." Not surprisingly, Jole is never depicted wearing a beard.

[8]"Whilst I gaze on Chloe trembling" appears in Allan Ramsay's *Tea-table Miscellany* (1724–1732), II, 5, in only 4 stanzas. That Jole, a man who has no passion for the ladies, would invent another 12 or 15 stanzas about the raging passion of a frustrated lover is humorous indeed.

to believe, tho' Mr Jole never showed it, or seemed to be vain of it, that he had a poetical Genius, and had added several verses to that ancient Song with his own accurate hand, Some of these verses are in themselves very Sublime and poetical, one of which, for its beauty and Singularity, I cannot ommit here quoting.

> Here there lies Interr'd a Squire
> Underneath this marble Stone,
> Who for Loving did expire,
> And he never Lov'd but one.

This verse in particular Mr Jole would sing with so lamentable a voice, as to draw tears from the eyes of the most flinty hearted, tho many affirmed that these tears flowed not from Commiseration, but from a certain gelastic conquassation.[9]

꽃꽃

As I talked but Just now of the fair Sex, it will be proper here to enquire, how far Mr Jole was ever engaged with them, he has lived always Single, having been, as it is thought, ever averse to the Clog of a wife, and a man of too much prudence and Solidity ever to keep a concubine, for this reason the world is not likely to be much entertained with his amours, and the transactions of his life would therefore afford very unfit materials for a novel; It being a question whether he ever permitted a woman to come nigher to him than arms Length, or a modest and decent distance, so as to hold Indifferent discourse, for, tho' he never showed any affection to the Sex, yet, he would deign to converse with them as rational Creatures, which showed, that he was too much of a christian to believe with some Philosophers, that women had no Souls,[10] but then he would behave

---

[9]Severe shaking caused by laughter.

[10]Hamilton is alluding to the traditional Turkish belief that had become commonplace in 18th-century England. See, for example, Samuel Butler's "Women": "The Soules of women are so small / That Some believe th' have

himself with the same Indifferent coldness, as one man does to another, or as one maid would accost another.

Yet, as man is a Sociable animal, and the most Savage and retired have at times their Darling companions, so, this celebrated Gentleman, Judging his own Species, unworthy to make constant companions and Intimates of, chose a Society of Cats for his friends, fellows and playmates, both at bed and board, and so far did his extraordinary charity and benevolence extend to those Cats, that he would deign to converse with them in the most familiar manner, giving some of them a christian like education, for he had some that he taught to sit erect, and clap their fore feet or paws together in a praying or begging like posture, he would stroke down their soft Skins, apply their mouths to his, give the females, Silk and velvet beds, in which to lie in, or deposit their kittins, and when, for fear of their multiplying too much, he would order some kittens to be drowned or buried alive, he was so tender hearted, that he would not see the execution, but shut himself up, and grieve for some time, as a tender mother does for her babes; . . . in fine the Great Nasifer, in the midst of his cats, looked like the Grand Signior in the midst of his Seraglio, and by means of his good discipline and advice, they were all so modest and well bred that when he entertained Company of the human Species, not one of those brutes would dare so much as to appear, or even to peep, but all retired to their proper Chambers, and appartments allotted for them.

Carlo Nasifer Jole, tho' he had no great communication with mankind, was thought to be a friend to human nature and a well wisher to Society, for, he always expressed a great aversion and hatred to thieves, rogues and villains, in such a manner, that, whenever he heard of any wretches accused of theft, rob-

none at all" (*Satires and Miscellaneous Poetry and Prose*, ed. René Lamar [Cambridge, 1928], 220).

bery or murder, he was for tucking them up, without the ceremony of a trial, Some Indeed said, that this proceeded from a rigid temper and cruel disposition, and therefore pronounced him a Mysanthrope, but I must beg leave to be of a contrary opinion.

In fine, Mr Jole was of a very Suspicious temper, cared not to trust any body, and was exceeding fond of power and authority, of which we shall see many Instances, in the Sequel of this History.

Chapter 5 ⚹ *The expulsion of the Batchellor's Cheese, an Instance of the amorous disposition of the Longstanding members.*

We have now discussed the primitive, Simple times of this ancient and honorable Club, and must bid farewell in a little Space, to that virtuous and heroic frugality, which prevailed in it at it's first Institution, for now Luxury began to peep from behind the Scene, and prepare for her pompous entry upon this Clubical Stage, and, Indeed, to carry on our metaphor, this bold actress took one great Stride at her first advance, and proceeded afterwards, with a *grand pas*, to expell Simplicity and plainness from the Club, and to Introduce, pomp show and extravagance, her constant pages and attendants, while another, her companion and coactor, with the like buskined pride, plaid the part of a momus or mimic, this was no less a person than Ceremony, as much a beau, as the other is a belle, whom we shall soon see also, showing his pragmatical front, upon the most conspicuous part of the Scene, and Introducing certain fantastical punctillios, forms and modes, by which he so disguised and poisoned the manners and behavior of the longstanding members, of this here ancient and honorable Club (as indeed he does those of all mankind, especially such as are in higher life, for he is never seen among beggars & Clowns,) that they did in no manner seem to be the same persons they were at their first Institution.

It was at Sederunt 10th July 18, Drawlum Quaint Esqr, being Steward, that the batchellor's Cheese was Expelled the Club, by an express Law, in which it was declared

> *Law XI.* That Cheese shall no more be deemed a dish
> of vittles, and therefore the use of it as such in the
> Club is forbid.

The Chief moover for this Law, was Nasifer Jole Esqr, whom we shall find afterwards by gradual Steps Introducing high relished dishes and dainties into the Club, he began first with rack punch, here madam Luxury first pop'd her head from behind the curtain, with her far fetched commodities, presently after this, come the bowl and tobacco pipe procession, then her adjutant Ceremony followed her beck; then an Iced cake makes it's appearance, . . . and thence Mr Jole proceeded gradually in his Schemes, and slap dash, there followed a whole troop of frecassees, ragous, hashes, soups, pasties, pies, puddings, dumplings, tarts, Gellies and Syllabubs, and it is thought, that it was by these artful Steps, that this politic gentleman raised himself to the presidential Chair, and advanced one Step, or Six inches above the other Longstanding members.

❋❋

While these matters were transacting in Club, the members had a visit from the Hon: Coll: Courtly Phraze, who . . . told [them] that he had Just now left the Company of the Ladies, those dear angelical creatures! . . . the Collonels discourse concerning the Ladies, put the members of the Club into an amorous vein, and there was not one there excepting Mr Jole, but resolved to have his Girl that very night; Drawlum Quaint Esqr, the Steward seemed to be more agitated by this amorous enthusiasm, than any of the other members, for, he went out of Club, attended by Loquacious Scribble M:D: and was resolved not to return, till he had blunted the edge of his desires, with some Gentle and kind Nymph, but, his resolution did not carry him thro' thick and thin, for, he was so terrified, at the Sight of a Superannuated female, who, upon his knocking opened her door to him, that all his tender Ideas vanished like Smoke, and taking to his heels, as if the Devil had been after him, he run faster back than he went forth, and took his Seat again in Club, quite out of breath.

It was not so with Laconic Comas Esqr, and Mr Secretary Motely, two Stanch Longstanding members, the first a widower, the other a batchellor, who, after the dismissing of the Club, went in pursuit of some fair Nymphs, who that night were assembled at a dance, and carried the Steward with them, but what their adventures and exploits were, we shall not relate here, as having nothing to do with the History of the Club, which is of too grave and Solid a nature, to admit of the detail and relation of amours, these triffles, properly belonging to Romances and Novels, and therefore cannot be any credit to True histories such as this.

Chapter 6 ❧ Some of the Members seized with a furor poeticus, and some account of the Baltimore Bards.

Much about this time, appeared an epidemical distemper in the Club, which broke out, no body can tell how, it was what Physicians might properly call a κακο-ηθεια or μαγιας ποιητικης,[1] malignitas poetica, or Furor poeticus, several of the members having been taken in an unaccountable manner, with fits of

---

[1] "Poetical wickedness or madness."

Rhiming, and writing of Rhimes, those that seemed to be most affected with it were Messiurs Sly, Motely, Blunt, Quaint and Scribble, tho' none were writers but the two last, however, the whole Club was in some measure touched with this malignity, so that they could scarce speak to one another, but in Rhime and Jingle, and even Mr Solo Neverout, sometime after, admitted a Member of the Club, who had never before shown the least genius or turn to Rhiming or versification, nay even made a Jest of it in his laughing way, and ridiculed all poets and poetasters, was so Infected as to break all at once into blank verse, and with great violence and vociferation, exclaimed to the Surprize of all present,

With dowble Lustre, Beckie's beauties shine.

And when he was desired to proceed farther, and make a Couplet of it, he bawld out in a furious manner,

Rise Jupiter, and snuff the moon!—

Upon which the company thinking he was crazed left him to himself, and urged no more questions. . . .

We have reason to believe, that this poetical Contagion took its rise first in the north, and therefore was of the frigid Sort, for, in the county of Baltimore, there appeared two Celebrated Bards, vizt: Bard Bavius, and Bard Mevius,[2] who, having broke out into most violent fits of Rhiming and versifying, Infected many people around them with the same distemper. . . .

The first bold Stroke that appeared of this kind was from the celebrated Bard Mevius, who, one day being In church, hearing the Reverend and pious Mr George Whitefield hold forth, was diverted in his attention to the Sweet words of that Inspired Saint, by some Ladies, who sat in a pew Just before him, with the whiteness and beautiful Length of whose Necks . . . he was so miraculously Charmed, that, Intirely forgetting where he

---

[2]On Bavius, see above, III, 4, n. 1. Mevius was another poetaster who incurred Horace's and Vergil's wrath.

was, he fell directly to Composing of verses on this delightful
Subject, and hammered out a very pritty epigram of eight lines,
the Stile and turn of which was so peculiar, that it is yet unequalled by any bard that has since appeared, and is really an
original, having never been paralelled in former ages, by any
of the Bards of Antiquity.[3]

Immediatly, upon the appearance of this amorous epigram,
. . . the critics were in an uproar against it, they took this poor
Bards performance all to pieces, as is the custom with Critics in
these our degenerate days, and discried more blunders and In-
accuracies in it than there were words, Some of the Longstanding members of the Ancient and honorable Tuesday Club were
among these Critics, particularly Messieurs Blunt, Sly, Quaint
and Scribble, who exercised the acuteness of wit and Genius
pritty Smartly upon this unfortunate Bard, and were Joined by
others, . . . from Criticising in prose, they went to Satyrizing
and Lampooning in Rhime, So the Baltimore Bards & the Critics of the Tuesday Club strenuously contended who should out-
rhime, and who should outcriticise each other, . . . and some
who thought them wiser than themselves admired much their
wit, while others who had no opinion of their wisdom laughed
at their folly and assurance, and condemned them much, as Idle
and mischievous, in trowbling people that thought no harm
with such poetical Jargon. . . .

It came at last to that pitch, that even the weekly Journal of
Mr Jonathan Grog, entituled the *Maryland Gazette*, was stuffed
with comments, Reflections and Satyrs on this unfortunate Bard
and his performances, so, that it is thought he must Infallibly
have sunk under the pressure, of this formidable hostile power
of Critics, had not an Invulnerable Champion, stood up in his
defence, vizt: the tremendous Bard Bavius, who was reckoned

[3]This elegant epigram and the lampoons Hamilton mentions in the following paragraph appear in bk. III, chap. 7, of *The History of the Ancient and
Honorable Tuesday Club*, where he continued the story of the conflict between
the Baltimore Bards and the Annapolis Wits for another chapter.

by many the compleatest bard of the two, and Indeed, the most extraordinary bard, that was to be found, far or near, and not to be daunted, or put out of countenance, by the conjoint forces of all the Critics put together.

This Illustrious Bard, was of a stern, Severe countenance, whose Severity and Sterness, was of great use to the other, naturally mild, modest and timorous, since he was much asisted thereby, in bearing the violence and fury of the Attacks made upon him, by his professd foes, the Critics and Bards of the Tuesday Club.

This Gygantic auxiliary Bard, mustering up all his force and straining the Sublime of his genius to the utmost, advised the other, to show the dignity of his muse, by outsoaring all those pitiful bards and Critics, that set up against him, and, that he should have his asistance, in whatever Subject he undertook, it was then resolved, by these two eminent Baltimore Bards, over a bowl of punch and a pipe of tobacco, to pen a Sublime panegyric on the celebrated toasts and beauties of their county, under the title of *The Baltimore Belles*. This piece was then Immediatly set about, and the Muses Invoked, and being finished by these rapid Geniuses in a few hours, was carefully revised, corrected, and wrote out fair, It was read by Bard Bavius, in a Sonorous and theatrical tone of voice, much approved of by both bards, and after a Second third and fourth reading, was left lying on the table for further perusal and consideration, or, rather to be exposed to the eye of the public, that it might meet with the applause it so Justly deserved; being such a specimen of the Sublime, as exceeded the execution of all Bards whatsoever, either ancient or moderen, since the days of Pindar.

❋❋

The news of this soon reached the Clubical Bards and Critics at Annapolis, together with a copy of the composition it Self, who set about it, tooth and nail, and gave it no quarter. One, under the name of Doctor Philalethes, published in the *Gazette* No 34 an Infallible receipt to cure the Epidemical and afflicting dis-

tempers of Love and the poetical Itch.[4] Soon after, another
Learned Physician, who stiles himself Doctor Polypharmacus,
in *Gazette* No 41 publishes another recipe,[5] and seems to be
diffident of the efficacy of the former, according to the humor
of great Physicians, who commonly prefer their own Nos-
trums, to those of all the faculty besides, this Learned Gentleman, describes Bard Bavius, under a violent delirium or *furor
poeticus*, excited by a *febris Amatoria*, . . .[6] on the Doctor's first
feeling his pulse, he exclaims thus.

> A well turn'd praise requires the nicest Skill,
> And he who writes ill natur'd must write ill.

And again, upon being asked how he did, he bawls out

> Then let the Muse her tuneful numbers raise
> And praise the beauties for the Sake of praise.

❊❊

Upon this the Doctor applies cupping Glasses, as he says, to his
head, and gives him a large dose of hellebore, which procures
a copious and fætid Stool, after which the Bard exclaims

> Maria sings, now bid the Muses hear
> Or Call Apollo from the Crystal Sphere.

Polypharmacus on this, suspects a calenture, plies him with
cooling Glysters to Relieve the encephalon, and Claps Sina-
pisms to his feet, and soon after, he breaks out thus.

> See, Lovely Risteau![7] happy, hapless Maid!—
> Happy the man whom this fair Maiden loves,
> O happiest he, whom this fair maid approves,
> Great is her worth, yet useless and unknown,
> Or useful to her charming Self alone.

[4]This notice appeared in the *Maryland Gazette* (hereafter, *Md. Gaz.*), no.
34 (Dec. 17, 1745), 3–4.
[5]See *Md. Gaz.*, no. 41 (Feb. 4, 1746), 4. "Doctor Polypharmacus" and
"Doctor Philalethes" could well be Hamilton and his brother John.
[6]"Amorous fever."
[7]Catherine Risteau was the wife of Thomas Cradock.

The Phrensy of a Baltimore Bard

This last, the Physician observes, is a most remarkable Instance of the Bathos, and by this, he percieved that the Violence of the Distemper abated, and gives him his famous remedy, which he calls his *Neutrum quid*. . . .[8]

Soon after this Bard Bavius wrote his celebrated Letter to the City of Annapolis, which he Intends as a kind of prose Dunciad, Introducing all his critics and opponent Bards in some Ridiculous Character or other, here he learnedly criticises on the term *Neutrum Quid*, and, assuming the Character of a Physician himself, he proposes a Remedy, or *Methodus Medendi*,[9] so very much out of the common road, that never any thing like it was seen either before or since, nor, I believe, ever will be, in this transient world, the piece it self being Inimitable, and extraneously extravagant, in short, to cure those frantic poets, as he calls them, Mr Jonathan Grog . . . was to put them into his press or typographical machine, and, an operator with a Spatula was to extract excrementitious matter from their fundament, while Parson Sly was to sing a Psalm, to Comfort them under the operation; in this prophylactic dissertation our Bard displays his profound skill and knowledge in Chemistry, by absolutely pronouncing Doctor Polypharmacus a dunce, for using the term *Neutrum quid*, which he says is in it Self Stark nonsense, as Intending something that is only chip in porridge, or neither Chalk nor Cheese, then he slides into a Learned Enquiry into the nature of Ordure and excrement, to which he elegantly compars the works and compositions of his Antagonist Bards.

This Learned Epistle made some noise for a time among the wits and critics, particularly of Annapolis, and produced several learned criticisms, dissertations and essays; and certain critical and Explanatory Notes were wrote upon it in the names of Martinus Scriblerus & Hurlothrumbo,[10] the first in a grave, the other in a Burlesque Stile. . . .

[8]"Something that is neither of the two."
[9]"Method of healing."

Bard Bavius, the only person now aimed at (since his associate Mevius, had altogether retired and absconded,) was also
attacked by another wit, who appeared in the *Maryland Gazette*
No 47, under the Character of an advertiser;[11] This wit assumes
to himself, the name of Jehoiakim Jerkum, and is thought to
have been personated, by one or more of the Longstanding
members, of the ancient and honorable Tuesday Club, takeing
upon them the Character of a Master advertising his run away
Servant; Bard Bavius is mentioned in this advertisement, under
the names of Bard & Bavius, he is described as a fellow dis-
ordered in his Senses, wearing a String of Bells about his neck,
carrying with him several Stollen materials from the works of
Pope & Prior, together with abundance of Trash of his own. A
nasty Fellow, whose discourse turns chiefly on excrementitious
Subjects, of uncertain parentage, and therefore, in himself an
original, praising for the Sake of praise, and Censuring for the
Sake of censure, apt to bewray himself in company, thro' a re-
laxation of the *Sphincter ani*, and then lay the blame on others,
an Enimy to the Presbyterians, tho' himself a Muggletonian,
the profit of his poems for one hundred years to come, is offered
to those who go on the *Chace* after him, and apprehend him, as
it appears to be a difficult thing so to do, besides what the Law
allows in such cases.

This Burlesque advertisement, utterly silenced Bard Bavius,
and consequently, the other Baltimore Bard, whose Champion
he was, and effectually cured that pestiferous *furor poeticus*,
which had for some time raged in Baltimore, and set many
people a quarrelling, and as many a Laughing, and, the mem-

---

[10]Martinus Scriblerus was a pseudonym sometimes used by Pope (the *Memoirs of Martinus Scriblerus*, a prose satire against false learning, was published
in the second edition of Pope's works [1741]). *Hurlothrumbo* was the title
of a popular burlesque (1729) by Samuel Johnson, a Manchester dancing
master.

[11]See *Md. Gaz.*, no. 47 (Mar. 18, 1746), 4.

bers of the ancient and honorable Tuesday Club, that were concerned in this conflict and victory, valued themselves much upon it, as having largely Contributed to the peace and quiet of the public, nothing being more destructive to the good order of Society and private families, than the Scribble of the *Poætæ Minorum Gentium*,[12] whether Panegyrical or Satyrical, handed about either in Manuscript, or from the press.

Chapter 8 ❧ *The Election and Cathedration, of the Honorable Nasifer Jole Esqr, President.*

We are now come to that period, where we must bid adieu to Clubical Liberty, for, as the end of the Roman Liberty, was at the time of their admitting a perpetual Dictator, so, the period of the Liberty of the ancient and honorable tuesday Club, was, at their election of a perpetual President.

It may be well observed here, how artful men will gain upon the opinion and affections of a people, when they observe a mild, easie deportment and behavior towards them, and when they heap benefits and favors upon them unasked. This was the very case with Nasifer Jole Esqr, and the long standing members of the ancient and honorable Tuesday Club; This gentleman wore a complacent and mild countenance, always adorned with a Smile, and like Cæsar of old, flattered the people, that by gaining the ascendant over their affections, he might the more easily seize the Tyranny into his own hands, and govern their persons as he thought fit, neither did he spare any bounty

[12]"Lower-class poets."

in the way of entertaining, for, at the very first time of his being Steward, he Introduced into the Club that expensive Liquor called rack, . . . at the second time of his serving Steward, which was Sederunt 23d, he added an Iced cake to the entertainment, which was dealt about in Luncheons to the members, curiously wrap'd up in clean white paper, this Cake, this fatal Cake, Compleated the Catastrophe of the Clubs liberty, and, as Esau sold his birthright to Jacob, for fair words and a mess of porridge, so this unhappy Club, bartered their Liberty to Nasifer Jole Esqr, for an old Song, Rack punch, plumb pudding, four pound of Candles, and an Iced Cake!

But tho I condemn the conduct of the Club in this affair, yet, that I may do Strict Justice to that great and Illustrious personage, Nasifer Jole Esqr, I am Sincerely of opinion that the Club could not have pitched upon a milder or more Complacent governor than he, for, at all times, he has shown himself benign, gentle and easie to be entreated, and, excepting only in that nice point of giving up the least article or particle, of his valuable prerogative and privileges, of which he is Justly tenacious, he has spared no pains to humor the Club, in every thing they desired, as will be plainly seen in the Sequel of this History. . . .

It happened then, upon the memorable 26th of November, 1745 O:S: at Sederunt 24th, Mr Secretary Scribble being Steward, that the Club resolved to Chuse a perpetual president or Chairman, and The Illustrious Nasifer Jole Esqr, was proposed by Mr Smoothum Sly, as a proper person for the presidential Chair, But, Capt: Bully Blunt stood up, and opposed it, telling the Club That he did not know that Nasifer Jole Esqr, or any esquire whatsoever, had any Juster claim to the Chair, than any other member or Esquire, That, he humbly conceived, without the least grain of Vanity, that, he himself being also an Esquire, deserved as much that eminent place and office, as any Longstanding member in this here Club, . . . To this a member made reply—That if corpulency and enormous Size of body was a qualification for the Chair, Captain Blunt in that respect only was Sufficiently qualified. . . . It was also observed by the same member, after alittle pause, That Captain Blunt, was not at all in a proper dress, for such a Solemn ceremony, as that of being elected a president, for, granting that he was every other way worthy of the place, yet, the Dirty night cap, the long beard, and the greasy banyian, was by no means a propper apparel, in which to ascend a presidential Chair. Upon this, Captain Blunt Retired, and, in a few minutes after, to the Great Surprize of all the members, appeared, dressed out in his regimentals, as fine as if he had Just been taken out of a band box; . . . but all this fracas prov'd in vain; for, on putting about the vote, the members gave their voices for Nasifer Jole Esqr, and Captn Blunt had no other vote but his own, and Nasifer's, who modestly gave him his. Upon this Nasifer Jole Esqr, with great modesty declared to the Club, his Insufficiency for this high and dignified office, and Solemnly protested that it was a thing he by no means desired, and wished it had pleased the members to bestow it upon a person more Qualified for and worthy of the place. But this was only like Cæsar's putting aside the Crown faintly, when offered him by Mark Anthony, and Indeed, these professions with most of the members passed for words of course, and bare formal and complimentary Speeches.

❊❋

Then was he led by two members, vizt: Mr Smoothum Sly, and Mr Secretary Scribble, to a Semicircular Smoking Chair, which happened to be in the Room, and set down in it with his back to the door, which Capt: Blunt perceiving, Invidiously thrust open the door, and, his honor getting hastily up, the Chair was overset, and, to the Surprize of every body, there Tumbled out a Close Stool pan, which as good luck would have it, had none of its proper contents in it, thereupon, Capt: Blunt, observed with a Sneer, That the President had made a Shitten entry into his office, and he hoped he would make the like exit.

Thus, was this great man exalted to the office of perpetual

The unlucky adventure at the Cathedration
of the Honorable Carlo Nanfer Jole Esqr.

president of this ancient and honorable Club, and to this day, has kept his Seat Steadily in that Chair, and we shall now see him make a considerable figure thro' the Course of this History, sometimes ruling in peace and quietness, sometimes in the midst of disturbance and hurly burly, sometimes exalted, sometimes depress'd, by his Inconstant and unruly Longstanding members.

BOOK IV

From the Cathedration of the honorable Nasifer Jole Esqr, president, to the first grand Anniversary procession.

Chapter 2 ❧ *Of a great Club Ball, and matters of Gallantry, with the Clubical Character, of Nasifer Jole Esqr.*

I have heard it said of a certain orator and Rhetorician, who used in his time to mount the rostrum with a *bon grace*, and hold forth with a *grand eclat*, that what puzzled him more than any thing else, in his oratorial and Rhetorical compositions, and exercises, was how to make a good conclusion, or ending, for, as to the exordium, or beginning of an oration, it was as easy as to whistle, and he could flourish it away in that part after a very Sublime manner, but how to end or conclude, or indeed where properly to stop, without making many an Impertinent circumbendibus, was the difficulty, *hic labor, hoc opus;*[1] that is, it required the art of hocus pocus.

The Honorable Nasifer Jole Esqr, now president of the ancient and honorable Tuesday Club, was just in the same Situation as this orator and Rhetorician; he had begun, alas, with too great Success, to Introduce excess and Luxury in matters of eating and drinking into this here Club, and it would have been

[1]Hamilton has purposely botched a passage from Vergil (*Aeneid* 6.129): "Hoc opus, hic labor est" ("This is the task, this is the work").

well, had he stopped there. . . . But, at Sederunt 25th Decr: 10th 1745, The Club being held at the house of Jealous Spyplot Esqr, Steward, The Chair of State being prepared as ordered at last Sederunt, and set forth, at the head of the Club Table, the Honorable Nasifer Jole Esqr made his appearance, in a flamming Suit of Scarlet, a magnificent hat, bound round with massy Scolloped Silver lace, a fine large and full fair wig, white kid Gloves, with a gold headed cane, and I cannot be certain whether or not he had a Silver hilted Sword, with a beautiful Sword knot of Ribbons, white Silk Stockings rolld, large Shining Silver Shoe buckles, his coat and vest edged round with gold twist, . . . in this luxury of dress did he ascend the chair of state, and looked like a flaming comet in his perihelion, the laced hat resembling the resplendent body of the Star, the flaxen wig the tail, and the other sparkling parts of his dress, the Shining constellations surrounding it. . . .

Thus did this great man, Inconsideratly Introduce the Luxury of dress, into this here ancient and honorable Club, and we shall soon find some of the Longstanding Members Imitating him in this, and, such as never knew before, any other than a Simple plain dress, members wont to come to club *sans ceremonie,* with night caps not over clean, Slouch hats, ragged round the brim, long beards, banyans and greasy wrappers, in laudable Imitation, of their worthy predecessors of the Ugly Club, now we shall find, turning beaus, and Indulging themselves in all the extravagance of dress and finery, appearing in regimental Suits, long flowing black gowns, bands, and full bottomd wigs.

The extravagance of the members went so far at this Sederunt, being extremely elevated at seeing their honorable president exalted for the first time in his Chair of State, as that the following order was made, vizt:

"That on Tuesday, the 31 of December instant, there shall be a ball held at the Stadt house, for the entertainment of the Ladies, at the common expence of the Club. . . ."

O Luxury! O excess! whether wilt thou arive at last, wilt thou not, now thou hast begun, go on in an unwearied round, 'till thou hast utterly ruined and anihilated this ancient and honorable Club?

❋❋

The ball then was held at the time appointed, which happened to be an extreme cold night, and therefore the better for dancing, there were a great many Ladies and Gentlemen, and most of the members of the Club attended, the Cake was froze, but the wine and punch retained their Liquidity, the Longstanding members that chose to dance, danced; and those that chose not, looked on, and drank a bumper now and then to expand the Animal Spirits, . . . there were danced many minuets, country dances & Jiggs, and, there was as much bowing, cringing, complimenting, Curtsying, oggling, flurting and Smart repartees, as is usual on such occasions, and the Reverend Mr Sly, tho the gravity of his Cloth, would not permit him to dance, yet he made by much the Smartest figure, in Squiring the Ladies, comparing them, as they stood in a row, to the milky way, . . . and abundance of other droll witty and facetious repartees, puns, dowble entendres, and gallant Sarcasms passed, 'till that Gentleman, being called upon, by a lady to dance; he pretended to step aside alittle for his hat and gloves, but took care to abscond, and not make his appearance again that night upon the dancing Stage. In fine, every thing was conducted with great elegance, and mirth prevailed in the company, nothing being wanting to compleat all, but the presence of his honor the president, who, by his absenting that night, showed that he was not altogether pleased, with this piece of Gallantry.

As we have given in a preceeding part of this history, the private Character of his honor the president, we shall here give a small Sketch, of what we may call, his clubical Character.

❋❋

His chief foible was ambition and love of power, a fault peculiar to great men and heroes, this appeared by his extreme desire to grasp as much of that, as he possibly could, by his endeavoring to have all matters transacted in the Club, Solely by his own authority and Influence; by his enforcing and procuring Laws, to lodge the whole governing and managing authority in his own hands; by his extreme tenaciousness of the privileges already granted him, and vehement desire to have more added to them.

❀❀

He was very fond of punctillios Ceremonies, and distinguishing badges of honor, thinking they contained in themselves something very edifying, expressive and Significant, and the long Standing members soon finding out this weakness, in a Course of a few years, loaded him with ceremonies, and ornamented him with a superfluity of pompous accoutrements, till at last they effectually cured him of this malady, for he smelt a rat, and grew sick and tired of these farces as will appear in the Sequel.

❀❀

Vanity was none of the least of his foibles, and it was thought he had some opinion of the Elegance of his form and features, for, he generally chose, when in the Chair, to sit opposite to a large looking Glass, and to turn and wriggle his body into different attitudes, in order to show himself to himself to the best advantage, to stroke down his face and beard, adjust the foretop of his wig, and to affect a complacent Smile and Smirk of the countenance, tho' at times, when Speeches were made that displeased him, or Snappish replies or retorsions were given him by the Chancellor, there followed an elongation of countenance, and a droping of the Lower Jaw, which some of the members called his timber Countenance, which would have afforded no uncommon hint to the famous Hogarth.

❀❀

But this worthy and honorable Gentleman, if like other mortal men, he had his little foibles, he was at the same time endued with very great qualities, of which, his forgiveness, long Suffering, and Surprizing patience were none of the least; often has he been Insulted, and affronted even in the Chair, by petulent and Saucy long standing members, and as often has he bore it with heroic resolution, and Surprizing composure of mind; once was he dragged out of it, pulled about the room, tossed and hursled from corner to corner, his ruffles tore, his ensigns of State threatned to be burnt, he himself called a traitor, a tyrant, nay even an old fool, yet after all this, could this great man forget and forgive. . . . Often, while he was racked with the excruciating pains of the gout, has he walked, trotted and run about in great anguish to serve the club, often has he Immerged his feet in cold water, to the great peril of his life, merely to overcome the attacks of the gout, that he might be able to do the Services of the Club, often has he neglected his own affairs, for the affairs of the Club, and has lost many a night's rest, and wore out his Spectacles in perusing and examining Letters, commissions, petitions, remonstrances, Songs, poems, odes, Summons, epigrams, accrostics, Club conundrums, and other Clubical papers of great Importance and Significancy, to the danger of his eyesight health and understanding. . . . In short, his good qualities were so many, that he was the admiration of all members, and all Clubs, and were we to lose, this great and worthy president, heaven only knows when or where we could procure such another.

Chapter 4 ※ *The Introduction of set Speeches into the Club, and the members that made the Greatest figure that way.*

So Inherent is vanity in human nature, that it seems to be Inextricably Incorporated and Ingrained with it, so as that it cannot be separated or Extracted, by the most Subtile Chemistry, wash'd away by the strongest Suds or purged off by the purifying fire of purgatory itself.

This Inherent principle of vanity appears in nothing more, than the great desire most men have to Speech making, and engrossing to themselves a great share of the talk in all places of rendezvous, such as Coffee houses, Taverens, Teatables, but more particularly in Clubs.

The first long standing member that was seized with this pestilent itch of speech making, was the Secretary, who was one, not the least stocked with vanity, in this here Club. . . .

The Secretary executed the Laborious part of his office tollerably well, by entering all the proceedings of the Club in the book of records, but then, his natural vanity, or opinion of his own self Sufficiency appeared glaringly even in this the execution of his office, for he often would, without the advice of his honor the president, or the Club, enter matters, in what manner and form he pleased, which was often the Cause of great disgust and heart burnings betwixt his honor & the Longstanding members, since the president often urged and mantained, that the Secretary had no business to enter any thing there, but by his order and direction, and, that nothing relating to what the members did or said, had any title to a place in these Records, but his Actions and his Sayings alone should be entered, while on the other hand, the members thought, that their proceedings, debates and determinations, had as good a title to a place in the records, as the acts and Sayings of his honor the president; Thus the Club and the President differed among themselves, and both with the Secretary, who, notwithstanding the many grave and Sharp rebukes, which he had from the honorable Chair, and checks and threatnings from the Club, went on in his usual way and would still enter matters as he pleased, an Instance of perverse obstinacy as well as of vanity and Self conceit, and Indeed, a positive and wayward humor, was none of the least failings which this club officer could be charged with, by which he often Introduced confusion into the Government of this here Club, thereby drawing the Indignation of his honor

Loquacious Scribble Esq.
Secretary & orator of the anc: & hon: Tuesd: Club

Nostri ab archivis consortii, aspice Scribam
Qui tua verba, Jole! Stylo perenni arat:
Nec non facta tua lepido Sermone perorat,
Nestor a quem lingua vincere posse putes.

From the archives of our club, look upon the Scribe
Who plows out your words, O Jole! with eternal pen
And also recites your deeds in elegant style,
Whom you consider able to defeat Nestor at talking.

the president upon himself and the members; This Secretary was also of a Scheming, plotting, Restless disposition, and his plots and Schemes, tho generally carried on, under pretence of doing honor to the President, and for the advantage of the Club, yet, for the most part, terminated in mischievous purposes and attempts, either to make tools of the Longstanding members, or to derogate from the honor and prerogative of the honorable Chair, at least, this Gentleman was much belied by his honor and the Longstanding members, if he was not a Sly, cunning, Insinuating, deceitful, mischief making member, the continual Author and promoter of Brawls, wrangles, Jealousies, Grumblings, heartburnings, hubbubs and hurly burlys in this here ancient and honorable Club, . . . however, this may be said in his commendation, that he was a very constant and punctual attendant on the Club, and spared no pains to do every thing for its interest and advantage, where it did not Interfere or clash with his own, or stand in the way of his ambitious Schemes, to advance his own Influence in the Club, and make himself a person of weight and Importance, and in this indeed he resembled many other Secretaries and politicians, who, In Indifferent matters can give very good advice, but whenever Self is to be served, that must of necessity be done, tho every body else should go to the devil.

At Sederunt 29th febr: 25th 1745/6, Capt: Seemly Spruce being first deputy in the Chair, and Capt: Bully Blunt Steward, the Secretary stood up and Informed the Club that he had a discourse or Speech to deliver, and craved permission to deliver it; this Speech we must observe, had been prepared of his own head, without orders from the Club, to which he was in all probability prompted by his vanity, having surely this opinion of himself, that he had an excellent knack at Speech making, and that the Club could not otherwise than be mightily entertained and Instructed, with this Sort of Exercise, he had leave given him to deliver this discourse, tho' not without some grumblings from Capt: Blunt the Steward; . . . Damn the Speeches says he, we meet together in this here Club to smoke, Chat, and put about the bowl, and not to hear and make Speeches, however, being permitted to deliver this Speech, he put himself into a proper attitude for it, and Imagining that he had Cond it by heart, did not use his papers, but began to repeat it with a tollerable good grace; his Subject was the advantages reaped from Society, and some encomiums on Clubs, a thread bare and trite Subject, but put together in a tollerable Stile, The Secretary had gone thro' one half of this oration, smoothly enough, without hesitating, and the Longstanding members had given a close attention to it, when an odd Circumstance happened, which made the orator stop short all of a Sudden, and obliged him to fumble in his pockets for his papers, . . . the occurrence was this, Drawlum Quaint Esqr, a Longstanding member, was more attentive than any one else to this harangue, and the better to swallow what was delivered by the Secretary sat with his neck streeched out, his mouth wide open, motionless, every limb of his body remaining as still, as if he had been a piece of Sculpture, and, in his right hand he grasped his tobacco pipe, the extremity of the Stem about two Inches from his mouth, . . . this figure struck the Secretary, (happening to turn his eyes that way) in such a manner, that it obliterated at once, from his memory, all that he had been saying, and all that he had yet to say on the Subject, so finding himself at a Stand, and that he could by no means recover himself, he stoped short for some time, and had recourse to his papers.

The Club seemed to approve of this Speech, at least they did not condemn it, and they so well liked of this custom Introduced by the Secretary, that they ordered Mr Drawlum Quaint, to prepare a Speech to entertain the Club at next Sederunt, . . . and we shall soon find some other members excelling this way, vizt: Mr Solo Neverout, Capt: Serious Social, Mr Jealous spyplot & Mr Smoothum Sly, and even his honor the president

Mr. Secretary Scribble delivering a Speech in Club—

himself in a remarkable manner, display'd his Rhetorical and oratorial learning, in an elegant Speech that he delivered to the Club, which we shall relate in it's proper place.

※※

At Sederunt 30th March 11th 1745–6, the Revd Mr Smoothum Sly being deputy in the Chair, and Capt: Seemly Spruce Steward; Drawlum Quaint Esqr, Delivered a long Speech to the Club, the Subject of which was honesty, this Speech was delivered without notes, but was very sarcastical and Severe, the Gentleman took almost all professions, offices and callings to task, allowing a very small portion of honesty to any Station in life, particularly to Sheriffs and other public officers, tho he seemed to be very partial with regard to the Gentlemen of the Law (the orator being himself a Lawyer) this longstanding member had a peculiar action when he spoke, which attracted the Eyes of the audience, and fixed their attention as much as the Subject on which he harangued, he kept his body still and motionless, his head and Shoulders stooping forwards, extending his neck to a considerable length, his right arm streched out, with alittle bend of the elbow, the forefinger of his right hand in a pointing posture, wch he moved gently up and down, his chin, when he made a pause, dropping down on his breast, his left hand under the waste band of his breeches, and, when he had occasion to stop in his discourse, (which was pritty often) to consider of what he was next to say, he would like many orators spit or hawk, or Cough, or yawn, and, for these excellent qualities in oratorial action, as well as for his elegant Stile and phraze of *this here* and *that there*, he was soon after promoted, to the honorable place of Speaker to the Club, . . . the Satyr of this Discourse was chiefly pointed at Mr Neverout, then Sheriff of the County, who, at a preceeding Sederunt, undertook to prove that Mr Quaint was Dead, which argument he managed so artfully and Sophistically, that he seemed to Convince the Club that he really was a dead member, and they actually voted him such, Mr Neverout, the same night Elevated

with his Skill in argumentation, tho' Indeed, he had borrowed
most of his reasoning from the Celebrated Isaac Bickerstaff
Esqr, in his famous controversy with Mr Patridge,[1] . . .
thought he could go farther in displaying his great abilities, and
exhibit a Specimen of his poetical Genius, the occasion was this,
Mr Quaint had wrote a Satyr on him and some others, which
he entituled the *Reverend Scout,* In which was a relation of an
adventure of Solo Neverout Esqr, Mr Secretary Scribble, and
Mr Slyboots pleasant, who had one night a Set meeting with
some Celebrated Nymphs of the town, at one of these polite assemblies, called twopenny hops, . . . these Gallants and their
Nymphs were observed from a low window in the Street, by
two Scouts or spies, who, having Informed Councellor Quaint
therewith, he wrote the aforesaid Satyr, In which he distinguishes Mr Neverout, by the name of *Littlebreeches;* Neverout
still resenting this, was resolved to answer it in the same Satyrical and poetical Strain, but never compleated any more than
one Couplet, which he made in Club, and was as follows.

> Whilst at the window, stood two prying pimps,
> Scratching and wishing, for the Buxom Nymphs.

❋❋

These two great geniuses for sometime contended together with
weapons of wit, and, we must own, that Councellor Quaint at
last got the better, for, he gave the first provocation and had the
last word to himself, this noted oration of his intirely silencing
his antagonist. ❋❋

[1]Hamilton is referring to Jonathan Swift's "A Vindication of Isaac Bickerstaff Esq; Against What Is Objected to Him by Mr. Partridge, in His Al-
manack for the Present Year 1709," especially the passage beginning:
"Without entering into Criticisms of *Chronology* about the Hour of his
Death; I shall only prove, that Mr. Partrige is not alive" (*The Prose Works
of Jonathan Swift,* ed. Herbert Davis [Oxford, 1939–1968], II, 162).

Chapter 6 ✖ *The Creation of Sir John Oldcastle knight of the Club, and the privileges thereunto annexed, & the appointment of the master of Ceremonies.*

❧❧

At Sederunt 38, July the 8, 1746, Jealous Spyplot Esqr being Steward, his honor in a high presidential dress, ascended the Chair, and it being very warm weather, he first of all pulled off a voluminous fair wig, which covered two thirds of his face, and laying it Carefully, together with his hat and gloves under the Seat of the Chair, he drew from his pocket, a fair, clean, white Linnen night cap, which with profound gravity, he drew over his pericranium and ears, then pulling out a large Roll of paper in folio, and a pair of temple Spectacles, he wiped the latter with a fair Cambric handkerchef, first breathing on the Glasses to clean them, and then he saddled his nose with that catoptrical machine, and turning over the papers he put them in order, and looking round him for a little while, he fixed himself in a proper posture in the Chair of State, and, while two of the long standing members, vizt: the Secretary and Mr Neverout, held a candle to him on his right and left, behind the great chair, he, with great Solemnity, and a Clear distinct voice, without much action excepting only alittle nodding of the head, pronounced an elegant oration, of about half an hour in Length, the Subject of which was wisdom; the Stile of this oration was much like that of a Sermon, and some censorious people did not stick to say, that the very marrow and Substance of it, was taken from a Sermon composed by one Doctor South,[1] but this much

[1]Hamilton is alluding to "For the Wisdom of This World, Is Foolishness with God" (1 Cor. 3:19), sermon 9 in Robert South's *Twelve Sermons Preached upon Several Occasions* (London, 1692).

might be urged in vindication of his honor the president, whom
I would be loath to accuse of plagiarism, without better
grounds, that it is a very common thing, for Great and Sublime
Geniuses to agree in Sentiments, so far, as even to use the same
words, when writing or speaking on the same Subject, and
therefore, from this very reasonable Supposition we may conclude, that his honor, and the aforesaid Doctor South, expressed
themselves in the same manner on the same Subject, without
the least Intercourse, or Communication one with the other, but
what gave a Colour for this malicious Insinuation, were some
seeming Slips his honor made, in pronouncing of some words
used by the said Doctor South, such as *Chous* for *Chaos*, which
made some rashly conclude, that his honor the president, did
not understand the meaning of these words, but how Silly and
groundless is this Insinuation, seeing it has always been customary, for great Geniuses to alter not only the Common Orthog-
raphy, but also the Common pronounciation of words, Just as
they please, which being Imitated by persons of small Genius,
has for ever been the principal cause of the Instability and fluctuation of our Language.

The first Symptoms of Joy, that broke out among the members,
upon this gracious condecention of his honor, appeared in their
Extraordinary liberalities to the [Club] box, which looked like
the Largesses of a British parliament to the Crown, after a most
gracious Speech from the throne, among others, Slyboots pleasant Esqr, contributed one pistole, the secretary four Shillings
and Sixpence, and the Sum now in the box, amounted to five
pounds, three Shillings and Sixpence, an Immense Sum, to be
collected in so short a space as half a year.

At these proceedings Capt: Blunt, seemed to grumble and be
uneasy; being, as he said, Justly alarmed, at the growing power
of the Chair, on which, his honor the president, having some

reason to be afraid of the Influence of this Old Standing member, Saluted him, by the title of knight, and Champion of the Club, under the name of The worshipful *Sir John Oldcastle,* knight of the Ancient and honorable Tuesday Club, and ordained, as a principal privilege of his noble office, that he should sit at the right hand of the Chair; Sir John, could not help showing, thro' the wonted gloom of his warlike countenance, some Satisfaction and Joy, at this unlooked for promotion, but pretended at the same time not to be satisfied, and refused to take his place, unless ushered in a proper manner, upon this, his honor Immediatly nominated and Created the Reverd: Mr Smoothum Sly, Master of Ceremonies, or Sir Clement Cotterell, to the ancient and honorable Tuesday Club, who Instantly rose from his Seat, took the Worshipful Sir John Oldcastle by the right hand, and placed him upon the right of the presidential Chair, . . . Thus did this Club, Inconsideratly permit the raising of great officers among themselves, and putting them above law, and hereby were Instrumental in establishing an Intollerable Tyranny over the long standing members, by strengthning the already overgrown power of the Chair, which occasioned a deal of trowble and perplexity, to this here ancient and honorable Club, as was wisely forseen and foretold by Jealous Spyplot Esqr, a Sagacious Oldstanding member, who always opposed these mad proceedings, and seldom Judged wrong in these cases.

漱漱

Chapter 7 ❧ *The Creation of the Speaker of the Club, & his privileges, and also of the Chief musician and his privileges.*

No more blue Stone good Doctor, is an old proverb, of which, I was never able to learn the first broacher, but waving such enquiries, my design in Introducing it here, is only for the Sake of the application, when any proceeding or piece of conduct, has been found hurtful to those who have practised it, or to those upon whom it has been practised, there follows an uneasy Sensation in the Suffering persons, much like that occasioned by the application of causticks in Surgery, and therefore they have the same reason to call out, no more of this, we feel the Smart of it too much already; One would think, that the ancient and honorable Tuesday Club, had already Sufficiently smarted, by the late proceedings of the chair, in creating two great officers, and had very good reason to exclaim, No more officers, good Mr President; but not a word of complaint on the matter, they were too much benumned and stupified, to feel the twinge that was given them, and Instead of exerting themselves to put a Stop to these proceedings, they allowed another state officer, and another officer of the Commons to be palmed upon them, so that it was likely that in a short time, the whole club would become State officers, and officers of the commons, and so all the Crew, being Quarterdeck men, as the Saying is, there would be no hands left to heave out the long boat, and therefore, the Ship of this Clubical common wealth, must of Consequence soon founder, or become a wreck.

❦❧

[At Sederunt 45th, October 14th, 1746,] the Secretary, in the place of Mr Quaint, delivered an extempore speech, which chiefly consisted in Encomiums upon Mr Quaint as a Speaker, of which Speech the Club approved, and he had the thanks of the same delivered from the mouth of Mr Quaint.

Hereupon, Drawlum Quaint Esqr, In consideration of his uncommon Talent at Speech making, was unanimously constituted and appointed, honorable Speaker of the Club, by his honor the president; this piece of mischief, the Secretary was principally concerned in, and we shall always find this petty officer, in the sequel of this history busying himself in mischief, and contriving schemes and projects, to set his honor the president and his Longstanding members together by the ears. He was a cunning, Sly and conceal'd operator, for advancing the Authority of the Chair, and, tho the honorable the president, always took him for an enimy to, and an underminer of his prerogative and privileges, yet, it will appear in the course of this history, that all his actions, designs and plots (under a mistaken policy to advance himself) had a tendency to establish a tyrannical power in the Club.

[At Sederunt 48 Novr: 25th, 1746,] Solo Neverout Esqr, being gifted with an excellent musical voice, entertained the Club with a Song, which, as it became the Subject of frequent contests and trials of Skill, between his honor the president and him, which should sing it most musically, and apply the best air to the words, we shall here give a transcript of it.

Club Song, sung by Mr Neverout[1]

> When Cloe we ply,
> We swear we shall die,
> Her Eyes do our hearts so enthrall.
> But 'tis for her pelf,
> And not for herself,
> 'Tis artifice, artifice all, all, all,
> 'Tis artifice, artifice all.

[1]"When Chloe we ply" appears in Allan Ramsay's *Tea-table Miscellany* (1724–1732), II, 63–64.

The maidens are coy,
They'll pish, and they'll fie
And swear if you're rude they will bawl,
But they whisper so low,
By which you may know
'Tis artifice, artifice all, all, all,
'Tis artifice, artifice all.

The wives they will cry
My dear, if you die,
To marry again, I ne'er shall,
But less than a year
Will make it appear,
'Tis artifice, artifice all, all, all,
'Tis artifice, artifice all.

❧❀

This song Mr Neverout performed, so much to the satisfaction of the Club, that they determined according to the following entry, which appears upon record.

"Solo Neverout Esqr: on account of his uncommon talent at Singing, is, by unanimous consent, appointed Chief Musician *con voce* of the Club, and, that, as often as he votes, he is to sing it in a musical manner, else his vote to go for nothing."

❧❀

Chapter 8 ❧ *The laudable custom of epistolary writing Introduced into the Club, the title of high Steward, and the first grand Anniversary procession.*

Human wit (if I may be allowed the expression,) is an active and restless principle, it can never be kept quiet or still, but will always be nibbling, if any of my readers object to this proposition and these terms of art, in stiling wit a principle, I shall only tell them, that they must even take the proposition and terms as they stand; I never having had leisure enough to study Logic or Metaphysics; but as I endeavor, never to use reflections foreign to my purpose, so, I think I have brought in this short apothegm, much *a propos*, in this particular part of the history, for we now find the epidemical distemper of Speech making and declaiming, thrust out of doors by the members, and the whole Quantum left of that *Cacoethes*[1] lodged in the honorable the speaker, who at times was very sparing of it, and dealt it out in small parcells to the members as occasion served. What then must take place of this declaiming humor, now ceased among the members of this ancient and honorable Club? for, it cannot be supposed, that their wit can lie fallow or Idle, no, it must have something to nibble at, or a crust to chew, and accordingly we find the humor of Epistolary writing take place among the members of the Club. . . .

The first essay of this kind from his honor, was at Sederunt 53 February 24th 1746/7, Dumpling Gundiguts Esqr, being deputy president, and Smoothum Sly Esqr high Steward, (the first who bore that title) when a letter directed to the Secretary, from his honor, and another to Mr Sly giving him the title of high Steward, were produced and read in Club.

To Loquacious Scribble Esqr,
Secretary to the Tuesday Club, These,

To be opened, and read to the Gentlemen when they are all met.

Gentlemen,

As I cannot be at the Club this night, have appointed Mr Spyplot to take my place in the Chair, not doubting but my choice will be agreeable to you all, and as I understand some of

[1]Evil habit.

the members, will not be able to come, it's probable you'll post-
pone the resolves of the last Club to our next meeting, and if
the Reverend Signr: Lardini, one of our worthy honorary
members, be with you, as have heard he will, Mr Speaker
being absent, must desire the favour of Mr Secretary to make
my compliments of congratulation on his appearance in Club,
after so long an absence—I wish you very merry, and hope
you'll meet with nothing to obstruct it, I respectfully Salute
you, and am Gentlemen,

> Your most humble Servant
> *Nasifer Jole.*

P:S: I understand that Mr Spyplot is not in town, so, if he does
not come in time, have appointed Mr Gundiguts to take the
Chair in his room.

The Letter to the High Steward was as follows.

To the Revd: Mr Smoothum Sly, high Steward
of The Tuesday Club, These.

Sir   Febr: 24th 1746/7
   I Just now received your message, per the Negro Man, and,
in answer to it's contents, as I cannot be at the Club this night,
have wrote to Mr Secretary Scribble, To signify the same to you
and the other Gentlemen at meeting of the Club, and am, Sir,

> Your humble Servant
> *Nasifer Jole.*

❋❉

The Stile of these letters is so peculiarly neat and elegant, that
we cannot ommit transcribing in this history all letters from his
honor, that are now upon record relating to the Club, since the
ommission of this would be an Irreparable loss to posterity, who
must certainly profit, by this patterne of stile and politeness.
The terms in these letters—*have appointed,* for I have appointed,—*as have heard,* for, as I have heard—*per the negro*

man, for by the negroe man, show plainly that Mr Jole had
studied the mercantile Stile, and made himself perfect in that
elegant and ornate manner of writing.

❦❦

As the Anniversary of the Clubs Institution, happened upon
thursday the 14th day of may next ensuing, the Club adjourn'd
it self to that Day, no anniversary committee being appointed,
but, the honorable the president, whose privilege and turn it
was to serve on that day, thought fit to adjourn farther 'till Tuesday the 26th of may, when his honor said, probably Green peas
and Gooseberries would be in Season, which would be a great
addition to the Anniversary Supper; It was accordingly celebrated on that day, being Sederunt 58th, with abundance of
pomp and Solemnity, the Regular members, and four of the
Honorary members, vizt: the Revd Messrs Broadface Round,
and Lardini, Mr Merry Makefun and Capt: Huffbluff Surly,
waited upon his honor the president, at his own house, ornamented with their badges and Ribbans, and went with his honor
in Solemn procession, marching two and two, his honor and
Sir John Oldcastle leading up the Van, and Mr Protomusicus
Neverout, and Secretary Scribble, closing the rear, to the house
of the honorable Mr Speaker Quaint, where the Anniversary
feast was kept, his honor and his longstanding members, thus
marching along, . . . were Sufficiently stared at, as they passed,
by persons of all Ranks and degrees, who seemed to be as much
astonished, as the mob is at a coronation procession, or any such
Idle pageantry, This was called the first grand anniversary
procession, and the only one, ever honord, with the presidents
presence.

❦❦

The honorable the Speaker, was desired by the Secretary, in the
name of his honor the president and Club, to open this grand
Anniversary meeting with a Speech proper upon the occasion,
but Mr Speaker, not being in the humor of Speech making,
like many other grandees, who are either above doing the duty

of their office, or utterly unqualified for it, desired to be excused, and requested the Secretary to officiate for him, which the Secretary did, directing his discourse to Sir John Oldcastle in the Chair, and to the other members of the Club, and then in particular, to the Speaker and Chief musician, congratulating the Club, on it's entry on the third year of it's Institution; to this Speech, the honorable the Speaker returned a short answer of thanks. By these opportunities, of exercising his elocution, the Secretary found means of making himself a considerable person in the Club, and at last, acquired such a knack at making speeches, that in spite of opposition, he worked himself into the office of orator to the Club, and became thereby the author and Instigator of much mischief and discord in the Club, as will be made appear in the course of our History.

BOOK V

*From the first grand
Anniversary procession,
to the foundation of the
Eastren Shore Triumvirate.*

Chapter 1 🦌 *A Chapter of Triffles, and concerning Clubbical Critics and Anticlubarians.*

Were it not for triffles, says a certain philosopher, (which I know only by hearsay) the world would be but very scurvily entertained, and life would hang on us like a heavy Clog, . . . whoever doubts of this doctrine, let him read the works of Solomon, that Royal preacher, whom I look upon to be a philosopher of no mean degree, that knew well the nature of triffles and vanities, among which he Classes all Sublunary enjoyments, after having himself had a taste of all.

Triffles and vanities are but Synonomous terms, and therefore, all that passes in this transitory life, this petty scantling of time, which we have allotted us to peregrinate thro' this absurd worldly wilderness, and to rant our Comical, or (as some are pleased to call it) tragical parts out upon this terrestrial Stage, is but of a triffling nature, why should any saucy, pert, demure, pricise, finical coxcomb of a Clubical Critic, to say no worse of him, nay, any Chuckleheaded, unexperienced, raw, Saucy Jackanapes pretend to say, that this our famous History, is more triffling than any other history, or this our ancient and honorable Club more triffling in it's constitution, government, model, form and Conversation, than any other Society whatsoever, great or small, be it Empire kingdom, Commonwealth corporation or Club.

But, to particularize alittle, what did Cæsar Conquer for? a Triffle; . . . what was the Grandure of the Roman Empire? a triffle a vapor, an evanescent Smoke; . . . what is the learning and wisdom of philosophers? a triffle; what is the Splendor, equipage and pomp of great princes? a triffle; what are Crowns, triple Crowns, Coronets, mitres, . . . truncheons, Stars and Garters? all transitory, vain, perishing triffles, bawbles, toys, in which the great babies of this world delight; What is a great man, attended by his Levee of pimps, liars, flatterers, Sycophants, parasites and hungry dependants? a damnd Superlative, unequalled unparalelled triffle, a paragon of triffles, the Sum Substance, essence and cause efficient of all the other evanescent triffles about him, since he contains them all, and they him, since they think by him, act by him, live by him, move by him, breath by him, and by him they have their being, not as rational men, which god made them, before they mangled god's work— but as fools, prigs and Coxcombs, which their foolish patron molded them into. . . . What are all human Enquiries, learned discourses, Dissertations, explications, comments, paraphrases and Annotations? Triffles! Triffles! the mockery of Learning, and the very Image of Ignorance. What are all the Charms of the fair Sex, all their allurements, all their Smiles, all their blandishments, all the pleasures in the lump, which they are able to afford? perfect, paultry perishing, good for nothing triffles. To sum up all, what is this Globe and all its Contents, compared to the General System of nature? an atom, a triffle, a thing of nothing; what the General System of Nature compared to endless space? a Spec, a triffle, a grain of dust; and what are all these to the Supreme Essence? more than a triffle, and less than nothing if possible.

Say then, ye wise men of Gotham, ye round heads of this world, with what face of Impudence can you assert, that this here History of ours, is a triffling History and this here Club a triffling Club, comparatively speaking, since there is not an ace difference between what you call Serious, Solid and rational, and all the triffles that you can ransac and cull out, in this our history, . . . which In fact are not more arrant triffles, than these other triffles that are to be met with in the histories of great Empires kingdoms, commonwealths, and in the Memoirs of the Characters and lives of mighty Emperors, kings, Generals and Commanders of armies.

Will you have the Impudence to say, that Julius Cæsar was a greater man than Nasifer Jole Esqr, because the first was Emperor over great territories, and the latter only President of a little paltry Club; Surely no, consider the Inscription, which Cyrus the great ordered to be put upon his tomb, and you'll find no difference between great Emperors and presidents of Clubs, The Inscription runs thus, *"O Man, whosoever thou art, and from whence soever thou comest, for I know thou wilt come, I am Cyrus, the founder of the great persian Empire, do not envy me this little portion of earth that covers my body,"* and pray does not an emperor take as small a portion of the Earth to lye in, as a president of a Club. . . . Again, will you pretend to assert with a grave composed countenance, . . . that the Roman, or the Russian, or the Turkish or the Persian or the Chinese Empires, are greater than this here Club, because they are Empires, & this here Club only a Club? Surely no,—and why pray? Why thus,—Is there any difference but in Size or Magnitude? are not the parts of a mite, as perfect as those of an Elephant, tho smaller? has not a mite its Sinews, nerves, arteries, veins, . . . Stomach, Intestines, genitals, legs, feet, toes, hair, Skin &ct: as well as an Elephant, and wherein do they differ but in magnitude of body? Has not the Tuesday club, it's president, State officers, officers of the Commons, Longstanding members,

honorary members, and an Empire or kingdom, it's Emperor
or king, prime ministers, rulers, nobles, commons &ct: and
wherein I pray do they differ but in bulk.

But take me along with you, ye conceited Sophisters, ye paultry reasoners of this world, Pray does not an Emperor eat, drink
and sleep as much as a president; does he not stink at times as
hideously as a president? does he not prevaricate, swear, cheat
and lie as grossly as a president? does he not tyrannize, oppress,
fornicate, whore, kill and massacre as much, nay more than any
president? . . . may he not be poxed as well as a president? may
he not have the plague, the hyppo, the palsey, . . . the Ripples,
the whiffles, nay the Itch as well as a president?[1] Nay, may he
not play the fool as much as a president? what then is the difference between an Emperor and a president, and in what does
it consist, a triffle, believe me, a very triffle, and not worth Contending for.

❊❊

I question not, but I shall be asked, why I should fall into this
odd Rhapsody, this rant, which they'll say looks as if it had been
hatched in Bedlam? but let me tell you my grave, Serious
friends, (whom I shall take the liberty to call by no worse name
than Anticlubarians,) that your ridiculous, Silly, and Idle remarks, uttered with a grave tho unmeaning face, and an Empty
head, against the Lawful recreations of Innocent mirth, and In-
offensive drollery, has been the occasion of all this rant, so, if
I have Committed any mortal Sin, at your doors I lay it, ye
Impertinent, precise, Stiff, Starch'd up, Cynical Logerheads.
I know you'll say, ye good for nothing wiseacres, ye mock
critics, and bungling molders of modes and manners, that such
Clubical pastime is beneath the dignity of rational creatures,
and wise men; but tell me, ye pragmatical dunces, . . . are you
never Employed about amusements less becoming a rational na-

---

[1] *Hyppo* is an obsolete abbreviation for *hypochondria*; *ripples* refers to a weakness in the back accompanied with shooting pains; *whiffles* refers to an attack
either of bragging or of farting, probably the latter.

ture, than these droll, facetious, gelastic and harmless Clubical recreations? do you never whore? do you never game? do you never swear? do you never lie? do you never flatter? do you never Idle your time away in insipid flat, childish and unprofitable Conversation? among fops like yourselves? . . . Wise men indeed! pray who made you wise men? on what ground do you claim that title to yourselves? is it on account of your knowledge? is it on account of your Learning? your knowledge is nothing, when compared to your vanity and Self conceit, and your Learning is Collected from broken Scraps of plays, Romances, Lewd authors,[2] title pages and hearsay, do you pretend to know more than Socrates, who, tho' the wisest of the Athenians,—of the greeks, and consequently of the whole world in his time, yet declared that *he knew nothing*. . . . But if you persist still, and say these Low clubical humors are Inconsistent with philosophy, pray what do you take Philosophy to be? . . . I tell you ye dunces, that there is nothing more gay, more frolicksome and (if I may so speak) more Jocose than Philosophy.

❀❀

But I shall leave you here, ye Incorrigible Anticlubarians, . . . ye Eternal trifflers, I shall bid you an eternal Adieu in this very place, and henceforth take no more notice of you than if you were not in being, or never had been hatched, which, had things really turned out so, would not have been a farthing's matter, either of profit or Loss to the world. . . .

Let me only conclude with this condolatory exclamation; Oh how I pity you, for your want of the true taste of life; for the want of that blessed humor, which set Democritus a Laughing, and Heraclitus a crying, . . . for, ye dry withered Stocks of human Society, Ye Statues and poppets in human form, you can neither laugh nor Cry in earnest, nature has absolutely denied you the power of both, and like a parcel of upstart mushroms, ye come into the world, and like a flitch of Smoked bacon, whose

[2]Unlettered, or untaught, authors.

Salt is soaked out, you go out of it, dry, dead, musty, Insipid and Sapless, having never in your lives enjoyed the Sweets and delights of clubical humors and recreations, without which life is not worth enjoying, but is a *tabula rasa*, or a *Cart Blanch*, or rather a blotted Scroll or Scutcheon, in which nothing of Sense or Significancy can be read or discerned. . . .

Chapter 2 🦟 *The accusation of the Speaker and Chief musician, and some other triffling occurrences.*

Socrates the Athenian philosopher, . . . being one day standing, or walking, or Lying or sitting, (it matters not how, or where,) under a plane tree, with the beautiful Phædrus, in a Sultry Summer's day, when the Sun shone bright, and the plains and the mountains and the fountains smoked again, while the Cattle stood under the Shady trees, . . . and switched their Sides with their tails to keep off the flies, and the Grasshopers Chirruped and sung, he took that opportunity to tell him a tale, how Grasshopers were once musicians, orators and poets, before the muses were born, and lived without meat and drink (as god knows many poor poets do now at this very day) and for that cause were turned by Jupiter into Grasshoppers, which is a creature, that like the Camelion, is said to live upon pure air.

It is very probable, that the honorable Mr President Jole, and the Longstanding members of the ancient and honorable Tuesday Club, remembering this tale of Socrates or some other such antiquated tale, thought, that their Orator, vizt: the honorable Mr Speaker Quaint, and their musician, the good Mr Proto-musicus Neverout, were like these ancient musicians and Orators, whom Jupiter turned into grasshoppers, that is, that the diet fittest for them was air, . . . for as they vended nothing

but air to the Club, in their vociferations, when the one sung
and the other declaimed, so they had nothing but air in return
for their Labor, that is Sound, of which air is the medium, excited either by loud laughing, or clapping of hands, by way of
applause. As for other rewards, they had not so much as the
value of one single farthing, to help, as the Saying is to keep
life and Soul together, this cold Comfort surely, together with
the notion of their being very great Club officers, and above
doing their duty, made them negligent and remiss in their respective offices, so that it was now a very rare thing, to hear
either a Speech from the honorable the Speaker, or a Song from
the tuneful Mr Proto-musicus; which attracted the hawks eyes
of that cunning and politic officer the Secretary, and gave
ground for an accusation brought against these two eminent
Club officers by him at two several Sederunts for negligence and
remissness in their respective offices, but these accusations were
little regarded by the Club, and in a manner slured over, the
reason of which probably was, that his honor the president was
Suspicious, (as he constantly professed to be) of the Secretaries
designs, Imagining, and perhaps with some reason, that this
Cunning menial Club officer, wanted one or other of these great
Club officers to be degraded, that he might step into his place,
as this is the common practice of great Statesmen and officers,
who generally envy one another, and the understrappers among
them are always on the Gape, for the places of those above them,
wishing and praying daily with great fervency, that they may
either be displaced, die, or go to the Devil, the Secretary probably might have some such designs in his Noddle, but then, it
must have been the honorable the Speaker's place he aimed at,
for, he was by nature so unfit for the other, that he knew as little
how to sing, as a bull-frog or a goose, and far less than a Swan,
Cricket or Grasshopper. ※《

At Sederunt 60, June 23d, 1747, Slyboots Pleasant Esqr, being
high Steward, the Secretary vented his Spleen against the Chief

musician, by accusing him of negligence in his office, as he had done the Speaker on the preceeding Sederunt, but the Club acquitted him, on account of his good performances, at other times, and as an acknowledgement of the favor, he entertained the Club, with [an] excellent new [Song]. . . .

New Song, sung by Mr Protomusicus Neverout[1]

When Orpheus went down to the regions below,
    Which men are forbidden to see,
He tun'd up his lyre, as old histories show,
    To set his Euridice free—To set &ct:

All hell was Surpriz'd, that a person so wise
    Should rashly endanger his life;
But, O ye good gods! how vast their Surprize,
    When they knew that he came for his wife.

To find out a punishment fit for his fault,
    Old Pluto had puzzl'd his brain,
But hell had not Torments Sufficient he thought,
    So he gave him his wife back again.

But pity succeeding, soon vanquish'd his heart,
    Being pleas'd with his playing so well,
He took her again, in reward of his art,
    Such power had music in hell.

It would seem by the above song, sung on such an occasion, that Mr Protomusicus Intended, not only to cox and sooth his honor the president, by as it were comparing him to the great Pluto, king of hell, but likewise made an excellent elogium on himself as a musician, by likening himself to Orpheus.

❊❊

[1]"Orpheus and Euridice" appears in *Calliope, or English Harmony,* 2 vols. (London, 1739, 1746).

Chapter 5 ❧ *Election and admission of Jonathan Grog Esqr.*

Magninus says, that a merry Companion is better than a Song, and, as the old proverb goes, *Comes Jucundus in via pro vehiculo*, a Jocular fellow to a man in the moaps is as a waggon to a Jaded foot travellar,[1] for mirth may be said to be the Nepenthe of Homer, Hellen's bowl and Venuse's girdle or Cestis. . . . The old greeks had their *Lubentiam Deam*, their Goddess of mirth, and the Spartans, Instructed by their Lawgiver Lycurgus, did *Deo Risui sacrificare*, sacrifise to the God of Laughter, after their wars especially, and in times of peace, which was practised in Thessaly, as appears by Appuleius Book 2d of the *Golden Ass*, who was himself made the Instrument of their laughter, why therefore might not the ancient and honorable Tuesday Club, after their hot disputes, and In their Calmer Intervals, by the Instruction of the honorable Nasifer Jole Esqr, their wise president and Lawgiver, make themselves merry, be Jocose, and execute their great gelastic Law, one upon another? And this we shall find they often effectually did, making use for an Instrument on these occasions, of Jonathan Grog Esqr, as the Thessalonians did of Appuleius, and, of the admission of this facetious Gentleman, we are now going to give an account.

❧❧

[On Sederunt 74th February 2d 1747/8,] upon a motion made by the Master of ceremonies, to Elect Mr Jonathan Grog of Annapolis, a member of the Club, he having made application, for the same to several of the members, the ballots, or Yeas and Nays were put Round by the Secretary, . . . and being found all Yeas, the Secretary was ordered to acquaint the said Mr Jonathan Grog of this, by writing, desiring his attendance at next Sederunt. As

---

[1]Jean-Chrysostome Magnen (fl. 17th century), a French physician and philosopher, was the author of *Democritus reviviscens* (1646), to which Hamilton is referring.

this gentleman, will in the Succeeding part of our History, make a very considerable appearance, as a longstanding member of this ancient and honorable Club, holding no less than five offices at one and the same time, vizt: those of purveyor, punster, punchmaker General, Printer and poet, which were signified, for brevity's Sake, by five capital P's thus, Jonathan Grog Esqr, P.P.P.P.P. it will not be amiss here, to give an Iconographical description of his person, and a Scetch of his Character.

This Gentleman is of a middle Stature, Inclinable to fat, round faced, small lively eyes, from which, as from two oriental portals, Incessantly dart the dawning rays of wit and humor, with a considerable mixture of the amorous leer, in his countenance he wears a constant Smile, having never been once seen to frown; his body is thick and well set, and for one of his make and Stature he has a good Sizeable belly, into which he loves much to convey the best vittles and drink, being a good clean knife and forks man, tho' no Glutton, and his favorite Dish is Roast turkey with oisters, and his darling liquor of late is Grog, he professing himself to be of the moderen Sect of the Grogorians, . . . he is a very great admirer, Improver and encourager of wit, humor and drollery, and is fond of that Sort of poetry which is called Doggrell, in which he is himself a very great proficient, and Confines his genius chiefly to it, tho sometimes he cannot help emitting some flashes of the true Sublime, in his Club Compositions; puns, Conundrums merry tales and Jests, are the favorite Subjects, on which he Chuses to exercise his wit and talents, and we shall find him affording abundance of mirth to the Club, in his compositions of this Sort, in fine, to sum up all he is really a good humored, smooth tempered, merry, Jocose, and Innofensive companion, a man of the most happy Clubical Genius that ever was known, and a Great promoter Improver and encourager of Clubific felicity, for were there 50 Clubs in the place, he'd be a member of every one of them.

※※

Jonathan Grog Esqr. poet Laureat & pres of Ceres of the J.C.

Ecce poetarum Clubicorum facile princeps,
Qui de te Cole, Scripsit lepidos versiculos,
Dum hi Leguntur, nunquam tua fama peribit
Cole, nec Insignis gloria nostri vates.

Behold of Clubic Bards the prime
Who sings thee, Cole, in pleasant Rhime,
And whilst his rhime is read, thy fame,
Shall live, so shall our poets name.

Chapter 8 ❧ *A Letter of Condolance wrote to his honor the President, Election of four Longstanding members, and other trivial matters.*

It was with this ancient and honorable Club, as it is with humorsome Children, to whom they say have your Cake and eat your Cake, or some fractious people, to whom is applied the Scotch proverb, *you'll neither dance, nor hold the candle;* so, this Club seemed never to know when they were well, either with, or without the honorable the president, for, when he was present, it was nothing but contention, wrangling, Jangling and brangling, about prerogative and privilege, presidential authority, and Clubical Liberty, and when he was absent it was nothing but pining, whining and declining. It was now the Season of the year for his honor to be laid up with the gout, which Calamity occasioned his absence from Club at Sederunt 96th, therefore, the Club, before breaking up, ordered the Secretary, to write a condolatory epistle to his honor, . . . this was done in prose, as the poetical Genius of the Club, had not as yet broke out in its full Glory, but, on all the following occasions of the like nature, this Condolatory address was penned in verse, this Epistle Run as follows.

By order of the Deputy President and Club, January 17th 1748/9.

To the Honorable Nasifer Jole Esqr,
President of the Tuesday Club.

Honorable Sir,
It is with regret that we address your honor upon this lamentable occasion, an Occasion which affords more pain than pleasure, as the Subject is disagreeable.

That gratitude and respect, which is due from us to your honor, as our most worthy president, obliges us to express some marks of concern, for your honor's Indisposition, and therefore we have ordered our Secretary to write you this our Epistle of our proper Inditing and framing, by which, we mean to Intimate our good wishes for your honor's speedy recovery, and our Sincere concern, since that, by reason of Sickness, we reap not the advantage, of your Gracious and precious presence & direction.

Our Club is now, as it were in a State of Anarchy, the rudder wants a skillful pilot to steer this our Clubical vessel in a right course, the deputy president falls fast asleep in the Chair, Sir John, the Champion looks like a *Mope in the Moonshine*, the Ladies are but faintly toasted; music and Song are quite mute, mirth and laughter are no more, our eye-sight turns dim in the glimmering of the candles, so, that we may say, with a certain great and wise preacher, *those that look out at the windows are darkened, and all the daughters of Music are brought low.*[1]

We have only one thing left to Comfort us, which is, that the Indisposition your honor Labors under is not of so malignant and mortal a nature as to extinguish our hopes of again partaking and enjoying your honorable presence, and benign Influence, which, that it may speedily happen, is the earnest desire, and ardent prayer of, Honorable Sir,

From the Club Room,	Your most affectionate and
Jan: 17th 1748/9	dutiful members of your ancient
	and dignified *Tuesday Club*
	Signed p: order of, and in the
	name of the Club,
	Loquacious Scribble Secrtry

✳✺

The following Sederunt, being the 97th Janry 31, 1748/9, Capt: Seemly Spruce being high Steward, and Jonathan Grog

[1]Hamilton has patched together two lines from Eccles. 12:3, 4; the persona of Ecclesiastes is repeatedly referred to as "the preacher."

Esqr, by special Commission, deputy president, was one of the
most Remarkable that ever happened in this here Club, for election of members, Ceremony and pomp.

※※

Jonathan Grog Esqr, . . . having ascended the Chair, the Reverend Mr Sly, Master of Ceremonies, moved the Club, that the
following Gentlemen, vizt: Mr Huffman Snap, Jealous Spyplot Junior, & Mr Quirpum Comic, should be admitted longstanding members of this here ancient and honorable Club,
. . . upon which motion, Mr Deputy President presented the
Secretary with a Special Commission from the honorable Mr
President Jole, to authorise and Enable him, to proceed and act,
with full power in this election.

※※

Then Mr Huffman Snap, moved the Club, that if the honorable the president's Commission had not been confined to the
above Gentlemen, he would humbly propose to the Club, another Gentleman, viz: Mr Prim Timorous, who was desirous
of being admitted a member at this Sederunt, upon which, the
Club not presuming to proceed farther (a dangerous piece of
Complaisance) without the consent of the honorable Mr President Jole, dispatched to him two Special messengers, vizt: the
Reverend Mr Sly Master of Ceremonies, and Mr Secretary
Scribble, with a written request from the Deputy president and
Club, to Indulge them so far as to suffer them to proceed in his
election, which, the honorable Mr President Jole, Readily
Granted, with this further message, to be delivered to the dep-
uty president of the Club, to drink the healths of all the new
Elected members, singly, in these particular words, vizt: *That
each one might be a longstanding member of the Club*, and betwixt
each health, Mr Protomusicus was ordered to sing a new Song,
exerting upon the occasion, his musical faculties to the utmost.

※※

As Mr Prim Timorous, now admitted a long Standing member
of this ancient and honorable Club, was heretofore a member

of the red house Club of Annapolis, under the Celebrated Mr George Neilson, . . . and, as the same Gentleman will be seen, holding a Considerable office, in this here ancient and honorable Club, vizt: that of Serjeant at arms, to the Right Honorable the Lord President Jole, (as he was at that time stiled) it will be proper in this place, to give a short Scetch of his Character.

Mr Prim Timorous was a person of a middle Stature, Inclinable to a slender make, of a mild Complacent Countenance, much given to smile, tho for the most part he carried in his look, a Sedate and Stayd gravity. He was by no means of a Loquacious disposition, for he loved better to hear others speak, than to hold discourse himself, he was always fond of Jocular and merry company, tho' he never attempted to be Jocular and witty himself, yet, he had this Singular good quality, that he could bear a Joke passed upon himself with great good nature, and was by no means one of that morose Set, who, because they cannot be witty or arch upon others themselves, will not bear a Jest from others, but are perpetually taking offence, looking grim, and Surly, upon the least Smart repartee or bob, which they think is pointed at themselves, Mr Timorous could bear very well to be plaid upon, and would Join heartily in the Laugh, when the Jest hit him full in the teeth, and his Laugh had something peculiar in it, his ha, ha, has, measuring such equal time as he breath'd them forth, as do the clicks of a short pendulum Clock, . . . and while he laughed in this manner, he would Clap his hands & stamp with his feet, regularly at every ha, ha, like one beating time to music, which afforded much pleasure and mirth to the company; he was very tender mouthed, when he adventured at any time to talk Smutty, and seemed to mince his words in such a manner, as if he was afraid to utter them, for which reason, he never could find in his heart, to pronounce Certain naughty english words, and paultry monosyllabs, that are used as toasts by our moderen rakes, . . . but would always express his meaning in a Circumlocutory way, tho' no man loved better than he to hear bawdy discourse, and at all times, when such discourse happened to be Introduced, he would listen to it with all his ears, and laugh at it in his Solemn way, . . . Mr Timorous, was, to sum up all, a good naturd peaceable Companion, neither giving offence to any body, nor taking offence at any thing, and none better qualified than he, to take him in a lump, for a good Club's man.

Chapter 9 ❧ *Sublime Club Letters, The tryal and acquittal of Sir John, the Gelastic Law executed on the Secretary.*

Musical Instruments, we are told, may be tuned up to a certain pitch, to which being kept, they have a pleasant and agreeable effect, but beyond this they occasion a discordant Jarring, and become highly offensive and grating to the ear, and the Strings at last start and fly. So in Clubs, the Constitution is capable of being exalted to a certain pitch, and no farther, without being unable to support it's own weight, and at last tumbling to pieces. When the presidential power is kept within Certain bounds, and he Contents himself with few, and those moderate titles of honor, when the State officers do their duty, and exceed not their Commission, when the officers of the commons stand up Strenously for Clubical liberty, when Club Law is duely executed, and Justice done Strictly on offenders, and matters of expence do not run too high, then all goes smoothly and Swimmingly on, and the Society flourishes, but, when the Chair aims at great power, and assumes great and Sonorous titles, such as *My Lord, Lord president, Lord presidential, your Honor, Honorable,* and *right Honorable,* titles, which Venerable presidents of Clubs have no more business with than our Reverend Bishops and Cardinals, now a days, who Call themselves the Successors of a parcel of poor and needy fishermen, have with *your Eminence,* *your Grace* and *your Lordship*,—when the State officers prove loose, dissolute and obscene in their conversation, and set themselves above punishment and the Laws, when the Longstanding members quietly submitt to oppression, and unwarrantable power, when enormous crimes and trespasses are slur'd over, and all Sort of Luxury and extravagance encouraged and countenanced, when pimps in office, are flatterd and Cajoled, by worse pimps out of office, then *Actum est,*[1] the Clubical State may for a little time make a great noise and Show, but suddenly, like a fair blossoming tree upon the Coming of a blast or frost, all its pride and Glory tumbles to the Ground.

This we shall soon find to be pritty much the case with this here ancient and honorable Club, which, now in its highest glory, strained to be higher, and thus, breaking the strings, Sinews or nerves of the Constitution, every thing ran precipitatly to decay, and, tho' a dissolution did not Immediatly Happen, yet, was the beauty, order and Strength of it much Impaired, by means of Superflous ceremonies Introduced, high sounding titles, badges of honor, Seals, medals, Caps of State, Canopies of State, and the like useless trumpery, which, like the Gewgaws used in the Ceremonials of Religious worship, that divert the attention of the populace, or great mobile, from the Substance to the Shadow, so these farcical, clubical conceits, divert the minds of the members from more rational pursuits, and set them on the hunt after pitiful bawbles. The first Remarkable appearance of this Clubical madness, broke out, in the Stile of some letters to his honor the president, wrote in so extraordinary a Sublime (such I am Sure, as Longinus never delivered any rules for)[2] that they quite turned the presidents head, so,

[1] "That does it!" (a phrase typical of Seneca).
[2] Longinus (ca. 213–273) was generally considered to have been the author of the treatise *On the Sublime* until 19th-century scholars more accurately traced its authorship to the 1st century A.D.

that he began now, not to know, which end of him was upper-most, for, at Sederunt 99th, Huffman Snap Esqr, being high Steward, the following letters to his honor were read in Club.

※※

To the Honorable Nasifer Jole Esqr
President of the Tuesday Club.

Most Honorable Sir,

Unpractised in that polite art and Demeanor, so natural to the members of your honor's Tuesday Club, and utterly unlet-tered and untaught in the ornate diction and peculiar Nitidity of Stile, conspicõus, in the Epistolary and congratulatory com-positions, addressed to your honor upon occasions like this which is the motive of my now writing, It may seem to your honor somewhat bold and assuming in me, to presume address-ing your honor, upon this occasion, and in this manner, espe-cially before having passed thro' your honor's Solemn Cere-mony of Confirmation, . . . but, seeing I am as yet a novice, and an unconfirmed member, I hope, if I make any blunder, in Stile, or propriety of address, your honor and the Club, will humanly overlook, and not attribute my trips to design, rude-ness, or Ill manners.

I design this evening, to do myself the honor and pleasure, of attending your honor's commands, at your honor's house, to serve as your honors willing and Chearful, tho unworthy and unqualified high Steward, where, when that Solemn minute ap-proaches, when I shall stand with my other fellow novices, be-fore your honors august Chair, to be, as it were Inaugurated, confirmed and consecrated, an effectual and true Standing member of your honor's ancient and honorable Tuesday Club, I earnestly beg your honor, to give Command to your honor's Master of Ceremonies, to Instruct me particularly in every Cir-cumstance, relating to the deportment and carriage to be ob-served, when in this Solemn and awful Situation, that I may not, to the dissatisfaction and disgust of your honorable and an-cient Club, and my own Shame and Confusion, be guilty of faults or blunders, or any Sort of misbehavior, thro' Ignorance or Simplicity, and, by this gracious Condecention, a permanent, and never to be forgotten obligation, will be conferrd upon, Honorable Sir,

Anap: 28 febr: 1748   Your honors most humble
                                           Most obedient, and
                                           Most dutiful Servant & H:S:
                                           Huffman Snap.

After Reading of this very polite and high strained letter to his honor the president, another to the worshipful Sir John, from the same hand was produced and read.

To the Most Redoutable Sir John,
knight of the Tuesday Club.

Most puisant and Invincible Sir John,
    Dreadful and horrendous have been the feats and atchievements, performed by the magnanimous knights of old, who, by their unparallelled Chivalry, shook mountains, burst rocks in twain, knocked down Dragons and Griffins, and made mere popets of Gyants, and all for the Sake of some fine fair Lady, whom perhaps they never saw. . . . But oh! ye Sempiternal astripotents! what a more Sublime field and excellent foundation, has a knight of such a Society as our tuesday Club to work upon, what an Infinite number of heroic actions and Glorious Exploits, must spring from such a groundwork, such an excellent foundation, when operated upon by a magnanimous genius like yours, for what knight I say, what emblazon'd Champion, either ancient or moderen, had ever such Subjects to exercise his valor upon and act in defence of, as the honorable the president, and longstanding members of the ancient and honorable Tuesday Club! for, such an honorable president and such longstanding members, I believe, never were heard of, seen or known, either to antiquity or these baser and Latter times, neither do I believe, shall Expecting posterity, ever be so happy as

to behold such a president, such members, and above all, such a magnanimous, epouvantable and Invincible knight.

After this well adapted prelimination, I am next to sollicit you, most Invincible and heroic Sir John, to do me the honor and dignity of your knightly presence this evening, at the house of our honorable President, where I am to have the Glory of officiating for the first time as high Steward, and I doubt not but your magnanimous presence, will Inspire into me that courage and undaunted Spirit, which will be necessary, when I stand before the honorable presidents august chair, to be Inaugurated and confirmed a perpetual Standing member, of our Ancient Tuesday Club, I am the more bold in demanding this of you, as I know you glory, in being the valiant champion of our Tuesday Club, and the protector, of not only the whole bod thereof under the honorable the president, to whom good manners and duty require me to give the first place, but also of every particular member, and especially of persons timerous and untaught like myself, and, as I hope your magnanimity will Indulge me so far, I am, Most Invincible and Tremendous Sir John,

Annap: 28 febr: 1748   Your worship's most humble
                             Servant and dutiful Squire
                             Huffman Snap.

This Letter is upon the right Clubical Bombast Stile, and savors pritty much of many Dedications wrote by certain finical puppies of authors, to patrons of very little merit and Significancy, at least, patrons of far less worth and Importance, than the worshipful Sir John knight and Champion of the Ancient and honorable Tuesday Club.

※※

The Secretary then, delivered to his honor and the Club, two Indictments against Sir John, . . . which he was ordered to read aloud, upon which Sir John, stood up, and with a bold and Intrepid countenance said that he was ready and prepared, to give a categorical answer to all Indictments, and Libels whatsoever, which Mr Secretary or the Club should bring against him. Then the Secretary proceeded to read the first Indictment in Law latin.

Indictamentum Imum

Tuesday Club Ss:

Socii Societat, Annapolit, diei martis, anglice *The Annapolis Tuesday Club* super honorem suam present, quod dom, Joannes, eques Societat, alias, domd, Joannes Oldcastellius eques Societat, anglice dict *Sir John knight of the Club, otherwise Sir John Oldcastle knight of the Club,* nuper de Civitat, Annapol, in Comitat, predict, homo pernicios, et Seditios, pravæ mentis, et turbulent, disposition, machinans et Intendens contra honor, et dignitat, domin, presidis, . . . vi et armis, rautose et riotose, assaultation, fecit exicrabilem, in Cathed, et honor, dict, dom, presid, Craterum Certam, anglice *A Punch Bowl* pretu quatuor Solidar, in manu tenens Impudenter audacter, et Insolenter, crater, dict, ori suo admovens, primam post ceniam Compotavit tostam contra Leges hujus Societat, quæ Confirmant dom, nost, presid, hanc privilegiam compotand, prim, post Ceniam tostam, et hanc contumeliam perpetravit, et assaultation. . . .

After Reading this Indictment, Sir John said, "Hum, Hum, a fine Rigmeroll indeed! who the devil understands one word of all this Stuff"—Then the Secretary read the English Indictment as follows.

Indictment I

Sir John, You stand Indicted by the name of Sir John, otherwise Called Sir John Oldcastle, in the parish of St Anne in the County of Annarundel, knight of the Tuesday Club, for that you, as a false traitor, . . . endeavoring and Intending with all your might, the peace and Common tranquillity of this our

Tuesday Club to disturb, and the Laws of the same established to overthrow, and to pull down and bring into Contempt, our said Serene president and his Chair, and the said honorable Chair, wickedly, maliciously and devillishly to usurp, you, the said Sir John, otherwise Called Sir John Oldcastle, knight of the Tuesday Club, and late a State officer of the said Club, . . . at a place called Batchellors hall, before the said President, in the person of his deputy, Solemnly sitting and sleeping in the presidential Chair, and in the presence of several of the Liege members of the said Club, . . . drank the first toast after Supper, against an express Law of this here Club, which has given that privilege, of drinking the first toast after Supper to the honorable the president alone, and this contempt and open assault, you, the said Sir John, . . . with force and arms, rautously and riotously, Impudently, audaciously and Insolently, hast perpetrated, against the aleigeance, due to the honorable the President, and setting a bad example to your fellow members, to commit the same Insolence, and against the peace of his said honor the president, his Chair and dignity. What say you Sir John, are you guilty of the matter wherewith you stand Charged or not Guilty.

Sir John would not plead, but looked very Sour and Surly first at the Secretary, then at his honor the president and then at all the Longstanding members round him, every one of whom remained mute, as it is thought thro fear.

The Champion however was not altogether silent during the reading of the Indictment, for, at the words, *Late a State officer of the said Club,* he Interrupted the Secretary and without rising from his Seat spoke to the following purpose.

"*Late a State officer!*—pray Sir, why *Late a State officer?*— Mr President Sir,—I have the honor to sit here at your right hand—I say Sir at your right hand in quality of a State officer, of this here Club, and, I beg leave to affirm Sir, that I was not only late a State officer, but also actually *Now a State officer,* and permit me also to take notice Sir, that it is altogether Irregular,

nay Illegal Sir, to proceed against the nobles by way of Indictment, but, had I been guilty of any crime Sir, I ought to have
been Impeached, and here I boldly appear Sir, and claim the
privilege of my peerage, being, I assure you, not alittle Surprized, that you should countenance such Illegal and audacious
proceedings, against a person who has the honor to be Champion of this here Club [here Sir John laid his hand upon the hilt
of his broad Sword] and prop of the Chair, and must beg leave
to say further, Sir, that you need not be Surprized if the Chair
should suffer a violent Shake, since you permit the underminers
and Sappers to approach so nigh your own foundations, by dig-
ging under my props."—Then Sir John frowened & was silent.

The Indictment being read, and Sir John refusing to plead,
Mr Attorney Spyplot, council for Sir John, stood up and spoke
as follows.

"Mr President Sir, (here he took a pinch of Snuff)

I should be sorry—humph—That Mr Secretary should be
allowed to prefer Indictments, in this here Club, Just when and
how he pleases, and desire to know Sir by whose authority, and
by whose advice and Instigation, this here Indictment, or rather
libel Sir, has been trumpd up; for Sir, If we do not enquire into
this, it is my opinion Sir—ah hey ho, [here Mr Attorney
youned] it will be a dangerous affair, and I humbly Conceive,
Mr President Sir, It concerns us a—a haunch—a—a haunch—
a—a haunch [here he sneezd thrice] all Sir, for Sir, if Sir John,
a Noble and State officer of this here Club, is laid open to these
attacks libels and Insults, none of us, Longstanding members
of the commoners, can reckon ourselves safe, and gi' me leave
to say, Mr President, Sir that your honor's Chair may be in
danger, for which Mr President Sir I should be very sorry"—
here Mr Attorney Spyplot sat down.

※※

The Secretary then read the Latin Copy of the Second
Indictment.

※※

To which Indictment Sir John said "Pish and phogh! prithee ha' done, there's too much of this Stuff, this is worse than the other, by Jupiter."

The Secretary then read the English Indictment as follows.

Indictment II

Sir John, you stand Indicted by the name of Sir John, otherwise called, Sir John Oldcastle, of the parish of St Annes in the County of Annarundel, knight of the Tuesday Club, for that you, as a pernicious, Seditious, depraved and turbulent knight, . . . did take into your hands, a certain punch bowl, of the value of 4 Shillings, charged with a certain Liquor called punch, and drank the following execrable, abominable, detestable, horrible, dreadful, Immodest, contumelious and damnable [here Sir John with great violence exclaimed ha! ha!] toast, which you, the said Sir John, . . . expressed in the following English words, viz: *To the pious memory of Sally Salisbury's* ———[3] against your aleidgeance due to our Lord the president, and setting a bad and pernicious example to your fellow members to be guilty of the same, and against the peace of our said Lord the president his Chair and dignity. What say you Sir John, are you Guilty &ct:

⁂

Sir John then addressed himself to the President and said "as to this last Indictment Sir, 'tis a parcell of damnd Stuff,—but as to the first, I protest, that had I not promoted drinking toasts In the Club, the whole members, as well as the deputy president, would have fell fast asleep."

It is plain from the management of these trials, that Sir John bullied and Intimidated both his honor the president and the

[3]Sally Salisbury (or Sally of Salisbury) is the alias of Mrs. Sarah Priddon, a fictional whore and the central character of Capt. Charles Walker's *Authentick Memoirs of the Life, Intrigues, and Adventures of the Celebrated Sally Salisbury* (London, 1723). Hamilton's draft, which reads "To the pious memory of Sally Salisbury's C—t," is a bit more explicit.

Club; and that they were much struck with a pannic fear at the bellicose Countenance of this Club heroe, . . . and to verify this observation, I must not ommit this circumstance, that Sir John after quashing the second Indictment, filled a bumper, and In the face of his honor and the Club, drank again, *viva voce*, the same filthy toast, for which he had been but Just Indicted.

༺༻

The Secretary again protested against the proceedings of the Club, in their quashing the Second Indictment, and being taken up short, by his honor, and some of the Longstanding members, was attempting to speak farther in his own defense, when the Gelastic Law was put in execution against him in an Illegal tumultuous and Clamorous manner, without any Signal given by the honorable the president.

༺༻

Chapter 10 ⚜ *Grand proposals in Club by the Secretary, Creation of a poet Laureat, Canopy of State added to the Chair, Speech of Sir John on that occasion, The master of ceremonies leaves the Club, election of a new master of Ceremonies, election of a Club Orator.*

An honest Emulation for precedency in learning or virtue, is always commendable (I say an honest emulation, because I would make a distinction between learning and virtue, and what are frequently mistaken for them, Pedantry and Hypocrisy, by which many rogues have Imposed upon the world,) and an ambition to excell in such excellent things, as are worth excelling in, is a glory to him that possesses it, 'tis *Ingeniorum Cos*, the whetstone of wit, and has been the cause of the rise and grouth of many a heroic action, as well as Club, on this noble and virtuous emulation (tho at first but mere banditti and Ruffians) the ancient Romans, laid the foundation of their great empire, which rose at last to such a height, as to outbrave every enimy but Luxury avarice and ambition, under the Insatiable Tyranny of which last, it fell and never rose again.

When the Ancient and honorable Tuesday Club, kept within decent bounds, as to expence, pageantry, Show, and presidential power, when they exercised their learning and bright parts in making of Speeches, penning of Letters, and striving, who should excell in this Laudable exercise, evading flattery and bombast in their Compositions of this Sort, they flourished, prospered, and grew up to that pitch of Grandure, in which they appeared at this very period, but when the power of the Chair was streched to an extraordinary extent, and the long-standing members strove one among another, who should have most favor and Influence with the honorable Chair, then the glory power and Character of the Club began to decline. But the prime cause of this declension of the grandure of the Club, was the emulation and contention among the State officers, and the officers of the Commons about precedency, which, like the Contentions between the Patricians and Tribunes of the people at Rome, laid the first foundation for Tyranny and Arbitrary power, and, the Secretary, an ambitious and turbulent officer of the Commons, was one of the Chief fomenters and promoters of this mischief, for, when he found that he could not advance himself in the Club, or gain the favor of the honorable Chair, by flattering Speeches, Orations, and fustian bombast letters, he went to work another way, and tried what might be done, by making great and valuable Presents to the Club, Introducing certain Seals, Medals, Canopies of State, Shields or Scutcheons, caps of State, Conundrums, and the like tinsel trumpery, which, we shall find in the Sequel raised great disturbance in the Club, set his honor the president, his State officers, and longstanding members together by the ears, and, this politic officer, at last compassed his ends, in a great measure, by picking up and securing to himself, whatever he could snatch, in these General hubbubs and Club hurly-burlys.

At Sederunt 100 March 4th 1748/9, Jealous Spyplot Junr Esqr being high Steward, and Huffman Snap Esqr, by commission, deputy president, the Secretary offered to make the Club a present of a Seal, cut in Silver, expressing the proper design and motto of the Club, to be used by the honorable the president, in the Sealing of Commissions &ct: which the Club accepted of, and the Secretary undertook and promised accordingly, to have this Seal done and finished at London, as soon as could be, committing the Care of the same to Capt: Comely Coppernose, (this evening entertained as a Stranger by the Club, according to ancient Custom) who in a little time Intended to go for England. ❀❁

Then the Secretary moved the Club, that there should be badges of Silver, prepared for each Regular member of the Club, weighing half an ounce each, dowble gilt, with the proper Signatures and mottos of the Club Imbossed, or raised thereupon, to be fixed upon ribbons, instead of the Card badges now used, and that the said badges, should be ordered to be prepar'd and done at London, upon this motion of the Secretarie's, the yeas and nays were put round, and it was unanimously agreed to; the Secretary then received orders to commit the Care of this to Capt: Comely Copper-nose, who undertook to have it done in the cheapest and the neatest manner, at the Common expence of the Regular members of the Club, The Secretary moved next, that blank Commissions should be printed, for the use of his honor the president, which was agreed to, and the Club, ordered Jonathan Grog Esqr, to print the same.

At the time of making these motions by the Secretary, the Club did not forsee the designs of this politic officer, in broaching them, but, the violent heats and disputes, which the Seal, these Badges, and these Commissions occasioned afterwards in Club, made them Sorely repent that ever they had agreed to these motions.

On Sederunt 101, Quirpum Comic Esqr being high Steward, and Laconic Comus Esqr deputy president by Commission, the Club met again in the School room, the ancient place of meeting of the Ugly Club, and the Songs of, *Stand Around my brave boys*, and *Bumpers 'Squire Jones*,[1] were sung by the deputy, at the express Injunction and Command of his honor the President, who had made it a Condition at the bottom of his Commission, to sing these Songs, besides which the deputy Complimented the Club with a Voluntaire Song, which as it was a favorite of his we shall here give a Copy of.

Club Song, sung by Laconic Comus Esqr D:P:[2]

She tells me, with Claret, she cannot agree,
And she thinks of a hogshead, whene'er she sees me,
For I smell like a beast, and therefore must I,
Resolve to forsake her, or Claret deny.

Must I Leave my dear bottle that was always my friend,
And I hope will Continue so, to my life's end,
Must I leave it for her, 'tis a very hard task,
Let her go to the Devil, bring 'tother full flask.

Had she found out my Chloris, up two pair of Stairs,
I had baulk'd her and gone to Saint James's to prayers,
Had she tax'd me with gaming, and bid me forbear,
Tis a thousand to one, I had lent her an ear.

[1] Handel's "Stand Round My Brave Boys" was published in the *London Magazine* (November 1745), 560–561. "Bumpers Squire Jones" appeared in the *Gentleman's Magazine* (November 1744), xiv, 612.
[2] This song appears as "The Jolly Toaper" in Thomas D'Urfey, *Wit and Mirth; or, Pills to Purge Melancholy*, 6 vols. (London, 1719–1720), II, 83–85.

Had she bid me read homilies, three times a day,
Perhaps she'd been humor'd, with little to say,
But at night to deny me, my dear flask of red,
Let her go to the Devil, there's no more to be said.

The honorable deputy sung this Song very pathetically, passion appearing in the twist of his features and glare of his eyes, especially, when he pronounced these words, *let her go to the Devil,* by which his hearers might easily know, that he was himself a dear lover of his bottle, and this was really the Case, for Mr Comus, tho he would talk but very little upon any Subject, yet, when the bowl or bottle came to be the Topic of discourse, he held forth very emphatically.

This evening was produced, a curious distich, wrote upon the envelope of the Club's badge, sent to the high Steward by Jonathan Grog Esqr, to the following purpose.

To Mr ⊞

Inclos'd I've sent your Tuesday badge,
To night, you'll see, how well 'twill fadge.[3]

The Club approved so much of this distich, that they Immediatly Created Jonathan Grog Esqr *Poet Laureat of the Club,* and thus made a new officer.

At Sederunt 102, april 11th 1749, Prim Timorous Esqr, being high Steward, a magnificent Canopy appeared fixed upon the presidential Chair, in the Shape and model of a large Scallop Shell, and upon the forepart of it, was erected an oval Shield, with the proper devices and mottos of the Club, curiously delineated thereupon. . . .

Sir John, after having taken his Seat as usual, at the right

[3]How well it will suit you, or agree with you.

hand of the Chair, and deposited a naked Sword upon the Club table *in terrorem,* casting a fierce eye upon this new Canopy, with a frown in his countenance, addressed the president, and spoke as follows.

"Mr President,

I cannot help taking notice of some Innovations here, which I presume, have been contrived and Introduced, without advice or consent of the Club, pray Sir, may I presume to ask, by whose authority, advice and expence, this Sumptous and noble canopy, has been affixed to the Chair, for Sure I am, that I, tho a person of rank and consequence, in this here club, was neither consulted, advised with, nor Concerned, in preparing, ordering and erecting this seemingly Superflous ornament."

Before his honor could make any reply to this bold harangue of the knight's, the Secretary politicly moved, that the Club should proceed to business of more Importance, and the enquiry went no farther at this Juncture.

The Reverend Mr Smoothum Sly, late Master of the Ceremonies, and an old Standing member of this Club, having departed the City, the office of Master of Ceremonies by his leaving the Club, became vacant. These two Important offices, of Speaker, and Master of Ceremonies, being therefore, at this time vacant, the Club resolved at this Sederunt to elect new officers to fill their places, but when the Club was proceeding to this Election, a question was started, whether the title of Speaker, should be changed for that of orator, yea or nay, and, the ballots being put round, it was carried in the affirmative, eight yeas & three Nays.

Then Laconic Comus, Huffman Snap, and Jealous Spyplot Senr: Esqrs, were set up as Candidates for the office of orator, and the Election was carried in favor of Laconic Comus Esqr, who, accordingly, after Supper, took his place at the left hand of the Chair, as Orator and State officer of the Club, and privy Councellor to the Chair.

The Club then proceeded to the election of a master of the

Ceremonies, and two questions were put, after the following Gentlemen were proposed, as Candidates for the office, vizt: Jealous Spyplot Junior, Jonathan Grog, and Quirpum Comic Esqrs, The first question proposed, was, whether Jonathan Grog Esqr, as already enjoying several offices and titles in the Club, vizt: Poet, punster, Printer, Punchmaker general and Purveyor, . . . was to be burdened with any other offices in Club, or was a proper person to stand Candidate for another office, yea or nay, the ballots were put about, and, it passed in the negative, nine Nays, and two Yeas; upon which the Club by balloting, Chose Quirpum Comic Esqr, master of Ceremonies, who took his place accordingly, at the right hand of Sir John, after the Club had been long delay'd in their proceedings in this Election, by a dispute upon some nice distinctions, fomented by Mr Protomusicus Neverout, a gentleman remarkable for raising objections, where no body else could find any.

As Quirpum Comic Esqr, will at times make a Considerable figure in this Club History, both in the Quality of an officer and private Member, it will be proper in this place, to give a short Sketch of his person and Character.

Quirpum Comic Esqr, is of a middle Stature, and wears on his Countenance a remarkable droll Cast or turn, altogether undescribable by words, there being as it were a Jest in the very turn of his features, posture of his mouth, mold of his nose, and cast of his eye, his disposition is comico-serious, or rather Seriocomical, having more of the Grave than Gelastic in his air, for he is seldom or never seen to laugh, tho' he has a Surprizing power, or faculty of setting every body else a laughing, which he does by his Superlative grave air, and *Judgematical countenance* that he puts on when talking of the most trivial or rather Clubical matters, and the queer Clubish gestures, which he uses while he speaks, which by the bye is but seldom, for he is not very fluent of tongue, he never speaks in Club, but it is much to the purpose, that is, his discourse is exactly adapted to the true turn and Nature of Clubical conversation, and always excites gelastic Commotions, in the muscles of every face but his own, for he never was but once observed to laugh in Club, and that was at the extravagant Speech and gestures of Mr Protomusicus Neverout, attempting to talk greek, . . . when the over exercised faculty of Risibility, had like to have made one half of the Longstanding members expire.

❀❀

After Supper, Mr Orator Comus, repeated the same Question, which had been started by Sir John, before Supper, with regard to the Canopy of State affixed to the Chair, demanding by whose authority and orders it had been made? To which the Secretary made answer, that he had some considerable time agoe, received some money of his honor the president to be applied to the use of ornamenting the Chair, and that by means of this money, and a small addition of his own, he caused that canopy to be made and prepared, with which answer, Sir John, the orator, and the Club seemed satisfied. Thus we see this ambitious officer erecting his batteries on all hands, but a little while since, he attempted to corrupt the Club, by offering to make them a present of a Seal, and now is endeavoring to corrupt his honor, by covering his venerable head with a Canopy of State.

❀❀

Chapter 11 ❧ *Celebration of the fourth Anniversary, Speech on that Occasion by the Secretary, foundation of the Eastren-shore Triumvirate.*

This ancient and honorable Club, having now arrived at its greatest pitch of glory, grandure, and magnificence, very grand preparations began to be made for Solemnizing the ensuing anniversary, that every proceeding might be transacted with that dignity and State, becoming so noble a president, such noble State officers and noble Commoners and Longstanding members.

❀❀

[Upon May 16, 1749,] at Seven o'Clock in the evening, the members proceeded accordingly, to meet his honor the president, and were Joined in the way by Prim Timorous Esqr; The honorable the president graciously advanced to meet them about ten paces from his own gate, and did each member the honor of a Salute by manuquassation. The members, before they entered the president's gate, Invested themselves with their badges, and walked in decent order to his honor's back yard, the way being strow'd with flowers, and the Club flag display'd, after sometime staying in the yard, they removed into his honor's great Saloon, and the honorable the president mounted the Chair.

❀❀

After some debate, whether the Secretary should be permitted to deliver any Speech, it was concluded that he should, and he rising up, made a profound obeisance to the Chair, and delivered the following oration.

Anniversary Speech, delivered by the Secretary

❀❀

Mr President Sir,

Not only myself, but all these here Longstanding members who now hear me, I shall be bold to speak for them and in their name, have a Singular pleasure and Satisfaction in seeing your honor possessed, of that there dignified Seat and office in this here Club, we have found by experience, Sir, that our Constitution has hitherto florished and prospered under your honor's benign management and oeconomy, for we all know, and must own that your honor's administration has more of the Sweet than the bitter in it, and has all along been carried on, with that even temper and Steadiness as to preserve an equal balance, between too rigid a Severity on the one hand, and a Supine mildness and

Indifference on the other. Neither can we accuse your honor of partiality or respect of persons, for some of our first rate grandees, have found the resentment of the Chair, when Just cause was given, as effectually, as the most Inconsiderable of our commoners,—we have continued now Sir, for four years, a regular, harmonious and polite Society, under your honor's discreet conduct and direction, and, as we are all conscious that you are the fittest person among us to possess that there Chair of State, and exercise the office of Supreme Governor of this here Club, so we wish you may long sit there, and Continue to bless us for many anniversaries to come with your wholesome and mild government.

Worshipful Sir John, knight of the order of the Tuesday Club,

Most Dignified and eloquent Mr Orator Comus,

I address you both in particular, as dignified State officers of this here Club, and the main props and Supporters of the honorable Chair.

It would be Impudence in me, to pretend to advise gentlemen of your rank and dignity, that Innate Generosity, that Inbred Spark of virtue and honor, which qualifies you for the high offices you hold in this here Club, together with the opinion you cannot but Justly entertain of the honorable the president's high merit and deserts, must prompt you to exert your powers and talents to the utmost for the Support, defence and honor of his chair and dignity.

Sir Clement Cotterell,

Mr Protomusicus and

Mr Poet Laureat,

This occasion affords each of you an opportunity of putting your best foot foremost, the first in setting every thing in order, that might, without his care be misplaced, the next in warbling forth melodious and melliflous notes, to Charm our ears, and captivate our Senses, and our Sublime Son of the Muses may now pindarize it, in praise of the honble: the President & Club.

Gentlemen,

This present meeting Commences the fifth year of the Æra

of our Society, and I hope, as it has hitherto florished and Increased, it will still continue so to do, not only for five years,
but for fifty times five, that the name and being of so worthy
and polite a Club, as this of ours, may not be lost to posterity,
and unknown to future ages—In fine,

Mr President and Gentlemen,

This is not a time to speak much, but to act well and as becomes us upon this occasion, without many more words then,
in order that our meeting here, may be as agreeable as the occasion Requires, permit me to make this motion, that our discourse and conversation be regular, orderly, free, humorous
and Jocose, without reflection, without passion, without reserve, without Clamor, without noise, and also that this Speech
and Motion of mine, may have your kind and Candid reception, as it proceeds from a heart full of good will and benevolence to the Society, and to conclude, let our Songs be in tune,
our puns and repartees *a propos*, and not too poignant or Satyrical, our toasts loyal and Amorous, our Stomachs keen, to relish
the elegant fare prepared for us by his honor the president, on
this Joyful occasion, and our punch bowls always replete, with
fragrant and nectarious liquor, for this Cordial Juice, taken
with temperance and moderation [here the Secretary took the
punch bowl in his hand,] lightens the Spirits, enlivens the wit,
and will conduce not only to make me a more fluent orator, but
you more Jolly and benevolent Long standing members.

❅❅

Then the Reverend Mr Smoothum Sly, late a regular, and now
an honorary member of the Club, standing up, spoke as
follows.

"Mr President, Sir,

I am to Inform your honor, that there is a Club now a forming upon the Eastren Shore, of which I have the honor to be a
member, this Club is yet in its Infancy and is not as yet perfectly
modelled, but we hope that in time we shall bring it to bear,
and I am Commissioned from the Gentlemen of that Club, Sir,

to pay their respects to your honor, and the Longstanding members of this here ancient and honorable Club, for, as you have acquired a great name far and near, by your wise and Just Conduct in that there Chair, as president of this here worthy Club, so, they having heard of your fame and Character, have a Just respect for you, and beg you would kindly receive their compliments, from my mouth, and Covet much your acquaintance and Correspondence, and to be regulated by your advice and direction."

❈❈

Then the Secretary standing up, remarked as follows.

"Mr President Sir,

I think the gentlemen pay this here Club, a piece of respect which they highly deserve, nor ought we to be remiss in returning their compliments, and we hope, as our Laws are allowed to be well framed and penned, and our constitution settled on a firm basis, that these Gentlemen, of that there other Club, will not think it beneath them, to consult our body of Laws, in order, the better to form a plan for theirs, as the Republic of Rome of old did that of Greece, when they sent for the tables of the grecian Laws, tho' I would not have you Inferr from this, that either they are as great as were the ancient Romans, or we as wise as the ancient Greeks."

At the close of the Secretaries Speech, Sir John, frowned and said—"Sir!—Sir!—I make bold to affirm, that we of this here Club, are as great, and as wise as any body, not excepting either Greeks or Trojans."

This was the first foundation of the worshipful the Eastren Shore triumvirate, a Society, which we shall find in the Sequel, intirely dependant upon, and subjected to the honorable Mr President Jole, and his ancient and honorable Tuesday Club, and thus began the power Influence and Jurisdiction of this great and Illustrious President and Club, over the other presidents and Clubs in British America.

❈❈

BOOK VI

From the foundation of the
eastren-Shore Triumvirate,
to the Creation of the
Chancellor.

Chapter 3 ❦ *Commotions in Club,* *the Records In danger of being burnt,* *Confirmation of a deputy Secretary.*

Turbulent and ambitious Spirits, when they cannot by open
practices and mere compulsion obtain their ends, often employ
cunning and artifice, and place their whole Confidence in that
Cursed Machiavelian maxim, *Divide et Impera;* Thus, some
wicked politicians, who pretend to act for the good of the public, keeping still a Steddy eye, upon one little pitiful, diminutive point, vizt: their own private Interest and advancement,
will clear their way, thro all difficulties and rubs, by exciting
the fury of party and faction, among those whom they Intend
to make their fools or gulls, and like the dog in the fable, pick
up the bone, while their fellow Curs are a fighting. . . .[1]

Thus, the Secretary, that ambitious, restless, and turbulent
Club officer, still aiming at the Dignity of a State member,
which he seemed resolved to procure at any rate Cost what it
would, after having by his cunning practices, . . . undermined
and overset Mr Orator Comus, and in a manner wheedled him,

[1]Hamilton is recalling Swift's "Republick of Dogs," in *The Battle of the*
Books (*The Prose Works of Swift*, ed. Herbert Davis [Oxford, 1939–1968],
I, 141–142).

into the Surrendry of his honorable office, made long strides to get into that dignified place himself, and because his cunning and artifice failed him at that Juncture, as we shall see in the relation of what follows, he endeavored all he could to set his honor the president and the Club together by the Ears, in order to try if he could not succeed by that means.

At Sederunt 108, after Mr Orator Comus had made a Surrendry of his office, the Secretary moved to the Club, when he found that his ambitious expectations were quite frustrated, by the Club's proceeding, in abolishing the offices of Orator and Speaker, into one of which he expected to be promoted, That he should have an asistant in his office allowed him, for he alledged That his was, of all offices in the Club the most trowblesome, especially, since he had been obliged, by an order of the honorable Chair, to make dowble entries. . . . Upon this, the Secretary delivered the book of Records to his honor the President, declaring That he would not receive it again, till his request was granted.

In making this motion, the Secretary had two ends in view, first to put the Club Into an uproar and confusion, and then to force them, as it were by this Surrendry of his place to chuse another Secretary, and by some means to get the orators office revived in Club, so, that having removed the objection of his Enjoying a multiplicity of offices, he might the more easily step himself into that honorable place, but the Club made a timely discovery of his policy in this affair, and would by no means Listen to his proposals, however, the motion that he made, so far answered his purpose, as to excite a very hot dispute in Club, some taking one part, and some another, . . . The Reverend Mr Muddy, who was gifted with a mighty Stentorian voice, was heard above all the rest, and his honor the president was not heard at all, it being only known that he spoke by the quick motion of his lips, his turning his face first to the right then to the left of the Chair, and his waving the book of records up and down, which he grasped in both hands, it was for sometime a

Club Hubbub, concerning the Records.

Confused medley of broken Sentences and words, like those heard in Groenland upon the coming of a General thaw, as Pray Sir—nay Sir—I say Sir—by your leave Sir—what!—must I Con- —no by G—therefore—pox on it—patience alittle— here Club—Judgematic—holla!—damn the book—burn the—hey, hey!—and such like unintelligible Jargon, while the Secretary like a Sly bitch, sat silent all the time Laughing in his Sleeve, and expecting what the Issue of this general confusion would be, in short, it seemed, as if the Longstanding members would go from words to blows, while the Loud laugh of Mr Protomusicus Neverout, Joined with the hoarse and Stentorian bass of the Revd Mr Roundhead Muddy, and the mingled Clamor of the other members, made the most horrid discord that ever was heard.

When the general clamor was hushed, some proposed that his honor should appoint a Committee, to burn the book, and not only destroy all the Records of the Club hitherto made, but keep no more for the future, this procedure some were of opinion, would tend to the final dissolution of the Club, and therefore it was warmly opposed, and his honor the President, foreseeing, that by this one rash resolve, if he should unadvisedly give in to it, at the Instance of his privy Councellor and right hand man Sir John, who was warm for this motion's taking place, he should lose all the Security he had for his prerogative and authority, notwithstanding that his resentment would have prompted him to do any thing to thwart the Secretary, declared himself openly against this proceeding, and, by his honor's prudence and moderation, the precious book of records, was thus snatched from the devouring flames, and the memorable transactions of this ancient and honorable Club, from eternal oblivion, which, had they been lost, would have been an Irretrievable Dammage to posterity, and have occasioned a Lamentable Chasm or blank, in the Journal De Sçavants, or Republic of Letters.

At Last Quirpum Comic Esqr, Master of the Ceremonies stood up with a grave Staid and Serio-Gelastic countenance, and adjusting his wig, and stroaking down his face and Chin, addressed his honor as follows.

"Mr President, Sir,—hem—

Tho I have heretofore, at the risque of my ears—hum—hum—served your honor's turbulent and ungrateful Secretary, in quality of his deputy without commission or order from your honor or this here Club, . . . yet to show your honor, and these here longstanding members, that I bear no Spite or animosity, to this here turbulent officer, and that I have a Sincere regard, for the peace and wellfare of this here ancient and honorable Club, I freely, and of my own accord offer my Service to act as his deputy with your honor's and the Club's permission, which—hum—hum—It is my duty to pay a regard to, and thus put a Stop to all his noise and Complaints for the future—hum—hum."

❀❀

Chapter 4 ❧ *Letter of Cats, danger of a dissolution of the Club, The Master of Ceremonies leaves the Club.*

Tho Jesting and Joaking, is often a very pritty Innocent and entertaining amusement, when Introduced with proper prudence and discretion, . . . being like a game at Shuttle Cock, where the volatile and feathered witicism is bandied about from hand to hand, with great Glee, vivacity and agility, which alighting upon any of the bye standers or players, by reason of its light Substance, being Compounded only of Cork and feathers, neither hurts nor bruises, yet have I often known that a Joke or Jest, tho' volatile and light enough in it's own nature, would occasion abundance of Enmity and ill blood, and even outragious quarrells and blows both wet and dry, where the Shuttle Cock, (to Carry on our metaphor,) lighted upon a tender Skin or an Inflammed or excoriated part, or in a word galled an old Sore.

This makes it necessary, that in passing Joke or Jest, the quality of the Jester and the quality and temper of the Jested, or to speake in the manner of our Learned Lawyers, the *Jestor* and *Jestee*, must always be maturely weighed and Considered, In order to evade an ensuing mischief; The Disposition of the But must be known, whether he be a person, that understands raillery, and also the nature and texture of the Jest it self,—Should the Jestor, for Instance, be a man of a Low degree, and the Jestee a Grandee, should the Jestor be a young Smart, and the Jestee an old Coxcomb or Choleric Don, should the Jestor be a poor fellow, and the Jestee rich, should the Jestor be a reputed wit, and the Jestee an arrant dunce, it is by no means safe for the Jestor to exercise his talents upon these occasions, and in these cases. . . .

Hence I conclude, that it is a very rash, and Inconsiderate thing, to pass Jests upon Emperors, kings, popes, Lords, proud prelates, powerful fools, noble pimps, wealthy blockheads, Whores and presidents of Clubs. The mischievous and almost fatal effects of an unlucky Jest, to this here ancient and honorable Club, the occasion of this preamble, shall be related in its proper place in this very Chapter.

❧❦

I come now to relate a transaction, seemingly triffling in itself, which notwithstanding, occasioned such a difference between his honor the president and the Club, as that it had well nigh ended in a final dissolution of this ancient and honorable Society, it was a Letter wrote to his honor the President by the high Steward Mr Quirpum Comic, at Sederunt 112, September 5th 1749, which was Intended for a Jest, but not being properly Seasoned with discretion, or applied to a proper person, proved a mischievous Jest, Mr Comic being a Single man, and no house keeper, intended to hold his Club in the School Room, the ancient place of meeting of the ugly Club . . . , his honor had an objection to this, alledging that a place where School boys met, was not at all proper for such wise men as the Long-standing members of the Tuesday Club to assemble in; besides, he objected to the place, on account of its Nastiness, and professed publicly and openly, that if the Club was held there, he would neither come himself, nor appoint a deputy, . . . Quirpum Comic Esqr, the high Steward, In order to please his honor *If possible,* had the room Cleaned, well sweeped and scrubbed, with mops, brushes, dusting Cloths brooms and Rubbers, and all in decent order for the Reception of the Club, . . . This Possibly might have brought his honor in some measure to comply, had the high Steward gone no farther, but he being in some degree nettled by his honor's unreasonable and uncivil behavior, could not restrain his rash and unadvised hand, but wrote his honor a Satyrical letter, which I cannot call by a more proper name than the *letter of Cats,* this letter was not suffered to be recorded, but the passage in it that gave offence, was nearly to this purpose, "That he [the high Steward] Intended to hold his Club in the School room, and, that his honor might have no objection to it, on account of the nastiness of the room, he had swept it clean, and taken care to whip out all *Cats* and dogs, Cats especially, as being a vermin mighty apt to breed fleas, and to piss about, and excite a very disagreeable perfume." This was the pinch, not only talking in such a Slighting manner of Cats, his honors favorites, but besides, there was a Sting in the tail of this observation, which was contained in the Implication, that his honors rooms were nasty, and perfumed with a disagreeable Odor, as he kept always a great number of these domestic animals about him, . . . this raised his honors Spleen and resentment to such a height, that he was heard to swear in his wrath, that he never would come nigh the Club again, or be any way concerned in it, and had his honor kept to this rash vow, here would have been an end and final Dissolution of this ancient and honorable Club. ※※

After Supper, Mr Secretary Scribble came into the Club & reported to the members, from the honorable the president, (with whom he had been for some hours in private Conference) his high displeasure at the high Stewards Letter, for which the members expressed their concern and Sorrow, and resolved to consider on ways and means, against next Sederunt, to accommodate matters to the Satisfaction of his honor the president, which the high Steward wisely foresaw was Impossible to be done without making a Sacrifice of him, for the good of the Common weal, and therefore like a wise and politic Statesman, he stood up with great gravity in his countenance, mixed with a small degree of Gelasticity, and declared His Intention to leave the Club, on account of the Great Inconvenience and trowble it was to him, to serve in his turn as H:S: he being a Single man, possessed of no house of his own, in which with Decency, to entertain his honor and the Club, and begged the members to Indulge him so far, as to take this his proposal in Good part; The members willingly & chearfully agreed to it, professing, That by their Constitution they were a free Society, and every man was at liberty to go and come at pleasure. Thus by this Impolitic Step, the Club lost a deputy Secretary & Master of Ceremonies at one blow.

Chapter 5 ※ *Petition to his honor the President from the Single females.*

The resentments of Great men, must at all events be gratified, and suffered at first eruption to have their full Spring, for, should the Inferiour powers, That is, the *profanum vulgus*, en-

deavor to confine it, like a Spark among gun powder pent up
and rammd down, it produces a violent explosion, which tears
and rends and drives every thing before it, with an Inexpressible and Irresistable fury, whereas, if it has free air, and is left
to its Self, it will either Spontaneously die away, or go off with
a puff, this politic maxim, the Longstanding members of this
ancient and honorable Club seemed not to be Ignorant of, when
to save their constitution, now In danger of a Lapse, they at
Sederunt 113 Septr 26th, 1749, Jealous Spyplot Junr Esqr,
being high Steward, gave way to the earnest desire of his honor
the president, to have the Letters of the Late high Steward,
which had given such offence, read, and Condemned to perpetual oblivion, a Just fate to all fomenters of mischief.

※※

After Supper a petition was presented, to the honorable the
president, from the Single Ladies of Annapolis, which was
read, and ordered to be entered, the tenor of which follows.

*To The Honorable Nasifer Jole Esqr, President of the
worshipful and ancient Tuesday Club, the petition and
remonstrance, of sundry of the Single females of Annapolis.*

Showeth,
    That whereas it has been observed by sundry persons as well
as your petitioners, that a Singular and Surprizing Success, has
all along attended such happy females, as your honor has been
pleased to pitch upon, as the toasts of the honorable Chair, every
one of whom in a short time, after having been thus adopted by
your honor, has Successfully and happily been provided, with
a much more Eligible State, than that of a Single Life,
    Your petitioners therefore, earnestly pray, that your honor,
instead of conferring your favors in so partial a manner, would,
in Commiseration of our desperate Situation, Include us all in
the circle of your favor, that the benign Influence of your hon-
or's maritiferous notice, may henceforth equally shine upon us

all, which benevolent Condescention of your honor, will have a tendency to multiply the Inhabitants of this City, as well as to better our present forlorn Situation.

> And your petitioners shall ever pray &ct:

The honorable the president was pleased to declare that he would grant this petition as far as lay in his power.

꙳꙳

Chapter 8 ꙮ *Admission of Philo Dogmaticus Esqr, Creation of the Chancellor.*

Hope is a passion by which all mankind are buoy'd up, be their Circumstance what it will, prosperous, or adverse, this Strange Phantom still haunts and attends them, . . . if they enjoy good fortune Hope still promises a better, if they Labor under distresses and difficulties, Hope whispers them, that they shall sometime or other be relieved; In fine this flattering power is still in view, unless when despair takes place, for this latter, being her mortal and sworn Enimy, she always takes flight at the Sight of his horrid front, as a beautiful modest and Coy virgin would fly at the Sight of a Rude rake or ravisher, and yet some people have as little ground or reason for Entertaining this flattering Phantome, as those who hope for the Millennium, have a chance to live to see those halcyon days, or those who fear the Sky will fall and smother the Larks, run a risk to be smothered and Crushed in their Company.

But tho this vain propensity, may often present us golden Scenes at a distance, and promise us relief in our greatest distresses and difficulties, yet such is the caprice of Lady fortune

In human affairs, or, to speak more Intelligibly, such is the Indiscretion and Imprudence of the bulk of mankind, that ten to one, those that hope for, and desire most, enjoy the Least of the good things of life, and many, who scarce ever hoped or expected a better fortune, than that they are at present possesed of, or ever longed after places and titles of honor, have them, I know not how, pop suddenly into their mouths to the great Surprize and astonishment of every one, . . . a remarkable Instance of this, we shall find in the case of the Reverend Mr Philo Dogmaticus, who, at one and the same Instant, as it were, was made a Long Standing member of this Club, Chancellor, State officer and privy Councellor to the Honorable The Chair, as also, keeper of his honors political Conscience, which transaction shall presently be related.

[At Sederunt 118 December 5th 1749,] the Secretary presented to the Honorable the president and Club, a petition from the Reverend Mr Philo Dogmaticus, who being desired to withdraw into an adjoining Chamber, it was read as follows.

To the honorable Nasifer Jole Esqr President, The honored Sir John knight, and the other worshipful officers, and worthy members of the ancient and honorable Tuesday Club.

Gentlemen,

As without Society, man would be the most wretched Creature upon earth, so to this he owes, tho' not his rational powers and faculties, yet the use and Improvement of them, . . . for without this, even reason it self would avail us very little, our nobler powers would Languish and perhaps be employed in mutual destruction, but Society, founded upon principles of right reason, directed by Just Laws, Impartially executed, under the administration of wise and virtuous Rulers, what a glorious Idea is it! what heart can conceive a greater blessing upon Earth! it is the very prelude, or rather type of heaven, where nothing is to be found but order, peace, love and all happy enjoyments worthy of the rational nature.

Wherever such well Constituted Societies are to be met with upon Earth, be they more public or more private, formed for more General advantage or the Comforts of a more private life, what wonder is it that men should wish and endeavour, to be members of such Societies, who, being prompted by a natural and reasonable Self love, wish themselves happy.

Moved by this principle, and the fame of this ancient, honorable and worthy Society of the Tuesday Club, the pleasures and benefits of which, I have also shared in, thro' that generosity, which has once and again Invited and admitted me, a Stranger among you, to the honor and pleasure of being a witness and partaker of your most ravishing Conversation, I humbly beg and petition, the honorable the president, the honored Sir John, knight, and the other worshipful officers, and all the Respectful worthy members of the ancient Tuesday Club, to perfect the honor they have already done me, by admitting me a member of it, and, however unworthy I may be at present, your noble examples, and Improving Conversation, will I hope, render me by degrees more worthy of such an honor, and lay under an Infinite obligation,

> Your most Loving, Devoted and
> Obedient humble Servant
> *Philo Dogmaticus.*

This petition being read, the ballots of yeas & nays were put round, and, the Reverend Mr Philo dogmaticus being unanimously elected a member of the Tuesday Club, Jonathan Grog Esqr, Master of Ceremonies and the Secretary, waited upon him in the next Room, acquainting him that he was elected a member, upon which they conducted him into the Club Room, where the honorable the president met him at the Door, and Saluted him with a hearty manuquassation, an honor, which was never done to any longstanding member, either before or since, and a happy Presage, or pompous prelude, to the great honors, that were soon to be heaped upon him.

Then Jonathan Grog Esqr, Master of Ceremonies, placeing

him nigh the presidential Chair, confirmed him in the following manner.

"Sir,

I as master of Ceremonies to our ancient and honorable Tuesday Club, with all the Ceremony I am master of, which mastery in Ceremonies, I acknowledge to be conveyd to me, by the authority of our honorable President, do Inaugurate, constitute and confirm you, Philo Dogmaticus Esqr, a good firm and Longstanding member of the Commoners, of this our ancient and honorable Tuesday Club, in token of which, I Invest you, with this the Club's badge, and here Solemnly present you, to the honorable the president, recommending it to you, to make your acknowledgements to the honorable the president and Club, in the handsomest and best Speech you can devise, upon this Important, and honorable occasion."

Then Mr Dogmaticus, standing in a proper posture and attitude, addressed the honorable the president and Club as follows.

"Honorable Mr President,

Honored Knight,

and all ye other worshipful officers, and,

Worthy members of the ancient & honorable Tuesday Club,

I Joyfully acknowledge the honor you have done me by my admission into your most noble Society, for which I return you my most grateful thanks, from a heart that shall always be devoted to the promoting of the honor and benefit of this Club in opposition to all Envious Rivals, and malicious Enimies, who can distinguish themselves only by reviling or detracting from that worth, which they must for ever despair of equalling.

May the ancient and honorable Tuesday Club, subsist and florish, while the Sun and moon Endures, and you my honored Superiors, and other worthy fellow members of it *Macti virtuti, omnique Genere foelicitatis estote,*[1] *Amen* and *Amen*."

[1]"Be honored with virtue and every kind of happiness" (first phrase echoes Horace, *Satirae* 1.2.31).

Mr Dogmaticus, having thus finished his gratulatory Speech, was Saluted by all round as a member, and took his Seat in Club accordingly. ❀❀

Then the Club proceeded to chuse a Chancellor, and keeper of the great Seal, and the Revd: Mr Philo dogmaticus, by a great majority was elected for that Important office, and the great Seal being Solemnly delivered to him by Jonathan Grog Esqr, master of Ceremonies, he in a handsom manner gave Thanks for the great and Important trust Committed to him, of Chancellor and keeper of the honorable the Presidents Clubical Conscience, solemnly promising a faithful execution of it, and then took his place appointed by the Club, on the left hand of his honor's Chair of State. . . .

Thus we find, in a most Surprizing and astonishing manner, this gentleman promoted to a great and new office of trust in the Club, on the very night, in which he was admitted a Longstanding member, without so much as applying or making Interest for it, which is a sign of either the great personal merit and Capacity of this gentleman, or at least, of the great opinion, his honor the president and Club had of his abilities and parts, but be that as it will, his honor never was so much mistaken in his man as now, . . . for he thought he had now got a firm friend to the prerogative and power of the Chair, but in a little time found himself most woefully baulked, for Mr Dogmaticus turned out to be a Zealous Republican, and a Stiff advocate for, and mantainer of Clubical liberty, and, we shall find this State officer, in the Sequel of our History, giving many a bold check to the petulence of the Chair, and occasioning many heartburns, broils, dissentions and Contentions, between his honor & the Longstanding members, and the principal author, exciter and fomenter of a great, dangerous & bloody rebellion, which broke out in the Club, as in due time shall be related. ❀❀

BOOK VII

*From the Creation of
the Chancellor & ct:
To the Introduction
of the Conundrums,
and the Chancellor's trial.*

Chapter 1 ❧ *General History of Conundrums, Puns, Riddles, Rebuses, Anagrams and Posies.*

Upon my entry into the Second Volume of this most prodigious History, methinks I am like one embarked, and ready to lose himself in a vast and Boundless Ocean, where I shall be tumbled about and carried to and fro, over restless and rolling waves, and scarce find any landing place, or the least prospect of *terra firma*, or land mark, whereon to fix my roving view. I am now to engage in a very Intricate and difficult task, That is, to give a short and summary History of wit and Humor, short and summary, I say, because I shall only skim the Surface, and take the Cream as I go along.

An accurate history of wit is what has been much wanted in the republic of letters, for, after Indefatigable Searches, and diligent Scrutinies, I cannot find any single author of our Clubical Class, that has treated this Subject in an historical manner, Some Indeed among the moderens, particularly the celebrated Mr Addison, has but Just transiently handled the Subject, and treated on Clubs *en passant*,[1] giving a few Specimens of the hu-

---

[1] Hamilton is alluding especially to *Spectator*s 9, 34, and 89.

mors and Conceits of these nocturnal assemblies, others more on the Clubical lay have exhibited curious collections of witty Sayings and Jests, witness the celebrated Tom Brown,[2] that prime Bard of Grubstreet, and that yet unparallelled paragon, Mr Ward, author of that Ingenious, smart and elegant piece, Intituled the *London Spy,* and those Inimitable poems ycleped *Matrimonial Dialogues*[3] . . . ; But not one of all these famous Grubeans, tho very equal to the task, has deigned to give us a detail historical and critical, of that distinguishing faculty of human Nature. I therefore, tho altogether unqualified, for so arduous an undertaking, and only a Star of the Second or third magnitude, among these Illustrious sons of Hesperus, shall humbly presume to lead the way, and open a door for abler heads, and Sharper pens, to treat this curious and new Subject.

❀❀

The first, and most ancient wit that we hear of Indeed is the Devil, who outwitted mother Eve, and persuaded her by certain quibbling Speeches and dowble entendres, to eat that Cursed *Apple* (as some call it) which empoisoned her whole posterity with Sin and misery. The admirable Milton, who has given us a beautiful and finished poem upon this very Subject, Introduces this ancient Rebel and deceiver, very much in Character, by making him an expert punster, we find him Calling gun powder in the act of Explosion, *Terms of Composition*, a breast work of cannon, *an open front*, and the confusion of the opposite Squadrons upon their discharge, he calls *a quick result to these terms.*—This is as plain punning as can be, and (if true) the most ancient Instance that is extant of it; In answer to these puns, Belial, his brother Devil, produces a whole String of them, he

---

[2]Thomas Brown (1663–1704) was an English satirist and author of the famous "I do not love thee, Dr. Fell" (see below, n. 8) and *Amusements Serious and Comical* (London, 1700), humorous sketches of London life.

[3]Edward "Ned" Ward (1667–1731) was an English author of Hudibrastic doggerel verse and coarse, humorous prose, including *The London Spy* (London, 1698–1703) and the *Marriage Dialogues* (1709).

calls the Shot, or Bullets, *terms of weight of hard contents*, which being *urged home stumbled many,* and those who receive them right, *had need to understand well from head to foot,* and, if not well understood, they serve *to show when the enimy does not walk upright;*[4] These ancient diabolical puns (with all reverence be it spoken to our Celebrated Poet,) would pass exceeding well, among our greatest Club wits and punsters in Christendom.

Immediatly after the General flood, we find Ham, exercising his wit upon his Sire Noe, passing Scurvy Jokes on his drunkeness and Nakedness, for which the old fellow, who seems not to have understood railery, bestowed a hearty curse on him and his posterity. There are many Instances in the Sacred archives, of great feats done by wit and Ingenious finnesse, Jacob tricked his brother Esau out of his birthright, Imposed upon his father Isaac, so as to get the blessing from his elder Brother, but herein he was asisted by the wit and Subtilty of a woman, vizt: his mother Rebecca, and, we often find, that the artifice and wit of a woman, excells all other, except only, that of the Old Serpent himself, . . . many more Instances might be mentioned of the like nature, but for brevity's Sake, I pass them over, only, I cannot help mentioning one more, and that is, of Sampson, Judge of Israel, whom we find puzzling the Philistines with a riddle, to answer which he allowed them Seven days, but all their wit could not unriddle it, 'till they were privatly Informed of it by his wife, who had wormed the explication out of her husband, under a promise (as is supposed) of Secrecy, . . . the Philistines, by the help of this explication, to the no small astonishment of the Riddle maker, explain the Riddle, upon which, Sampson turns punster, and tells them, that if they had not ploughed with his heifer, they never could have expounded his riddle, this shows us the great antiquity of Riddles and puns, and from thence we may draw this conclusion, that women in all ages of the world, were bad Secret keepers.

[4]*Paradise Lost,* 6.611–627.

Having given that preference, which is due to Sacred History, I now proceed to exhibit some Specimens of wit, out of profane writers, to wit, Poets, Philosophers, and Historians.

❊❊

Athens, which was of old, a celebrated Seat of the Muses, brought up, like an Alma mater, several Celebrated punsters, Riddle-me-ree men and repartee masters, The Learning of the Sceptics, (who had a Considerable School there) consisted chiefly in clenching and playing upon words, nor could their arguments, such as they were, finely spun, and nicely wove, (much like those of our moderen Metaphysicians,) be Successfully Carried on, without frequent use of the dubious and dowble meaning, and the quaint quibble, . . . to Learn this art, among other quaint and humorous accomplishments, Xenocrates shut himself up for several years, in this famous nursery of arts & Sciences, and returned again into the world an accomplished wit; a notable Instance of humor and drollery he exhibited, by getting to bed for one whole night with Lais, the famous Corinthian Courtezan, after whom, all the world, at that time ran mad for Love, or rather lust, and got up from her in the morning fresh and fasting, and, as Good a maid (as he affirmed himself) as when he went to bed with her;[5] this odd piece of humor in the Sage, afforded matter of laughter and wonder for nine days at least, to all the young Smarts and rakes of these times; Even Socrates himself, the Gravest, and most Sedate of all the Athenians, . . . condescended at times to mix in the Company of Strollers & Comedians, to drink off his glass with roaring Companions, and in frolicksome Clubs, to write fables, and tell witty tales. The known Story, of the Scurvey usage this

[5]Xenocrates of Chalcedon, a disciple of Plato and head of the Academy from 339 to 314 B.C., was known for his austerity and self-control. Lais was the name of at least two celebrated courtesans of Corinth and, eventually, a generic name for courtesan. Hamilton's sources for the story are probably Valerius Maximus (4.3.3) and Diogenes Laertius (4.2).

Philosopher met with from Xantippe his wife, the most per-plexing termagant and Vixen, that ever Contended for the Breeches, evinces this wise man's Strong turn for wit and hu-mor; after he had received, as an Eplogue to a Smart Scolding bout, from the hands of that Invincible virago, the discharge of a well replenished pispot right on his head, he said pleasantly, wiping and stroaking down his head, face, hoary beard and gar-ments, and shaking his reverend ears, that nothing was more common, after fierce winds, and loud Claps of thunder, than heavy Showrs of Rain.[6]

※※

The prince of poets Homer, who has been Called with great propriety the father of Poetry, shows himself to have been a compleat master of the Gelosophia,[7] (if I may be allowed the term) in his characters of Thersites the Buffoon, and Vulcan the Blacksmith, as also, in his history of the amours of Mars and Venus, . . . where the true Burlesque is exactly followed up, and seems much the same with that used at this day, by our Moderen Grubstreet Bards, and in our Club Conversa-tions. . . . Ovid, thro' all his works, abounds with genuine paragrammatical, or Rather *pragmatical* wit, and seems to have had the rarest knack at it, (Martial the Epigrammatist excepted) of all the Latin poets. An Instance of the wit of the last men-tioned poet, will not come in Improperly here with an Inge-nious translation of it, by a young Student, applying it, to one Doctor Fell,[8] his Pedagogue, or master, who it seems was a per-son, not much loved by his pupils.

[6]Hamilton is probably recalling the account by Diogenes Laertius of Xan-thippe's argument with Socrates, in which, after she scolds him, then drenches him with water (not urine), he wisely informs his companions that he knew her thunder would end in rain (*Socrates* 2.35).

[7]*Gelosophia* is Hamilton's invention for "the art of laughter."

[8]Dr. John Fell (1625–1686) was bishop of Oxford and promoter of the Ox-ford University Press. Although much respected in his day, modern readers

Non amo te, Sabidi, nec possum dicere quare,
Hoc tantum, possum dicere, non amo te.
Translated
I love you not Doctor Fell,
And why, I cannot tell,
I only this can tell,
I love you not Doctor Fell.

❀❀

Democritus and Diogenes, Both Philosophers of ancient Greece, seem to have been persons of a Strong turn towards Drollery, and Clubical wit, tho of opposite characters, The first being a merry, facetious and good humored companion and a hearty Laugher, the latter of a more Solemn turn, and humor more adapted for your hum-drum Clubs, tho as much a droll as the first. . . . But of all the droll fellows that ever appeared among these Philosophers, that Sage, (whose name I cannot now recollect)[a] in my eye, seems the most whimsical and burlesque, who, when he was Caught in the act of leudness with his doxy in the Streets of the City of Sparta, being reproved for it, was (as he pretended) very much Surprized at the Insolence of his reprovers, seeing (as he said) that he was employed about a very Laudable work, for the good and advantage of Society and posterity, vizt: *The planting of men.*

Having thus cursorily traveled thro antiquity and given a slight Scetch of the State of wit among our ancestors, I should now take a Survey of the moderen State of wit, which I shall do in as brief a manner as I possibly can.

The Gothic Incursions had for some centuries, buried polite Learning and Arts, in a huge Chaos of Barbarism, Stupidity and Ignorance, so, that there was not to be seen or found in any

---

remember him most as the butt of Thomas Brown's poem. Fell, dean of Christ Church, had expelled Brown but said he would remit the sentence if Brown could translate Martial's 23d epigram (first book). The translation Hamilton provides is roughly the same as Brown's.

[a]This is told of Diogenes.

place, not even in the Cells and Cloisters of the monks, where the small remains of learning and wit, fled at first for refuge, the least Sign of a Genius for any Sort of wit or Ingenuity. Those who devoted themselves to a monastic life, a State of Leisure and Inactivity, Instead of Bestowing their leisure time, of which they enjoyed a great deal, in useful Studies, did nothing but eat, drink, whore, loll, saunter, sleep, and mutter over a rabble of unintelligible prayers. In this State of Torpor was the drowsy world for a Considerable Time, till Mahomet the Great took and sacked the City of Constantinople, then a Swarm of Greek monks poured in upon Europe, and bringing along with them, such of the writings of the ancients, as were saved from the fury of war, fire and desolation, curiosity prompted some to pry into and study these writings, upon this, wit began again to raise her disconsolate head, and the first grand task she applied herself to, was commenting and expatiating upon the writings of that Great Philosopher Aristotle, this was for a great while the labor of Duns Scotus and the Schoolmen,[9] who were the broachers of a Sort of Learning, very Intricate and obscure, which dealt chiefly in *abstracted notions, Entities, Identities, quiddities, Substantialities, consubstantialities, Transubstantialities, Spiritualities, materialities,* and a hundred other Sesquipedalian terms, then was Introduced the *Ars dialectica,* together with *Barbara, Celarunt, Darii, ferio, Baralipton,*[10] and other such Barbarous terms, which sounded in vulgar ears like the names of so many Infernal Devils. By this art, a man could in a Sylogistical way prove very clearly, that *a man was no horse* or *a horse no man,* and vice versa, *a man was a horse* and *a horse a man,* this Celebrated Science has since been of Singular use both in the pulpit and at the bar,—Then was Introduced also the *Ars metaphysica,* which could reduce nothing to something, and

[9]John Duns Scotus (1265?–1308?), known as Doctor Subtilis, was one of the great medieval Scholastic theologians.

[10]These words, nonsense in themselves, are a Scholastic mnemonic for teaching the patterns of syllogisms.

something to nothing, create many an *Ens rationis*,[11] and draw a parallel between abstracted Ideas and Substantial forms, making them walk hand in hand together by analogy, so as either to force your assent, or altogether deprive you of your Senses.

By the Sages of these Bright Illuminated times, many dark matters, or arcana of nature were discovered, Magic, that ancient art, was revived and new modelled, and, Instead of being conversant in the motions and revolutions of the heavenly bodies, and geometrical problems, as in the Days of Abraham, Zoroaster, Hermes and Ptolomy,[12] it consisted in drawing Circles, erecting Strange figures, Invoking certain devils by new Invented names, and putting the Body into antic dresses and postures. . . . Then many elaborate Tracts were wrote *de Secretis naturæ*, after the Stile and manner of the great Albertus Magnus, who, in those days composed an Ingenious tract, *De Secretis mulierum*,[13] in these profound writings were displayed many great arcana and Secrets, hitherto utterly unknown, such as how to know another man's thoughts, how to see into futurity, . . . how to prevent an evil eye, how to dream whatever you pleased, how to avoid witchcraft and fascination, how to exorcise the devil, and how to charm away distempers and cure them

[11]A Scholastic term, probably from Duns Scotus, meaning "something that exists only in the mind," as opposed to an *ens reale*.

[12]Zoroaster, the Greek name for Zarathustra (a figure of Aryan legend known to the Greeks as early as the fifth century B.C.), was credited with an immense number of works dealing with theology, astrology, and magic. Hermes Trismegistus, the name given to the Egyptian god "Thoth the very great," was the reputed author of philosophical-religious treatises and various works on astrology, magic, and alchemy. Ptolemy (fl. A.D. 127–148) was a celebrated mathematician, geographer, and astronomer whose major work, the *Almagest*, is a complete textbook of astronomy as the Greeks understood it.

[13]Albertus Magnus (1192?–1280), a German Dominican friar and great Scholastic philosopher (nicknamed Doctor Universalis), was known as a wizard, although he was not a professed alchemist; of his many works on chemistry and philosophy, the ones Hamilton cites are spurious.

by repeating of certain words, an Instance of which we have in
the Ingenious Invention of a Sage of those times,[14] which is a
Charm of words to drive away a quartan ague, vizt:

```
a   b   r   a   c   a   d   a   b   r   a
a   b   r   a   c   a   d   a   b   r
a   b   r   a   c   a   d   a   b
a   b   r   a   c   a   d   a
a   b   r   a   c   a   d
a   b   r   a   c   a
a   b   r   a   c
a   b   r   a
a   b   r
a   b
a.
```

This admirable Charm, has, as we are told been used with Success for a thousand times, but some how or other, in these our
degenerate days, has lost it's efficacy, probably from some necessary Circumstance being ommitted in the use of the Charm,
such, perhaps, as repeating it in a certain hour of the day or
night, or fasting, or in a particular posture of body, or dressed
in a particular attire, or with two Stockings on one leg, or with
a Jacket wrong Side outwards, . . . the ommission of any the
least part of which ceremonies, would render the Charm of no
effect.

※※

Poetry too, at this time, began to raise her mortified head, from
among the Rubbish of Ignorance & barbarism, and was so over-
joyed, that she began at once to carrol it, in pleasant jingle, and
delectable Rhime, which jingle, she has been so fond of ever
since, that she has never quitted it, . . . and, tho some old fash-
ioned fellows, such as Milton and Shakespear among the English, have dizened her up, in her ancient plain Stole of the

[14]*Abracadabra* is a cabalistic charm, supposedly derived from the initials of
the Hebrew words *Ab* ("Father"), *Ben* ("Son"), and *Ruach Acadsch* ("Holy
Spirit") and formerly used as an antidote against ague and other maladies.

Blank Rithmos, yet she still most affects the company and conversation of our Jingle Jangle men, and soft Sweet Rhimers, this attire, which she has of late appeared in, is utterly moderen, true indeed some of the ancients attempted . . . to put her in this dress, and were laugh'd at for their pains, particularly Cicero, when he took it in his head to turn poet, composed an admirable Jingling line so often quoted since his time, as an instance of his Strong genius for Poetry, *O Fortunatam, Natam me Consule Romam.* . . .[15] But Cicero, in the above recited instance, might have said the same, as the renownd Doctor Sydenham said, when a certain mode of practice, which he recommended, was laughd at, by his bretheren Physicians—"whatever you may now think, gentlemen, of this my practice, however you may please to redicule it, yet I know it will prevail and be in vogue, when all our heads are laid."[16]

✲✲

History likewise, in these enlightened times, received additions and Improvements which it never before had, and was dressed up in very fine and Gaudy trappings, to the Immortal Geniuses of that age, we owe, the new and rare Invention of Romance writing, a kind of History, altogether Novel, (hence some kinds of Romances are called *Novels*) and hitherto unknown, from these great Historians, came the Prodigious Histories of *Amadis De Gaul, Amadis de Grece,* . . .[17] and a hundred other voluminous pieces, equally witty amusing and Instructive.

[15]"O lucky Rome, born when I was consul!" (quoted in Quintilian, *Institutes* 9.4.41, for its bad scansion, and 11.1.24, for its immodest sentiment).

[16]Thomas Sydenham (1624–1689), "the English Hippocrates," introduced new methods of treating smallpox, agues, and other maladies as a result of clinical observation rather than theory. In the preface to *The Whole Works of That Excellent Practical Physician Dr. Thomas Sydenham* (London, 1696), Sydenham anticipates the negative responses his observations will draw, but not in the words Hamilton attributes to him.

[17]*Amadís de Gaula* is a 15th-century Spanish or Portuguese romance; *Amadís de Grecia* (1530), by Feliciano da Silva (fl. 16th century), is a Spanish sequel to *Amadís de Gaula.*

These were the Heroical Histories of the times. There were also the amorous Histories of *Cassandra, Cleopatra, Clelia,* & *Almahyde,*[18] all adapted to excite amorous and tender passions, particularly among the readers of the fair Sex, The ancient Kingdom of France was very productive of Inventions of this kind, naturally flowing from the volatile and sprightly Humor of that Gay people.

The pulpit, which poured forth Streams of excellent paragrammatical, or pragmatical wit, in those halcyon days, and sounded forth deep Mysteries, in a beautiful Ænigmatical Stile, is now turned into a rostrum, whence nothing is to be heard but dry morality. When, oh when, shall we again hear Paradise Called a *pair of dice*, all houses, *Ale houses*, Divines, *Dry vines*, & matrimony a *matter of money,* from that Learned Chair of truth; . . . when again, shall these blessed times return, when Ingenious punsters shall be promoted according to their merit, to places of honor and profit? when again shall our Theatrical performances overflow with that quaint punning, with which they teemed in the days of Shakespear and Ben Johnson. Heaven restore that happy time, when the true Paragrama shall again raise her head, and banish what is called Simple Nature, with her plain fanatic puritanical Dress, but, that I may not digress too much and run away from my Subject, I shall now proceed to the Critical part of this history of wit and humor.

The Species of wit, which is my proper Subject at present, is what I call true Sheer wit, and, as it is usual for Learned authors to define their Subject, before they enter fairly upon it, I

[18]The first two titles were written by Gauthier de Costes de La Calprenède (1614–1663), French author of several lengthy romances. *Cassandre* (1644–1650) concerns the daughter of Darius and wife of Alexander; *Cléopâtre* (1647–1656) involves a supposed daughter of Antony's Cleopatra. The second two were written by La Calprenède's equally prolific contemporary, Madeleine de Scudéry (1607–1701). *Clélie* (1654–1660) concerns the Clelia who escaped the power of Porsenna by swimming the Tiber; and *Almahide* (1660) is a story of the Moors in Spain.

shall here take some pains, to define that Sort of wit which is here treated of.

Mr Locke, Mr Dryden, and Sir Richard Blackmore, have all of them defined wit differently, and, as it is common for wits to differ, as much as Doctors, I (tho a puny wit) shall beg leave to differ from them all.

Mr Locke says, that "wit consists in an assemblage of Ideas, and Joining such of them together as have any fitness or congruity, with such variety and Quickness as to excite agreeable visions and pleasant pictures in the fancy."[19]

Mr Dryden Tells us that "wit is a propriety of words, and thoughts, adapted to the Subject,"[20] and

Sir Richard Blackmore Informs us very Gravely, and more like a Physician or Philosopher than a poet, That "Wit proceeds from a Concurrence of regular and exalted ferments, and an affluence of animal Spirits, rectified and refined to a degree of purity."[21]

Tho it does not become me to criticise upon great poets and Philosophers, being myself but an understrapper, yet I may modestly differ from them, and therefore, I reject the preceeding definitions as faulty, and shall give you one of my own framing.

Wit then, is a certain faculty, actuated by the fancy, which can out of Chaos bring order, and again reduce order to a Chaos, the materials it works upon, being the brain furniture of a poet or Critic of the Celebrated academy of Grubstreet, which Chamber and furniture exactly resembles a Lumber Garret, and its Miscellaneous contents, The operator *Fancy*, putting the

[19]Locke's famous definition of wit appears in *An Essay concerning Human Understanding* (1690).

[20]This quotation appears in "The Author's Apology for Heroic Poetry and Poetic Licence," Dryden's preface to *The State of Innocence, and Fall of Man* (1677).

[21]This passage appears in *An Essay upon Wit*, in *Essays upon Several Subjects* (London, 1716), 193.

broken pieces together, consistently or Inconsistently as she pleases, by which she always excites Gelastic motions in the Landlord of the said Garret or the wit himself, and sometimes in others, but more frequently in these others produces furious contorsions of the countenance, scornful frowns, and contemptuous grins and Sneers, this garret lumber being often full of spikes Snags, and crooked rusty nails, which being hursled about in a violent manner by the fantastical operator Fancy, are apt to gall, prick, fret and wound whenever they touch tender parts. This Fancy is a very Ingenious artist, and a fit Inhabitant for such a Lumber Garret, as a poet's or critic's Skull, for she has the knack of bringing together and uniting things that bear no relation or afinity to each other, things that are even directly opposite and contradictory one to the other, and thereby Creates such forms and monstruous Structures as are fit to frighten children, vizt: Chymeras, Sphynxes, Harpies and Centaurs; abundance of her freaks this way may be seen in the ancient Theology and mythology, and more glaringly in the productions of our moderen wits; In the first, are still to be seen, upon Stones and medals, dowble faced Januses, men and boys with wings and plumage, Serpents with human heads, . . . and a thousand other devices of the like kind; The moderen Inventions of this kind Indeed, consist more in productions of the fancy of a more abstract nature, and not comeing directly under the Cognisance of the Sculptor and painter, Such are these prodigious productions of human wit, called puns, Conundrums, Riddles, Rebuses, Anagrams . . . & posies, all which, I Intend to treat of in order as they stand.

A pun is properly the evolution of a Conundrum, as a Conundrum is the Involution of a pun, but this definition, like many others, would need a Comment or Explication, and, as the best way of explaining, is by giving examples, I shall here exhibit a pun and a Conundrum in their proper Shapes. A gentleman in a Tavern, speaking of a table, round which the Company sat, said: *This is not a Tavern Table,*—why so? said one of the Company,—because said he, there is never a *drawer* in it, The Table being without that convenience,—This is a genuine and proper pun, but, if the same gentleman had said, *Why are some tables like Taverns?* and any one had answered, because they have got *drawers* in them, this would have been a proper conundrum, or the aforsaid pun Involved. . . .

I have Sufficiently Enlarged upon the Conundrum with regard to the Etymology of the word in the foregoing part of our History,[22] and have little more to add concerning it here. . . . I might here give examples of several Celebrated conundrums Invented by the wits of our times, but I shall wave that for brevitys Sake, as I shall have occasion in this history to exhibit many of the Tuesday Club Conundrums, which, for elegance and propriety, excell all others, that have been Invented before or since; In fine, as a Conundrum, is a Species of the Riddle or Ænigma, because it is something Involved, that Requires an Evolution, or Explication, . . . I think some such figure as the following, would be a proper representation of the moderen Conundrum, which is a human head placed upon a large brawny pair of buttocks, this truely represents a Conundrum as a performance of wit which has two extremes, but never a mean, or middle part, and these two extremes are distorted, or turned the wrong way, so that to find a mean, or meaning for it, and turn the distorted parts into their proper situation or posture, is a trial of Skill in the person that resolves the Conundrum, this figure, might *ad libitum*, be depicted, either with a gelastic grin, or with a grave countenance, according to the Species of wit couched under the Conundrum, some Subjects being grave

---

[22]In book IV, chap. 1, Hamilton writes: "Every one, who understands the french Language, knows what is meant by the word *Con*, which, for fear of offence to modest ears, I shall not translate into English, it is derived then, . . . from this french word *con*, and two english words added to it, vizt: the words *under* and *him*, but the two last words for the ease of our polite pronouncers and writers have been contracted thus, *und'r'um*, and the whole Joined together make . . . the plain word *Conundrum*."

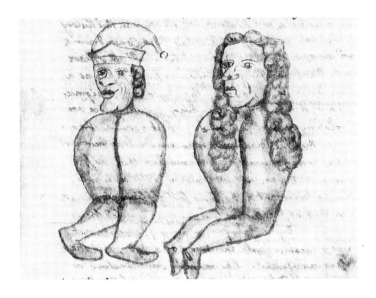

& Solemn, and others light and merry, . . . as for any other Significant matters expressed by this hieroglyphic, I mention them not here, that the critics of Succeeding times may have some Scope to work upon, for probably these Gentlemen, may discover certain Mysteries in it, which I, the Inventor, never once thought of, like many of our moderen Antiquaries, and medal Historians, who find out meanings in medals and old Inscriptions, which the Inventors never Intended.

Every old woman and School-boy knows what a riddle is, that being an usual entertainment by a winter's fire, a proper place for framing of Riddles and solving of them, so that it will be needless for me to give a definition of it here, these have been exhibited to the public, by our wits both in prose and verse, and the late Ingenious Dean Swift has given Specimens of his great Skill in this kind of Composition, in his poetical *Miscellanies*,[23] which, as they are in every bodies hands, I shall make no ex-

[23]Probably a reference to *Miscellanies in Prose and Verse*, 5 vols. (London, 1727–1735), of which the first volume has a preface signed by Swift and Pope, and the fifth has some titled riddles in verse.

cerpts from them, but shall here give my readers a Riddle of
my own framing, as an example, to let them see wherein this
piece of wit differs from the pun & Conundrum.

Riddle

My head is wavering and light, ⎫
And yet I serve to guide aright ⎬
All travellers that walk by night, ⎭
I have no knowledge of my own,
Yet Stores of learning I make known,
I oft require a pinch of Snuff,
And often vanish at a puff.

Any one, who has a moderate quantum of brains, may discover
that which is Intended by this Ænigma, and therefore I need
show him no *Candle* to guide him in his way.

❋❊

The ancients generally framed their Rebus in pieces of Sculpture or painting, or struck it on medals and it went by the Name
of Hieroglyphic. The moderen Rebus differs from the Ancient
Hieroglyphic in this particular, that it is done by circumlocu-
tion, or a prolix description, instead of exhibeting the Pigmata
or Iconographia. To give an Instance, suppose a Gentleman,
whose name is Thomas Codlington, was to be Hieroglyphized
in the ancient, or Rebused in the moderen manner, an ancient
operator would do it thus, first, draw the figure of any one volume of a Large book in folio, which makes *Tom,* . . . then represent the figure of an Ass, which Compleats *Tom as* or Thomas,
then after allowing a convenient distance between the figures to
distinguish the Christen'd name from the Sirname, represent
the figure of a Cod fish, then the said fish salted, dried, and
spread out, which is *ling,* and last of all, the picture of a Town,
and thus you will have *Cod ling town,* or Codlington, which
summed up makes Thomas Codlington; The Moderen method
to Rebus this gentleman's name, would be quite different, for

a wit of the present age, would employ many words to express only these two, and this he would chuse to do in verse, perhaps in the following manner.

> Of a high German critic take Volume the first,
> And a Creature with dullness & long ears accursd,
> A fish that in northeren Seas they do take,
> The same cur'd with Salt & then dried on a flake,
> A Rabble of houses, built all in a Cluster,
> Put them aptly together, a man's name you'll muster.

※※

I come now to the Anagram, which is only a proper Name transformed, by shifting the letters of it from their natural places to others, by which transposition and transmutation, is framed a word or a Sentence, which expresses some remarkable quality accident or action of the person, whose name is so anagrammatized, for example, let us take a man's name and a womans, such as Jasper Goswall, and Mary Carrier, they might stand Anagrammatized thus, supposing the first person to be a rogue and the latter a whore.

Jasper Goswall   Mary Carrier
anagram   anagram
A Gallows I press.   I marry Care.

These anagrams are of the Satyrical kind, but some are of the panegyrical Stamp, such as authors may compose for their patrons, and lovers for their mistresses, I shall give two examples of this Sort, the first passing a Compliment on a patron, the latter expressing a lover's Suffering for his mistress.

Robert Boonight   Elmira Damahoy
anagram   anagram
Right noble root.   Oh! I am realy mad!

And this is enough to show the nature of this kind of Ingenuity.

※※

The last piece of moderen wit which I shall Consider, is the posie, which may be called a dwarfish Sort of poetry, the lines being short, and consisting of few words, because these performances must be crammed into a small Space, that is, into a wedding ring or a pair of Garters, tho' there has been Instances of this kind of poetry upon Tavern Signs, and advertisements, two Remarkable ones of this Sort, are 1st That Ingenious Posie, which was Composed by a Certain Parson, at the Instance of a Taveren keeper, at the Sign of the Bell, at whose house he often Tossed off a Can of good beer, The Landlord desiring that the Inscription upon his Sign post might be a Loyal one, and also have some relation to the bell, the Parson composed the following Ingenious Rhime to be wrote under the Bell.

Dong ding
May the king
Ding dong
Live Long.

2d, that Quaint and Laconic advertisement, put up by a doctor on the Street door of the house where he Lodg'd.

In this place
Lives Doctor Case.[24]

The Tavern Inscription got the Landlord much Custom and the Parson Guzzled his pots of Beer Gratis, 'till like most parsons he waxed very fat and unwieldy, as for Doctor Case, The Singularity of his advertisement, much augmented his practise.

There are two Sorts of these posies, vizt: posies for wedding rings, and posies for Ladies Garters, Examples of both follow.

[24]The bearer of that sign is John Case (fl. 1680–1700), an astrologer who eventually styled himself M.D. and is mentioned by Addison, Pope, and others.

Ring Posies	*Garter Posies*
By Love I move.	Love ever Join Your heart and mine.
At heart I smart.	Who views your eyes Most Surely dies.
To you I bow.	Give me one kiss And Crown my bliss.

Many Examples might be given of posies, but these are Sufficient, to give the Reader a taste. And now having finished this Important Chapter, whose length I suppose, will the less Chagrin the reader, when he considers that this extensive Subject has been discussed in so small a Compass, I have nothing now to do, but to proceed with our History.

Chapter 4 ✖ *Complaint of Sir John, Club Conundrums and Jests.*

It is a question that has often been propounded by Philosophers, but never to my knowledge has had a Satisfactory resolution, vizt: whether there be any Remedy in nature to cure men of that Impertinent, Censorious and fault finding humor that prevails among them? It is Certain that every man has a particular failing, peculiar to himself, which he can by no means thorrowly conceal, . . . and the reason of this is that every man gives more attention to his neighbours defects than to his own; and, whatever contributes to render his neighbour's Character Ridiculous, he will paint it out in strong and lively colors, and Censure and Condemn him for it beyond all measure or modesty. To Cure this malignant humor effectually, a man need only with alittle more attention look Inwards upon himself, and ten to one but he finds a like or a worse picture there. The Carracatura then

Corresponding with his own features, or perhaps not so ridiculous or distorted, will probably, as soon as he perceives it, strike him so as to make him forbear, or at least behave with more Charity and moderation.

We have observed thro' the course of this History when we had occasion to touch upon the Character and actions of the Honorable the President, that his Chief foible was Love of power, and therefore, he used all the methods possible to make himself absolute in the Club, this was the Cause of frequent Brawls between him and the Longstanding members, who were very unwilling to submit to an unreasonable yoke. The late Created Chancellor Philo Dogmaticus, soon discovered this unhappy foible in his honor the President, and took an opportunity to Ingratiate himself with the members, by setting up as an advocate for, and a mantainer of their Liberties and privileges, and being an open free spoken man, and withal positive, and somewhat Rough in his behaviour, he failed not at all times to reprimand his honor the President to his face and use hard speeches to him, calling him a Tyrant, and an oppressor, as will be seen on many occasions in the Sequel, . . . but notwithstanding the Chancellors Specious pretences for Clubical liberty, and his professed detestation of Tyranny and arbitrary power, he was himself of such an austere Cast and disposition, that of all men he was the most unfit to be trusted with any degree of power or authority over others; which appeared by his boistrous and Tumultuous behaviour, which many times broke out with ungovernable violence, and, had he ever obtained the Chair, he would Surely have Turned out, a more arbitrary Tyrant than his honor the president, but being partial to himself, like most men, he never perceived that he possessed this foible to a greater degree, than his honor the President, for, to say the truth, when he reprehended his honor on this account, it was neither more nor less, than the pot calling the kettle black-arse according to the old proverb.

[At Sederunt 123 January 30th,] Sir John, knight and Champion of the Club, stood up, and made a complaint, That the Understrappers, or Subaltern officers of this here Club, had already received their Commissions from his honor the president, at a Certain Sham Committee, which he hoped the Club would examine into, and, that he, the Chief State officer of the Club, and the next person in dignity to the Chair, the defender and Champion of the liberties and privileges of the Club, . . . had been slighted, neglected, and used in an affrontive and Contemptuous manner, having had no Commission as yet, granted or offered to him, by his honor the President, . . . he therefore requested the Club, if they had any regard for his character and dignity as chief State officer, or any care for their own Safety and liberties, as he was their Champion, to give him Immediatly a Commission, and power to act as knight and Champion of the Club, otherwise, his Sword helmet and Coat of mail, might, for ought he Cared lye bye and rust, and this here ancient club be exposed to Continual assaults and Insults, without his trowbling himself about defending or protecting it.

The Club finding the Justice of these complaints and foreseeing the danger of these terrible threats, entered Seriously upon Consideration of the matter, and, after some warm debates, it was resolved, that a Commission should be drawn up for Sir John under the great Seal, and subscribed by all the members, this was a piece of machinery of the Chancellor's, who finding the terror the Club was in, at the boisterous threats and Stern looks of the Champion, took this opportunity to bring them to consent to this rash proceeding, and, to show, that he durst use the Great Seal, the badge of his office, without consulting his honor the President about the matter, this, he avowedly owned he did, to pull down alittle the presidential pride, and throw light upon his hardened, or darkened conscience, of which Conscience, he Justly reckoned himself the master or keeper.

※※

Then the Secretary was ordered Immediatly to draw up a Commission for Sir John, which having done, the great Seal was affixed, all the members present subscribed their names, and the Commission was Solemnly presented to Sir John by the Secretary, in the name of all the members, for which Sir John made a Champion like Compliment & bow.

❋❋

Supper being ended, and the king and Club Toasted, The Conundrums were Called for according to the order of last Sederunt, when Jonathan Grog Esqr, master of the Ceremonies, with great Gravity, produced in Club his first Conundrum, wrote out upon a Scroll of paper, which was to the following Purpose.

Conundrum 1st

To drowsy man, pray how can you Compare
A garment that is worn till quite thread bare.

After deep Consideration, and handing round the billet among the members, Huffman Snap Esqr gave in answer, Because they both wanted a *nap*, the Club declared it was a good answer, and Jonathan Grog Esqr, drinking a Bumper, to the prosperity of the Club, delivered in another Scroll of paper, wrote upon to this effect.

ans: 1st: The answer's easie, for we all must grant,
that Both, and each of them a *nap* does want.

Then he delivered his Second conundrum to this purpose.

Conundrum 2d

How shall I to myself compare
The watch which in my fob I wear.

The Club after deep consideration could not answer this Conundrum, and Jonathan Grog Esqr, being declared victor gave in his answer to the following purpose.

ans: 2d: Because that each of us Contains,
A great deal more of *Guts* than Brains.

There arose a learned dispute in Club, whether this last was a proper Conundrum or not, as there seemed to be no Clench, or playing upon a word contained in it, at last it was agreed that it was proper.

These Conundrums having thrown the Club into a grave humor, by reason of the Intense Study the members exercised to solve them, in order to raise again the flagging Spirits of the Longstanding members, it was proposed that toasts should be drank with epithets, which Epithets should Rhime to the name of the Lady Toasted—This is an exercise of wit, at times much used in polite Companies, for Example, suppose one should drink miss Smart, has gained my heart, or miss Price is cosy and nice, . . . after several toasts of this Sort, miss Hunt was proposed as a toast in Club, at which Laconic Comus Esqr The deputy President said bluntly, in his dry manner, *who? Miss Hunt? it will be no difficult matter to find a rhime to fit her name—* and was Just going to say more, when an universal Laugh broke out among the members, which was so violent and loud, that the like had never yet been heard in Club, even when the Gelastic law was put in execution with the utmost violence and Rigor, or, when Mr Protomusicus exerted his best at a horse Laugh, in short, it was astonishing to hear how they laughed, till the tears gushed out at their Eyes, and they lost their breath, and the poet Laureat, who loved with all his Soul, a Joke of this Sort, laughed till his wig tumbled off of his head, and his bare poll would have equally become a Laurel or an Ivy wreath, had any one Claped it on at that time, but Laconic Comas Esqr, looked very much amazed and said once or twice, *Well! damn it!—what then?—what then?*—Thus merrily ended the Sederunt 123, which was the first Sederunt of the *Conundrums*, and might properly be called the gelastic Sederunt.

Chapter 6 ❧ *Fatal Comasian Conundrum, Club Conundrums, Second Embassy of the Triumvirate.*

I am now to relate an adventure, which excited much uneasiness in Club, by first depriving it of one of it's best members, and next, disgusting one of the principal State officers. . . . [At Sederunt 126,] after Supper, when the Conundrums, business and toasts were all discussed, and, every Longstanding member expected to retire in peace, Huffman Snap Esqr, stooping down, picked up a paper, which unfolding, he gravely Informed the club, that he had found a Conundrum, which if they pleased, he would read to them, That they might exercise their wits upon it. There arose Immediatly a murmur in the Club, some Trick of the Secretary's being suspected by his honor and the members, The Chancellor seized the Conundrum out of the hands of Huffman Snap, and saddling his nose with his Spectacles, read from the Scroll, as follows.

Why is L——— C———'s mouth like a puppet Show?

Immediatly on the Reading of this Conundrum, the Countenance of Laconic Comus Esqr fell, and a Cloud overspread his visage, which made him look excessively murky, . . . the Secretary, who (however much blamed in this affair) was no further concerned, than that he had composed the Conundrum, and rashly mentioned it, in the hearing of some people, who took the advantage to make their fun of it, by promulgating it, contrary to his advice, fearing a fatal event from Mr Comas's Indignation, alledged, that the Chancellor, from a defect, in his eyesight, or Spectacles, or both, did not clearly see or discern, the Initial letters of the Supposed name in the Conundrum, that if he Examined more nearly, he'd find that the Letters were J:G: and not L:C: this he did, in order, if possible, to roll the Joke from Laconic Comas upon Jonathan Grog Esqr, who was a facetious man of a quite opposite humor to the former, and could bear a Joke the best of any in the Club, returning always *tit* for *tat*, . . . but this artifice of the Secretarie's would not take, tho' Intended to serve the Club, by preventing the loss of one of its best members, which at last was the fatal effect of this wicked Conundrum; The Club Conjectured, that the Letters L:C: must Intend Laconic Comas, but declined giving any Solution of it, tho there wanted not in the Company who knew both the Conundrum and answer, and who it pointed at, even before it was produced in club. But the Chancellor, taking off his Spectacles, and stroaking down his beard, with a Superlatively grave Countenance, told the Club, that, tho wit was not his province, yet he would adventure the Solution of it, and submit it to their Candid Judgement, and Clapping on his Spectacles again he read

Why is L:C's mouth like a puppet Show?

Then unsaddling his nose, and looking up, he said, "I answer— Because there is always *Punch* in it."

At this answer some in the Club Laughed, others looked Serious, and a few pretended to be astonished, Mr Comas looked more Sullen than usual, and rising up, requested his honor, that he might be allowed to serve the Club once more at next Sederunt as high Steward, the president, who had not as yet, laid aside his timber Countenance, asked Mr Comas, if that was all he had got to say? to which he answered, that he had nothing else to offer—The president told him Smartly—that he Surely had less brains than tongue, which was next to none at all, to let this Scurvy Joke pass upon him unanswered; this Sharp Rebuke, made Mr Comas's heart Rise to his mouth, and it was said that the tears gushed out at his eyes, this Tragical end, had this unseasonable Joke, and this Sederunt broke up in bad humor.

The next Sederunt was held upon the 10th of April, 1750, Laconic Comas Esqr, being high Steward, and nothing passed at it but the Conundrums; only that some observed, that the H:S: wore a very unsatisfied Countenance, and droped several hints, Intimating that this was his last Service to the Club, and Indeed it proved so, for he left the Society this very night, not being able to swallow, far less to stomach that pestilent and Satyrical Conundrum, published on himself at last Sederunt.

The Conundrums then being Called for, Jonathan Grog Esqr, produced his, as follows.

Conundrum 1

Why is the king's prick, in marking down a Sheriff like an Elephant?

Jealous Spyplot Esqr made answer, Because it *Stands*, Jonathan Grog Esqr, drank a bumper to the Clubs prosperity, and gave in his answer.

ans: Because it always *Stands*.

Then he delivered his Second Conundrum.

Conundrum 2d

Why are dried apples, like married people?

The Club, after Consideration gave it up, and Jon: Grog Esqr, gave in his answer.

ans: Because they are *pared* ⎫
　　　　　　　　　　　 paired ⎬ was declared victor.
　　　　　　　　　　　　　　　 ⎭

❋❋

I shall beg leave here to observe, lest it should escape the observation of the Reader, that there seems to be an uncommon
delicacy and Elegance in most of the Conundrums, composed
by Jonathan Grog Esqr, as may be seen in the one Just now mentioned, Concerning *The king's prick*, which is not only a perfect
Conundrum, but Contains also a delicate pun, as the word *Prick*
may be Interpreted various ways.

❋❋

[At Sederunt 128, april 17th 1750,] appeared Smoothum Sly
Esqr as ambassador from the eastren Shore triumvirate, the
Substance of whose embassy, was to deliver the Compliments
of that Society to the honorable the president and Club, and
to acquaint them, that a Club was formed and set on foot, on
the other Side the water, modelled Exactly after the plan of
the ancient and honorable Tuesday Club, and, that the Triumvirate, having had the Chief hand in forming the said Club,
they desired the Correspondence, Countenance and protection
of his honor the president, and the Ancient Tuesday Club,
under whose Government, they placed themselves. This was
soon granted, for neither his honor, nor the Club would refuse
a request, which had a tendency to exalt their own honor and
dignity.

The ambassador then proceeded to accuse Solo Neverout
Esqr, in the name of the said Triumvirate, for a disrespectful
answer he had given to Mr Merry Makefun, a worshipful
Triumvir, who, enquiring after the welfare of his honor and the
Club, The said Neverout, turned first round on his heel, and
made no reply, but, the Question being repeated, he answered
in a huffing manner, that he knew nothing of either, on which,
Mr Makefun, took a live Coal from the fire, and, as the said
Neverout, stood with his hand behind him, thrust it into his
fist, and burnt him in the hand for his Contumacy, but, as that
was not a Sufficient punishment, he requested his honor, in the
name of the said Triumvirate, to give orders to his Secretary,

to prosecute the said Solo Neverout Esqr, for the said Contumacy and Insult.

His honor the President hesitated a good deal at this report and request, and, while he pondered with himself, what to do in the affair, the Secretary, according to his usual forwardness and petulancy, expecting to distinguish himself in this process, and pick up some gleanings to serve his purposes, rose up, and began a Speech, in which he proceeded to accuse Mr Neverout, . . . the Secretary, thus rising up, had not spoke a dozen words, before Mr Neverout, with a very loud voice Interrupted him, but, he obstinately continued his harangue, and the other his loud and Clamorous Interruptions, in the Manner of a dialogue as follows.

Secr: Mr President, Sir, I here in the name of the Eas—

Proto: No accusation—no accusation—

Secr: —Eastren Shore Triumvirate—

Proto: No accusation—ho—no—

Secret: Triumvirate Commence pro—

Proto: Hollo—hollo—ho—no accusation—

Secret: Process against Mr Pro—

Proto: No—no—no—I say no—no accusation—

Secret: Protomusicus, for a contempt which—

Prot: No accusation—you ho—no accusation—

Pres: Mr Secretary, forbear, I command both of you to sit down and hold your peace.

Secret: Sir, it is the duty of my office to—

Prot: No accusation—ho—no accusation—

Pres: Prithee be quiet, let us have less of your noise, I order you this minute to be silent.

Chanc: Sir, you go beyond your authority, I humbly conceive that any member of this here Club, may have the liberty of speaking.

Pres: Not what, and when he pleases, without my permission.

Chanc: Pardon me Sir, I'd laugh at any man, would pretend to hinder me.

Pres: I would hinder you Sir, who am your President.

Chanc: Your president; Your fart Sir! I'd dispise such arbitrary and tyranical proceedings, and dare you to your face to restrain my tongue, whenever I have a mind to speak, and—

Pres: For the Lord's Sake ha' done, you talk more than comes to your Share—and nothing to the purpose,—I command Silence.

Chanc: You Command a fiddle Stick—what, are we to be under your tyrranical will in every circumstance?—no, we will have liberty of Speech in Club, and you shall know it.

Pres: Pish—pish—pray, if you have a mind to bawl, remove alittle farther from my ear, you tear it to pieces.

Chanc: No Sir, here is my place, and here I'll keep my Station—and will not submit to your damn'd tyrranny (here the Chancellor, bawled very loud, and looked very pale, as some thought, with real anger, tho' others Imagined his anger was purely Clubical)

Mr: Attor: Spypl: Why, Mr President Sir, I think it a very hard case, that any man should pretend to clap a padlock on my mouth in this here Club.

Pres: Hey! Sir, has your mouth been Locked all this time, and now you open it in this rude manner—

After this the noise grew so great, and all talked together in such a tumultuous manner, that the Club Scribes could not take down any more of this Elegant dialogue, and Mr Protomusicus came off with victory by the help of his honor the President, and looked with contempt on the ambassador, and by the mediation of the Club, the Chancellor and President were so reconciled, as to shake hands and drink to one another, This displeased some of the Longstanding members, who were fomenting the quarrell, but the president and Chancellor regarded them not, it being a rule with great men, when they please to make little men their tools and Instruments, once they have Compassed their ends, to put the same Standard value, upon their pleasure and displeasure, which Standard value, is Just nothing.

❧❧

Chapter 7 ❧ *Arrival of the Club medals, Celebration of the 5th Anniversary, Ode and Speech on that occasion.*

❧❧

The members of the ancient and honorable Tuesday Club, being mortal men, as much as the members of his majestie's privy council, the members of both houses of parliament, or in fine as much as the members of the most august Assembly or Senate, that ever met or will meet, . . . are alike subjected to the Seducing arts of flattery with the understanding and Senses of other mortal men, as has appeared in many instances of this our History, for we have seen here, how the arts of flattery have prevailed over his honor the president, and his State officers, so as to make them Judge erroneously, and perverted their understanding to such a degree, as that they could not comprehend how any proposition could be rational or Consistent with Common Sense, which had not a direct tendency to promote their power, Influence and authority in the Club; as for the Senses of his honor, and his Longstanding members in General, we shall find, in the following part of our history, how Grossly they were misled and Corrupted, by a vein of pomp, Show and magnificence, assumed in the Club, and what a powerful effect, this Species of adulation, in the Shape of Medals, Caps of State,

Canopies, Capations, and Solemn Grand processions, had upon their understanding and Judgement.

At Sederunt 129 May 1, 1750, Tunbelly Bowzer Esqr being H:S: the Secretary reported in Club, that he had received the Club Badge medals, from Capt: Comely Coppernose, the Club's agent at London, . . . upon the one Side of this medal was struck, the Emblem of liberty, sitting by an altar, upon the altar was the motto *Libertas et Natale Solum,* and Round the Edge of the medal, *Carolus Cole Armiger Præses,* which by an unacountable blunder of the Sculptor, was put instead of *Nasifer Jole,* or *Carlo Nasifer Jole,* . . . upon the reverse was a heart, with two hands Interlocked in the amicable Gripe, and in the Middle in Large Characters, *The Tuesday Club,* in *Annapolis Maryland, May 14th 1746,* and round the edge of the Medal *Concordia res parvæ Crescunt.*[1]

❀❀

Thus the Club, to perpetuate their memory, and that of their honorable president, were at the expence of strikeing a medal, in which piece of vanity they have Imitated several other Societies, and therefore are not Singular in this particular.

❀❀

Upon the 15th of May, 1750, according to the appointment of the Grand Committee, The members, regular and honorary, . . . convened at the Secretaries house, at four o'clock p:m: and an hour after, Invested themselves with their badge medals and proceeded to Sir John's house, who received them dress'd out in his regimentals with a bold martial air, and Introducing them into the Antichamber, Entertained them with Rich Lemonian punch, and Generous wine, at 6 o'clock, they dispatched a messenger, to his honor the president, to acquaint him of their comeing, and, in half an hour after marched out

[1] "Small endeavors flourish through unity" (Sallust, *Jugurtha* 10.6). For further information on the Tuesday Club medal, see Sarah Elizabeth Freeman, "The Tuesday Club Medal," *Numismatist,* XLVIII (1945), 1313–1322.

The Tuesday Club Medal.
Courtesy, Collection of the
Maryland Historical Society,
Baltimore, Md.

in Solemn procession, . . . the order of the procession was, as follows.

1. Jonathan Grog Esqr, Mr of Ceremonies, *Solus*
2. Sir John, Knight, & Philo Dogmaticus Esqr, Canc:
3. Slyboots Pleasant & Tunbelly Bowzer Esqrs, L:S:M:
4. Jealous Spyplot Junr Esqr L:S:M: & Capt: Dio Ramble, H:M:
5. Merry Makefun and Signr: Lardini Esqrs H:M:M:
6. Smoothum Sly, Esqr & Dr Polyhystor H:M:M:
7. Solo Neverout, Pro: Mus: & Secretary Scribble L:S:M: & rearmen

As the procession moved on in a Solemn and Stately manner, it was honored with a great number of Spectators of all Ranks from windows, walls, Balconies, and even the Sides of the Streets, were lined with Children and other Spectators, nay, the *Patres Conscripti,*[2] or members of the Great provincial Senate, deigned to come forth of the doors of their house and look on

[2]"Chosen fathers," the common address of Roman senators, as in Cicero's orations.

this gallant Show; for the Long standing members made a most Splendid appearance, with their dowble gilt badge medals— when the procession came within twenty paces of the honorable the president's gate, his honor made his appearance, and advanced to Salute them, on which the procession stoped alittle, and Jonathan Grog Esqr, pulling out the Anniversary ode, waved it in a Graceful manner, in his hand, by way of Salutation to his honor the President, his honor made several low bows, which were respectfully returned by the master of Ceremonies, who raised some dust in the Street, by means of the many Genteel Scrapes he made, to set off his bows, nor were Sir John, and the Chancellor wanting in their bows and Salutations, then, his honor, taking his place, between the two Latter, the procession went forewards, and passed thro' a gate, into his honors yard, the way being strowed with flowers & the Colors displayed as usual, . . . after sometime sitting in the yard, round a table Garnished with punch bowls, bottles, Glasses and Tobacco pipes, [the members] Translated themselves into his honor's great Saloon, which was beautifully Illuminated with Sconce lights, and set out with various garlands and flowers, and his honor having ascended the great Chair of State, . . . Silence

The Second grand Anniversary Procession.

was commanded by Jonathan Grog Esqr, Master of the Ceremonies, and the Secretary was Called upon to deliver the anniversary Speech, which he, standing up in his place, pronounced as follows.

Anniversary Speech

Mr President Sir,

Such a Surprize and astonishment as possessed the old hoary and Squalid anarch Chaos, when he was waked out of his eternal Slumbers, by the elucidation of the Celestial lights, when Creation first sprung, such a Surprize, I say, Honorable Sir, must at this Instant possess my Sensorium when I behold the members of this here ancient Club, Incumbent over those capacious bowls, replete with precious punch, most Splendidly elucescent, with those Glittering and Lumeniferous badges, like so many oriental and bright planets, Rising upon the watery deep, and adorning the azure Expance with their Immortal Irradiations! whilst you, Great Sir! like the Solar Center of this grand Clubicular System, dispence Inexhaustible Lustre to all, and, from your fountain undeminished, the whole emanation of light proceeds, the Splendor of our Longstanding members being nothing else, but the reflected glory of your honor, our most honorable president.

Sir John,

Thou Standing Sturdy pillar, and Robust butteress of this here ancient Club, who, as our mellifluous Laureat, has in Cibberian numbers sung, *with front terrific guards the awful Seat*,[3] whose valor, quickened and enlivened, by the Influencing beams, proceeding from that there exalted Chair, is an eternal fence and Safeguard to the Longstanding members of this here Ancient club, so, as that they can, with tranquill Security, . . . defended and protected sit here, and quaff nectareous draughts of Lemmonian punch and manducate the most delicious am-

---

[3]Colley Cibber (1671–1757), English poet laureate, is a constant butt of humor in the Tuesday Club. This passage does not appear in any of Cibber's more memorable works.

brosial Cates, from his honors Culinary *officino,* as also, with freedom, roll round the Ingenious pun, and well Involved *Conundrum,*[a] led and directed by the yet unequaled wit, and unparallelled acumen of our Laureat's genius.

Happy, we enjoy the Sweets of peace and plenty, under your valorous protection, and sit secure from all assaults and Insults, for—should any bold Intruder dare to break in upon our peace,

His bones Sir John,
Would fall upon,
And furiously, at every bang,
Demand a promt eclaircissement,

as our above said Sublime bard, has most elegantly expressed it,—Gird then, Sir John, your Sword upon your manly thigh, . . . lest dire destruction from the vigilant foe, should menace, and find us off our guard, for, at your voice Stentorian and terrific, and most horrendous frown, all enimies will fly away apace, even before the Lustre of your refulgent Sword, darts from the dark recesses of the Scabbard, to strike us dead with most horrific Glare.

Most honorable C[han]cellor,

Thou most profound, M[aje]stic, and pacific Stream of Salutiferous Justice, whose equal and Imp[ar]tial hand destributes balsamic and healing equity, to the Long[sta]nding members of this here ancient Club, that Infallible Traumatic Balsam, which heals up and Cicaterises the wounds, ulcers and Slashes, made in our Constitution, by the ill timed altercation, and vociferation of some longstanding members, whose ambition and desire of power in this here ancient Club has outrun their prudence and discretion. Thou Infallible Solver of all knotty points, that are, or shall be started in this here ancient Club, look here, upon the harmony and order that prevails among us, on this here Solemn and pompous occasion, and then, O take

[a]Here his honor the president, who was no friend to puns and Conundrums, stooped down, and whispered Sir John, at his right hand, saying loud enough to be heard, *I think we have enough of this Stuff.*

not all the Glory to yourself, nor Imagine it is Intirely the effect
of your wise and Just œconomy, but remember to stop, before
you go too far, and let not vain glory mislead you, for, as all the
wits and geniuses of this here ancient club, derive virtue and
power, from that there honorable Chair, so you, with all your
Stock of equity, must own, that, from that there fountain head,
it all proceeds, else, the waters of the Stream could never flow
so Clear & so majestic. . . .

Jonathan Grog Esqr,

Shall I address you as worshipful m[as]ter of ceremonies,
or as poet Laureat, to this here ancient Club, fo[r] both these
Eminent places you possess, the least of which great off[ic]es,
would be a multifarious theme, for a Club orator to En[la]rge
upon, worshipful, worthy and witty Sir, the order and decency
of this here ancient club, is by you supported and directed, by
you we know, and are Instructed, when and how we are to sit,
walk, address the honorable Chair, how, with an air to bow, how
to take our place in Club, and with what decorum there to de-
port ourselves, . . . with enchantment have we heard you pronounce, the Inaugurating Speech at the Confirmation of a new
member, vizt: "I as master of ceremonies, with all the Ceremony I am master of, which mastery in Ceremonies, I acknowledge to have received from his honor the President &ct:" words
elegant and well ranged, a trope as yet unequalled, an expression Inimitable—Shall I now address you as a bard—O for the
whole troop of muses from Pindus, to asist me here—Come
Thalia, come Melpomene, come Urania, come Clio, come
Polhymnia, come Euterpe, come Calliope, come Terpsichore,
come Erato, come altogether in a Group, and enable me to address this eminent Bard! . . . The Laurels shall for ever florish
upon your brow O Illustrious Laureat! so long as you continue
to sing the eulogium of his honor the president, and this here
ancient Club, and your bold Strokes, shall be remembered in
future ages, and read with admiration and astonishment, by
our Sons, and our Son's Sons, whilst a multitude of grateful
puns & Conundrums [here his honor the president frowned]
like rich balsams and Spices shall Season the whole of your

Compositions, and render your fame Savory & odoriferous to posterity.

Dignified Proto-musicus,

Rouse up now all the powers of Sweet music, warble forth the praises of his honor and this here ancient Club, our Laureat's verse will afford words in plenty, his honor the president will afford ample Subject, 'tis your business dignified Sir, to modulate Sound, . . . let us see this night, that notwithstanding the criticisms made upon your performances, by some Capricious members, that you can, upon such a Solemn occasion, outdo even your own outdoings, asist him O Apollo, to go thro' this arduous task, stand by him with your Melodious Lyre, that his voice may be kept in tune, & give him a Sip of Helicon, that his Spirits may not sink under the mighty burden of singing Solo, the Sublime Anniversary ode, Composed by our poet Laureat, thy favorite!

Gentlemen,

You the old Standing and longstanding members of this here ancient Club, Long and firmly may you stand, a diapente of years have you already stood, and I hope five hundred shall not see you fall, pray the Celestial powers to preserve the life of mighty Jole, for, by him you stand, and are supported as an ancient Club, and, when he goes, may it be at a long, late and distant day, and pray the gods to send us Just such another, if possible, but alas, we may pronounce with a Sigh, where is he to be found, I am afraid he is not yet born, and we need not expect him, till the return of the golden age, or the celebrated millennium, when, we are told, that all mankind, shall be as one Club.

You worthy Gentlemen, honorary members, of this here ancient Club, I greet you well, in the name of his honor the president, . . . welcome thrice welcome worthy fellow members, to share with us the rich fare, and Jovial mirth and Glee of this Solemn occasion, in a twofold Sense may you be called honorary, first, as this here ancient Club has done you honor in adopting you as members, Secondly, as being Gentlemen of worth and Character, you reflect an honor upon this ancient Society, and add to its Lustre and Glory, being so many Stars of the Second magnitude, in this our Clubicular System, for we must allow the old and Longstanding members to be the first rate Stars, that surround like Satellites the great Luminary of the Chair.

And now Honorable Sir, and Gentlemen, enough for Speech making, let us prepare to eat, drink, laugh, sing and be merry.

The Secretary having pronounced this Speech, (in which is exhibited the first Specimen of his knowledge of the Sublime in Club Speeches, and his fondness for the moderen method of Introducing the heathen Gods and Goddesses into his Declamations) his honor left the Chair, and the members went to Supper, and were entertained in a most elegant and magnificent manner, by his honor, altogether Suitable to this Grand occasion.

After Supper, Jonathan Grog Esqr, Poet Laureat was called upon to read the anniversary ode, which he did with a Clear and Audible voice, standing up in his place as follows.

Anniversary Ode, for the Tuesday Club

Set to music in three parts, and to be sung, and played on several Instruments, on tuesday the 15th of May 1750. Humbly Inscribed, to the honorable Carlo Nasifer Jole Esqr, president, and the Longstanding members of the said Club by

Their Humble Servant
The Poet Laureat.

Recitativo
Thrice hail Serene returning day,
Bright Day, outshining far, the rest,
In which the Tuesday Club, in may,
First rear'd her gay and Social Crest.

Phæbus has now five Courses ran,
The Laureat twice essay'd to sing

Great Jole's eclat, that glorious man,
From whence the Club's best blessings spring.

※※

Chorus
Fortune ever changing,
Now shall keep from ranging
   And with great Jole shall live,
For his refulgent glory,
Shall fill each pompous Story
   Whilst time and fame survive.
   Recitativo
Honor[a] and Justice[b] on each Side the Chair,
Behold, while Jole sits there in State
Secure. Our knight with courage rare
And front terrific, guards the awful Seat.
   Aria
For should a bold Intruder dare
T'assault the Club, or storm the Chair,
     His bones Sir John,
     Would fall upon
And furiously at every bang
Demand a prompt eclaircissement.

※※

   Recitativo
High in the chair with look profound
Illustrious Jole dispenses round
   Awful, but Just authority,
He with a Sage Important face
Most graceful fills his lofty place,
   Promoting mirth and Jollity.

※※

[a]The Champion.
[b]The Chancellor.

Aria
Let this glad evening crown the day,
    Let mirth abound
    And bowls go round
    To honor Jole,
    Our life and Soul,
And each Sad thought be Cleard away.
    Grand Chorus
Whilst Jole shall live to fill our Chair,
We ever shall be debonnair,
No turpid cares our Joy shall Rob,
Kind heaven Grant, that long he may
Remain in health to bless this day,
Long live, Long live the Tuesday Club.

This ode met with great applause, being composed in the right moderen taste, the machinery of it consisting chiefly in a group of heathen Gods and Goddesses, the Constant attendants of all Princes and great men, on their birth and wedding days, and therefore very proper ministers for honorable Presidents of Clubs, whose greatness no man can call in Question.

❧❧

Then several martial tunes were plaid Solo, Sir John knight and Champion of the Club, dancing several heroic and warlike dances, and honored the Chancellor so far as to dance a Jigg with him, while the latter laid aside the Gravity of his office, and play'd and danced at one and the same time, but Sir John making a fawx pas, he fell upon the Chancellor, had almost overset him, and broke the bridge of the fiddle.

❧❧

Thus in great pomp and magnificence, was this grand anniversary Celebrated, at the house of Mr President Jole, in North East Street, where, besides the Show and Splendor of the Entertainment, and the Instrumental music that was exhibited on this grand occasion, there was abundance of Eloquence displayed In various Speeches, made by the members, both hon-

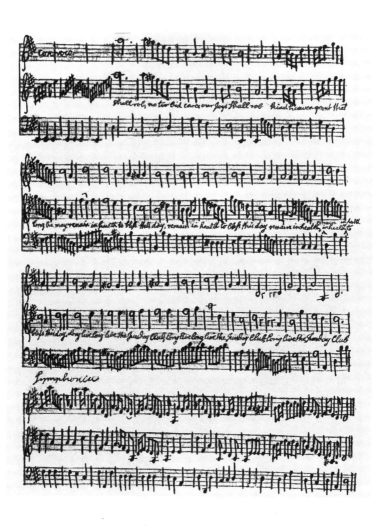

orary and Regular, . . . there was also a great deal of vocal music, for, after Mr Protomusicus had performed, most of the members sung, and the old Catch of Captn Serious Social was sung several times over, where is the following distich.

One bowl in hand, and another in Store,
Enough's enough, and we'll have one more.

On which his honor the president observed, that they might have 100 more, if they pleased, but Mr Merry Makefun answered, that they would not be quite so unreasonable or inconscionable, and sung it in the following manner.

Enough's Enough, we'll have ninety nine more. . . .

Thus ended the 5th Anniversary, in which the Club took upon them a deal of Grandure and State, and began to look upon themselves, as men of Great Consequence.

Chapter 8 ☙ *Deputy Chancellor's Commission, Impeachment & acquittal of the Chancellor.*

In all Societies whatsoever, there are, and must be, people that Lead, and people that are led. There are Cunning men and fools, blended together in Communities, and the Cunning and ambitious, will never be without their train of fools and Simpletons. This is the very nature of human Society, & is observed as often in Clubs as any where—Even among beggars, or those that are upon a level, there will be leaders, advisers, directors, and some that assume the management and Sway of the rest of the ragged fraternity.

From the Jarring or opposite interests of two or more ambitious men setting themselves up to be leaders or directors in Society, that monster *Party* takes it's origin, which is a plant, or rather weed of a monstrous quick Growth, and Choaks every useful vegetable near it, in fine, it effectually breaks the union of, and weakens Society, for union in any Society is Strength, and, if it does so, it is no promoter of the Common Good. . . .

These Political observations, occurr very naturally to a historian of (my) degree and Class, in writing the History of such a Society, as that of our ancient Tuesday Club, In this Club, we have found . . . a president, who for some time acted with the Sole power, till State officers were Created, which in some measure checked that power, and occasioned several Commotions in Club, Thence, party took its rise, and began to play her pranks, at last, two great Rivals, the President and Chancellor, appeared in the lists, and like Cæsar and Pompey at Rome, raised unextinguishable heats and Animosities, in this unhappy Club, both pretending to act for the General Good, tho' they had nothing less in their view, the absolute power over, and Sole Sway in the Club, being in effect, what they both aimed at, and it will appear at last, in this history, after many violent Struggles and Convulsions, that the Chancellor, like Pompey, being overcome, the Club, as the Romans did to Caesar, became Slaves to Nasifer Jole Esqr.

❀❀

[At Sederunt 132,] a Commission for appointing Slyboots Pleasant Esqr: Deputy Chancellor, from Philo Dogmaticus Esqr, who was obliged to be absent for some time on a Journey, was produced and read in Club, but disapproved of. . . . This Commission follows.

To my worthy and Trusty Friend,
Slyboots Pleasant Esqr, Greeting.

Necessary affairs, calling me away this day, from the honor and pleasure of attending the honorable and ancient Tuesday Club, whereof, I am by their distinguished and Superlative favor, an honorable member, in quality of Chancellor, and keeper of the Great Seal, and, it being necessary, that they should not be, without the asistance of so useful and Important an officer, I was willing and ready to supply their want at this time, of my acknowledged and Eminent talents of Judging in equity and preserving the tranquillity, peace and harmony of the honorable Club, . . . and, which is my peculiar and difficult province, being the keeper and director of his honor the president's political conscience, therefore, I do hereby committ to you, my worthy and Trusty friend, Slyboots Pleasant Esqr, . . . my full power and Commission, for me, and In my place, to act this night, the 12th of June 1750, as chancellor of this here club, meeting at your own house, recommending it earnestly to you, to act Impartially, without respect of persons, suffering no Infringement, either of the Just liberties and privileges of the members, or the prerogative of the Chair, at least, not without the same authority that Confered them, under which his honor knows that he holds them, and, I am satisfied, has reason and moderation to claim no further, knowing well that every creating power, has also an annihilating power.

[Seal]   Given under my hand and Seal
                          at arms at my Lodging in the
                          City of Annapolis, this 12th day
                          of June, 1750, and have sent
                          you also the great Seal, and
                          Instrument of the office.
                          Signed *Philo Dogmaticus*.

This Bold and daring attempt of the Chancellors, to Lessen the presidential authority, by taking to himself, a power of appointing his deputy, very much Incensed the president, & alarmed the L:St: members, as it was an open attack, upon the prerogative of the Chair, and a plain defiance of Club Law, . . . it was observed, at the reading of this Commission, that his honor the president assumed the most dreadful timber countenance, that he had been seen to assume for a great while.

※※

[On the 26th of June, Sederunt 136,] the Secretary was . . . ordered to read the Impeachment, against Philo dogmaticus Esqr, late Chancellor of the Tuesday Club, for high Crimes and misdemeanors.

※※

Articles exhibited, by the State officers and
Longstanding members of the Ancient Tuesday Club,
against Philo Dogmaticus Esqr, late Chancellor
& keeper of the great Seal for the said Club.

Whereas the office of Chancellor of this here Club, is an office of the highest dignity and trust, upon the Just and diligent execution whereof, the honor of the Chair, and the wellfare of this here ancient Club depends, and whereas . . . the said Chancellor, having continued in this high office, untill about the 12th of June 1750, puffed up with ambition, and a wicked desire of power, . . . did, Illegally, daringly and damnably, contrive, machinate and perpetrate, the following high crimes, treasons and misdemeanors, vizt:

Article I. That the said Philo Dogmaticus Esqr, at or upon the 12th of June 1750, or thereabout, being in the high office of Chancellor of this here Club, did, Secretly, Clandestinely, and as it were by Stealth, upon the very day, on which the Club was to sit, . . . convey himself from the place, Passing over in a boat, in the night, to the Eastren Shore, absconding from the Just wrath and Resentment of his honor the President, while his creatures and agents left behind, were Carrying on devlish machinations and plots against the honor & Dignity of the august Chair and the liberty and privileges of the L:St: members, of this here anct: Club.

Article II. That on, or about the 12th of June, 1750, the said Philo Dogmaticus Esqr, did most traiterously perfidiously and wickedly, directly contrary to the Duty of his office, . . . give up, deliver, and resign, the Great Seal of this here ancient Club, and the political Conscience of his honor the president, into the Care and keeping of Slyboots Pleasant Esqr, then H:S: by means of a Certain Illegal, unwarranted and false Commission . . . , in great Contempt, of the authority and dignity of his honor the president, and to the Irreparable prejudice of the L:S:M: of this here ancient Club.

※※

This Impeachment being read, no proof could be produced against the Chancellor, as to the first article, it appeared that he had Crossed the bay, at the time specified in the Impeachment, but he alledging, that he had gone about necessary business, and that he had left no Creatures behind him, to carry on plots, the Club by vote acquitted him of the first article.

※※

No proof could be brought, that the Chancellor had wrote the Commission, and so, by a vote, he was acquitted of the 2d Article, and Called to the Chair, when he came there, he eagerly snatched up the Great Seal, kissed it thrice, and laid it down again upon the table, with a respectful bow, and the members congratulated him upon his happy deliverance, and restoration to his honorable office, this prosecution stuck in the Chancellor's Stomach, and, tho he at present stiffled his resentment, yet, sometime after this, it burst forth in a violent manner, so as to shake his honor out of the Chair, and almost shatter the Constitution of the Club to pieces.

※※

BOOK VIII

*From the Impeachment and
acquital of the Chancellor,
To the Grand Ceremony
of the Capation.*

Chapter 4 ❧ *Extraordinary Club, appointed by his honor the President, Third Embassy of the Triumvirate, abolition and expulsion of the Conundrums, The Secretary created Club Orator.*

Tho' caprice be a foible most Incident to fools, yet at times wise men will suffer themselves to be ruled by it, . . . not only Individuals are sway'd at particular Junctures by this odd humor, but whole Societies suffer themselves to be ruled by it, and what would seem somewhat Strange, Societies that are composed of wise, Staied and grave members, and can boast of having men of wit and learning, . . . an example of this will soon appear, and that in a very Strong light, in the Conduct of the ancient and honorable Tuesday Club, both with regard to the honorable the president, and the whole posse of the Longstanding members, The first, in his Countenancing the Introduction of a *Cap of State*, which he had long agoe disapproved of, either thro an affected or real modesty, the Latter, in their creating the Secretary orator of the Club, in a manner against his will, and when he was far from soliciting for it, or trowbling his head about that promotion, which he had nevertheless heretofore, used all his policy and artifice to obtain, and (as we have seen) in vain.

On the 18 of September, 1750, by the Special order of his honor the President, was held an Extraordinary Sederunt of the Club, being Sederunt 139, when Tunbelly Bowzer Esqr, served as H:S: This Club was held upon account of weighty and Important matters to be Considered, the Eastren Shore Triumvirate having sent over Embassadors to the Club, which was their third Embassy since their Institution.

The Secretary being called upon to read the proceedings of last Sederunt, he was stop'd by Jealous Spyplot Senr Esqr, who rising up declared That according to a former rule or order of the Club, . . . the Club is not regularly formed, till the great Seal appears upon the table, and, as Huffman Snap Esqr, deputy Chancellor, had not as yet come to take his Seat in Club, and deposit the Great Seal before his honor the president, no proceedings ought to be read till that was done—on which the Secretary desisted.

This objection raised the Spleen of his honor the President to a very great degree, and Indignation appeared very plain thro' his timber Countenance, he could not digest the thought of the great Seal's being set up as his rival, and made a Check to his authority and power, nor could he sit easy in his chair, till this absurd order of the Club, (as he was pleased to call it) was revoked, which rendered him altogether a Cypher, or person of no authority.

Then the Revd: Mr Smoothum Sly, a Triumvir standing up in his place, delivered the Substance of the Embassy from the Triumvirate, addressing his honor the president and the Club to this purpose.

"Mr President Sir, and you the Longstanding members, and honorary members of this here ancient Club,

I am to Inform you, that, by the Late Inexpressible loss of

Mr Merry Makefun, our Eastren Shore Triumvirate, of which worshipful Society, I have the Honor to be a member, is reduced to two. We look upon you, honorable Sir, to be the head and father of our Society, . . . as we were originally nursed up, under your Paternal Care and protection, so, we deem ourselves to be your Children, and more especially, seeing we are also Composed of honorary members of this here ancient and honorable Club; we apply therefore, to you, honorable Sir, the *Original* of our health and mirth, to restore us again to our former State, by adding one to our number, and therefore, we humbly propose your honorary member, Mr Theophilus Smirker, to your honor, and the worthy Members of this here ancient and honorable Club, as a person worthy to fill up that vacancy."

❋❋

Thus we find how the Empire and Dominion of this ancient Club, had already fixed itself on the Eastren Shore, by their becoming arbitrators and Judges, even in the case of electing and appointing members, for the Worshipful triumvirate.

❋❋

The Conundrums being called for, after Supper, Jonathan Grog Esqr, produced his.

❋❋

Conundrum 1st

Why is a man with a moderate pox, like a finished Church bell?

After some Consideration Quirpum Comic esqr, made answer, Because he has a *Clapper,* which the Club allowed to be good. . . .

Conundrum 2d

Why is matrimony like Polyphemus's eye?

The Club gave it up and Mr Grog delivered his answer.

ans: Because it is a great *tye* }
               eye }   decl: victor.

This Conundrum was Condemned by the Club as Improper, and altogether Insignificant, upon which Jonathan Grog Esqr, after having been formally declared victor, by the Secretary, drank a bumper, tho' not obliged to do so by any Law or rule of the club, which Indicated either his Ignorance of the Club laws, or his great affection for a bumper.

***

It was then moved by Jealous Spyplot Senr Esqr and seconded by the worshipful Sir John, that the Conundrums should be totally abolished and expelled, as a Species of low wit altogether unworthy of the dignity of the Club, and, upon the vote's passing round, they were, unanimously abolished, and banished the Club for ever, to the no small Satisfaction of the Master of Ceremonies and the Secretary, whose Invention was already worn thread bare in this (as it was esteemed) low and vulgar exercise.[1]

***

There was at this Sederunt a very unexpected question started in Club, which was, whether the club should proceed to chuse an orator? This question passed in the affirmative and the Secretary was chose into that office, by a great majority, This office the Secretary persisted in refusing to accept, either as it is thought, out of an affected modesty, or, because he was not satisfied with the bare title and office, unless he enjoyed thereby, the Station of a State member; the President protested at first, against the Club's proceeding in this affair, but the Club were resolved to regard neither the Secretarie's refusal nor the President's protest, but forced the office upon the one and the officer

---

[1] Jonas Green and Alexander Hamilton each presented 32 conundrums in club (all 64 appear in the complete edition of *The History of the Ancient and Honorable Tuesday Club*). They each prepared 2 conundrums for any given night; Green presented his first, then Hamilton. As Hamilton admitted, Green was the superior "conundrumificator," which is why only his conundrums are represented in this edition.

on the other; and, tho' his honor consented at last that the Secretary should be Orator of the Club, yet he never would Consent to give him the distinguished title of a State member.

※※

Chapter 8 ※ *Disputes Concerning the Cap of State, History and Character of Coney Pimp Frontinbrass Esqr, Account of Sir Hugh Maccarty Esqr.*

Assurance is an useful Qualification, which Carries many men thro' the world, better than an honest and reputable calling. I have known some fellows, well stocked with assurance, tho' void of all Good qualities whatsoever, either natural or acquired, by this single talent alone, get mightily in favor with princes and great men, twist them round their fingers, and do with them what they pleased. . . . Wherever the person possessing this pushing and profitable quality introduces, or rather intrudes himself, he enters into the Spirit of the conversation in an Instant, . . . he laughs, weeps, looks dull, Sprightly, mourns and rejoices with the Stream, and in a minutes time is as well acquainted, and as free with every person in the Company, as if he had known him all his life. . . .

I should not have Introduced this chapter of our history, with this prolix preamble on assurance, had not his honor the president, and his ancient and honorable Club, after having so long managed their own matters, Intirely by their own wit and Understanding, now, at this unlucky period of our history, met with a person exactly of this character, In Coney Pimp Frontinbrass Esqr, who made his appearance at an Ill fated hour, in this here ancient Club, and by his devices and projects, contrived and furthered, Soleley by the force of assurance, put the whole Clubical System and Oeconomy, into such disorder and Confusion, as that the Constitution of the Club became thereby subject to Severe Convulsive fits, and not having recovered it's wonted Strength and vigor, even at this day, continues still in a Lamentable, broken and Crazy condition. . . .

At Sederunt 145, December 18, 1750, Quirpum Comic Esqr, being H:S: there arose in Club, some very hot disputes Concerning the Cap of State, which it seems his honor the president took it *in his head,* not to wear *on his head,* asserting That it was a Scandalous patched up bawble, and, that some nasty Slattern of a milliner, had not only Imposed upon the Good agent Capt: Comely Coppernose, but also in the Grossest manner upon himself and this ancient and honorable Club, in pretending to palm such a daub, and such a pitiful patchd up piece of work upon them, and, that if the Club Chose to dishonor themselves, with such a despicable rag as that there Cap was, they might get whom they pleased to wear it, but he never would disgrace his head with any such greasy trumpery.

※※

The Club began to Consider, what was to be done with the Cap of State, when a gentleman present, and Invited to Club as a Stranger, according to ancient Custom, by name Coney Pimp Frontinbrass Esqr, . . . humbly requested, That if the Club did not Chuse to use this here Cap of State, he might be allowed to carry it to New York for a great president of a Club there to wear, to which Club, he belonged, as a dignified member,—To this proposal the Club Consented by a vote, but his honor the President, protesting against this proceeding, the Gentleman very respectfully, Restored the Cap again into the hands of his honor, by no means presuming, tho' he had the Consent of the Club, to act against his honors will and pleasure.

Whereupon Sir John, in a bold manner seizing the Cap of State, Clap'd it upon his head, and wore it during the Remaining part of the night.

※※

As [Coney Pimp Fortinbrass] and his sham heroe, Sir Hugh
Maccarty Esqr, are very deeply concerned in the Sequel of this
History, I think it will be necessary to give here, a short Scetch
of the Character of each.

Coney pimp Frontinbrass Esqr, first Introduced into the ancient and honorable Tuesday Club, by the Recommendation of
the Honorable Philo Dogmaticus Esqr, the Club's Chancellor,
was, as he said, a native of Scotland, . . . he seemed to be a
person cut out for Travel, and in his time had seen many parts
of the world, he pretended to be a person of universal Genius
and universal acquaintance, and . . . there was no transaction,
great or small, but what he seemed to be acquainted with or to
have had a hand in. . . . As to religion, he set up for a Quaker,
and at times would be very Stiff and formal, and abound in *thees*
and *Thous*, but he would at other times forget this preciseness,
and hold forth, in as polite a Stile, as any pragmatical puppy of
the times, . . . he took a particular pleasur in finding out men's
foibles, and weak Sides, and then would expose and make fools
of them in such an artful manner, that they would not for a great
while perceive his drift, but Imagine all the time that he admired their parts and understanding; he was above measure for-
ward in thrusting himself into companies of all Sorts, and Immediatly mixing in the Conversation, with that freedom and
forwardness, as if he had all his life been in Intimate friendship
and acquaintance with every one in the Company, and the very
next Company he went into, he would make use of these person's
names and Characters not much to their honor or advantage,
especially if it would turn out any way advantagious to himself,
. . . in fine, he was one very well adapted to act the buffoon, in
every degree of life, of such a finished assurance, that he had
very few equals and no Superiors in that distinguishing Quality,
and we shall soon see, what disturbances he excited in the ancient and honorable Tuesday Club, by the Sole force of his Impudence, effrontery and buffonery.

Sir Hugh Maccarty Esqr, a Supposed great Club president,

whom Coney Pimp frontinbrass Esqr, first made mention of in the ancient and honorable Tuesday Club, calling him the President of a very ancient and Right honorable monday Club at New York, was, for some time believed to be a real person, and more Especially, by his honor Mr President Jole, who, upon his having so grand a description of his person and Character declared or delivered to him by the aforesaid Mr Frontinbrass, had Conceived a mighty great opinion of, and esteem for him, he, from the description, Imagining him to be a person of a very austere disposition, who had an absolute Command over his Club, and who would be obeyd at any rate, . . . but alas! the pleasure of that thought, did not continue long; for, after he had spoke much in praise of the said Sir Hugh Maccarty Esqr in every Company, and Conversation he happened into, falling into raptures, when he discoursed of that great Clubic heroe, he found, to his great disappointment and Grief, that this mighty Club magnifico, was no other than a mere *Ens rationis*, a Quixotic person, who never had any other place of existence either he or his Club, but the maggoty brain of the aforesaid Coney Pimp Frontinbrass Esqr, which discovery was made, by the great application and Assiduity of his Champion Sir John, who took Infinite pains to persuade his honor, of the nonexistence of this Phantasmical Club heroe. . . .

Chapter 9 ❧ *Sublime letters of Coney Pimp Frontinbrass Esqr, to his honor the President; The Frontinbrassian Articles drawn up and assented to; Creation of a Serjeant at arms, Coney Pimp Frontinbrass Esqr, made agent & plenipo for the Club In America.*

Human pride is Infinite or Incommensurable, it being Impossible for the Greatest mathematician or algebraist, to calculate the Length, breadth, height and depth of it; . . . from this principle of pride, so Ingrained in human nature, all men have been fond of taking to themselves great and lofty titles, and laid hold of every opportunity to attain to them. . . . Seeing then, that Great priests, great kings, and great men, at all times, have been so fond of pompous titles and designations, it will not at all appear Strange or uncommon, that Great presidents, should be Carried away with this prevailing principle of pride, and assume to themselves high titles, which many think they have no right to assume, we shall soon see an Instance of this in the Conduct of the honorable Nasifer Jole Esqr, presidt: of the anc: & hon: Tuesday Club.

At Sederunt 146 January 1, 1750/1, Solo Neverout Esqr being H:S: his honor the president produced in Club two letters which he had received from Coney Pimp Frontinbrass Esqr, honorary member, they were read, and put upon Record, as follows.

To The honorable Nasifer Jole Esqr,
President of The Tuesday Club, These.

Most Honorable Sir,

   The Idea of the Grandure and magnificence of your honor, has so filled my fancy, ever since I had the honor and pleasure of viewing your honor, exalted in that distinguished Chair of State, of the *Ancient and honorable Tuesday Club,* that it has quite occupied my thoughts by day, and my dreams by night—I am so swallowed up in the Contemplation of your honors Excellence and magnificence—so stuned with admiring your profound wisdom and Sagacity, that I am like one, Just come out of a dark dungeon, into the light and Clear Sunshine, . . . and tho' to distraction, I am astonished, yet, I cannot say I clearly see all your honor's excellencies and perfections—'Tis my most prevailing ambition, that I may, before I leave this place, be enabled perfectly, to comprehend your Grandure and dignity, and therefore, I would beg the favor, that your honor would permit me this evening, to wait upon your Refulgence, and thereby acquire a more perfect Idea of your presidential Highness, I am, with the utmost deference, and most humble, profound Submission,

Annapolis 20th Decr 1750   Your honors most devoted
                            Most obsequious Servant
                            Slave and Confounded admirer
                            Coney Pimp Frontinbrass.

   This letter, in the Strain of which appears, abundance of Impudence and affectation, Impudence in the gross Flattery that runs thro' the whole, and affectation, in the odd peculiarity of Stile and words, was thrown out as a bait by the writer to catch his honor the President, and his honor the President snaped at it and was accordingly caught, an Instance of the degree of Infatuation, the Club, by their repeated Compliments and flatteries, had brought this worthy Gentleman to, and a great example of the frailty of human nature, which, in the most Sagacious, can be so tempered and wrought upon, as to acquiesce, and give assent to the grossest lies and absurdities.

The design of this Letter was to procure a private audience of his honor the President, which accordingly was procured, and Coney pimp Frontinbrass Esqr was admitted into his honor's antichamber, . . . he found his honor in a dishabille, being in his night cap Gown and Slippers, Laconic Comas Esqr, Late a privy Counsellor of his honor, being in the Room with his honor, smoking a pipe of tobacco. . . . When Frontinbrass came first into the Room, he pulled off his hat tho a Quaker, kneeld down upon one knee, and humbly desired that his Lordship would permit him the honor of kissing his Lordships hand, on which the honorable the president, started from his Seat, looked somewhat Surprized, and pull'd up his breeches, Laconic Comas Esqr, swore a great oath, and Damnd the Impudence of Frontinbrass, however, he persisting in his request, his honor at last streched forth his right hand, and Frontinbrass Eagerly kissed it, on which Laconic Comas burst out, *O! God dam' you! you'r a fool by God!* Then his honor pull'd up his breeches again and sat down, and Commanded Frontinbrass to arise, which Command he obeyed—Frontinbrass then Entered into a Long discourse concerning *Clubific Felicity*, and the nature of Presidential power, endeavoring to demonstrate, that the first Intirely depended upon the unlimited extent of the latter, and wondered that his Lordship did not exert himself more arbitrarily in the Club, and advised him to keep the members more under absolute Command for the future. While these Speeches were making, Frontinbrass in directing his discourse to his honor, would always rise from his Seat, and his honor would rise also, and pull up his breeches, while Laconic Comas would, every now and then burst out into, *Damn the Nonsense, you'r both fools by God!*

❋❋

[After his second letter was] read in Club, Coney Pimp Frontinbrass Esqr honorary member, stood up, by permission, and

Private Conference of Frontinbrass with the Honourable Nauifer Sole Ear ————

addressing his honor, by the Title of *my Lord, . . .* humbly request[ed] That his Lordship would permit him to propose
some articles, for the right regulation and government of the
ancient Tuesday Club, which, he found to his great Sorrow and
Concern, was in the utmost confusion, and ready to sink into
anarchy and ruin.

Some of the members alledging, that this was a reflexion on the
Club, Coney Pimp Frontinbrass Esqr, pretended to take affront
at this, and was seemingly going to leave the Club in an abrupt
manner, but, before matters came to that extremity, his honor
the president, and the members, permitted him to retire with
the Secretary into another room, where, having drawn up Certain articles, they returned into the Club Room, . . . and presented the Articles to his honor, the president, and the Club,
requesting that they might Immediatly be taken under Consideration, and the members accordingly resolving themselves
into a Committee . . . chose Tunbelly Bowzer Esqr, Chairman
of the Committee, and, after considering them *articulatim*, delivered by the mouth of their Clerk, to his honor and the Club,
the following report.

Report of the Committee

Your Committee after mature deliberation have determined and
agreed, that all the articles contained in the Schedule presented
to your honor and the club, shall stand, with the amendments
thereunto made by your Committee, except the article 5to Running to this purpose, "That when any of his Lordships officers
misbehave, his lordship shall have a power to degrade them *ab
officio,* and appoint others in their Room"—which article, your
Committee has expunged.

Signed *Tunbelly Bowzer Chairman.*

The Articles Presented by Coney Pimp Frontinbrass Esqr,
allowed by the Committee.

Law XLIX. *1mo* That his honor the President, for the future,
in Club-time, shall be called my Lord Presidential.

2do That he shall have an unlimited power to do all the good
he can to his Club.

3tio Which Club, shall be called his Lord Presidentship's
ancient Tuesday Club, and every officer thereof, shall be Called,
his Lord Presidentship's officer.

4to That all Commissions shall be annually renewed and the
persons appointed, at the Sole pleasure, and by the nomination
of his Lord Presidentship, which shall be signified, by his Lord
presidentship's drinking to the person, by name and title whom
he Intends to promote.

5to [The 5th article, by order of the committee, and at the
particular desire of his Lordship, who modestly declined such
an extent of power, was left out.]

6to That on anniversary days, and every first Club night of
the new year, every member, shall have the honor of kissing his
Lord presidentship's hand, at the same time, offering the Compliments of the Season, to his Lord presidentship, this last article, to be an unalterable privilege of the Club.

7mo That every person admitted as a visitor, honorary, or
fixed member, may, as a privilege, have the honor of kissing
his Lord Presidentship's hand.

8vo That there shall be appointed from among the Commoners, an officer, called, his Lord Presidentship's Serjeant at
arms, who, by the order of his lord presidentship, shall take all
offending members into Custody, and them safely keep, in such
place, as his Lord presidentship shall appoint, during his Lord
Presidentship's pleasure.

9mo That his Lord presidentship shall have a mallet, to
Command Silence, on the Sound of which, The third time at
most, whosoever is refractory, shall be taken into Immediate
custody if his lord presidentship shall think proper.

10mo That every cause, that may be determined by his honor the Chancellor, may be carried by appeal to his Lord presidentship, who may finally determin the same.

11mo Lastly the above articles, are humbly offered with a Salvo, that all former, natural and political rights and privileges, of the State officers and commoners of this here ancient club, shall be Strictly observed.

❀❀

Thus were passed the Frontinbrassian Articles, by which, were Ceded to his honor the president (now his Lordship) more high privileges and powers, than had as yet been given him, since the first Institution of the Club; and tho' Jealous Spyplot Senr Esqr, who was concerned in drawing up the articles, had Incerted the Concluding Clause, as a Salvo for the liberties of the Club, and thought that he had by that means rendered the preceeding articles of little or no effect; yet the Club went into the Strict observation of every one of them, so much were they Infatuated and blinded to their own hurt.

❀❀

There arose some discourse in club, after the passing of the articles, concerning who should be appointed Serjeant at arms, during which, his Lordship drank to Prim Timorous Esqr, who was thereby constituted his Lordships Serjeant at arms, according to article 8vo. . . .

Then the Serjeant at arms proclaimed in the manner following.

O yes, O yes, O yes, all manner of persons, are Commanded to keep Silence on pain of his lordship's displeasure.

Silence being made, the Serjeant at arms proceeded to make another O yes.

O yes, O yes, O yes, it is his Lordship's pleasure, that all Commissions shall stand Good till further orders.

Then his Lord presidentship, Graciously granted to Coney pimp Frontinbrass Esqr, for his Signal Services to the Club, (or rather to himself in contributing to render him absolute) a full testificate, under the Great Seal and privy Seal at arms, of his being an honorary member of the Club, and also, constituting him agent and Plenipo for the Club at New York, and over all the British Continent and Islands of America.

Chapter 10 ⚜ *Lugubris Cantus, by the Club.*

※※

At Sederunt 147, January 15th 1750/1, Philo dogmaticus Esqr being, for the first time, since he was Elected into the Club, High Steward (an Indulgence which never was granted, to any of the Longstanding members, but himself, vizt: to be allowed to attend the Club as a regular member for 27 Sederunts successively without once serving) and Huffman Snap Esqr, deputy in the Chair, a letter was produced in Club from the high Steward to his Lord presidentship, which being read was recorded as follows.

To The honorable Nasifer Jole Esqr,
Lord President of the Tuesday Club.

My Lord president,
   Your Lordship's ancient Tuesday Club, being appointed to meet at my house this evening, I expect and request the honor of your magnificent presence, so necessary to the Solemnity, order and pleasure of our Society, I could, according to custom, expatiate upon your Lordship's distinguished and unparalleled Qualities for the high State *this here Club* has advanced you to, but that fact . . . shows your Lordship in a light that confounds all Imagination and, would make all Eulogical attempts, even from the God of Eloquence himself, an affront, or, if the good Intention of it, should save that misfortune to the author, from a person of your Candor and benevolence, it would reflect upon his understanding to offer any description or Commendation of

what, by the confession of all the world who have heard of the ancient Tuesday Club, and their Illustrious head, is both Ineffable and Inconceivable.

For my own Sake therefore, and not to offend your excellent perception and delicate ear, I restrain the Impetus, which, without that motive, would have been Irresistable, and beg leave to subscribe myself, my Lord,

> Your Lord presidentship's
> Most dutiful obedient Chancellor
> and humble Servant
> *Philo Dogmaticus.*

It may seem Strange to many, that this adulatory Epistle, this puffed up piece of fustian, should come from the hands of the chancellor, who was a plain spoken man & not in the least degree addicted to flattery, but his design in writing this letter, may easily be seen thro'. . . . The Chancellor knew very well, that the Honorable Nasifer Jole Esqr, was come to his akme of power and pride, and, like a ripened Impostume, he was Just ready to burst, so full was he of prerogative and lofty titles, and therefore he Judged wisely, that the adding a triffle more to the quantum would bring his overswoln Glory to a Chrisis, and break the Inflated tumor, for which reason, he wrote this letter with a design, Intirely to turn his Lordships head, that he might in this fit of Infatuation, the more easily pull him down, and it was not long after, that he effected this devlish project.

❀❀

The Club was then Informed by the Secretary, that his Lord presidentship was much Indisposed. The members began very much to condole their Case, . . . and the following mournful ditty or Poem was framed by the Conjoint muses of the Club.

❀❀

Lugubris Cantus[1]

In Imitation of Spencer, Author of the Fairy Queen.

The Members of the Ancient Tuesday Club
Sat, nodding oer their pipes, in pensive mood,
While, at each whiff, a heavy Sigh and Sob,
Burst forth, and eke of briny tears a flood,
The Chair, Bereft of Jole deserted stood,
Bereft of Jole, the Club's main prop and Stay,
For why, In Jole, was center'd all their Good,
And not a Sound was heard, but 'lake and wail a day!

✿✿

The Genius of the Club, beheld from high
To what dire dumps, the members sunken were,
She, from Olympus Top straitway did fly
And like a Ghost, in mids of them appear,
She ask'd of them, the Cause of all their Care—
What dismal hap, my Sons has you betiden,
Compose yourselves, forbear to gape and stare,
Your Piteous case I hope's, not desp'rate past abiding.

If my Celestial power, can you relieve,
On that Support you safely may rely,
Forbear, my Sons, forbear to sigh & grieve
—Oh! grieve we must (said they) If Jole should die,—
Woe's me (then did, Th'astonishd Genius Cry)
If Jole should die, your Glory's at an end,
But Courage, I'll back to Olympus fly,
And urge almighty Jove, the fatal Stroke to fend.

✿✿

She spoke and fled—the members all uprous'd,
With new born Joy, each Countenance was Crownd.
Her kindly words new Courage soon Infus'd,
And with a Smile the Sparkling bowl went round,
The hall re-eccho'd with a Joyful Sound,

[1]This "Funeral Chant" appeared in the *Maryland Gazette*, no. 299 (Jan. 16, 1751).

The genius of the Tuesday Club, appearing
to the Longstanding members —

And every lip dip'd deep into the bowl,
That soon all Grief in Joyful mirth was drownd,
And all the Joyful Song was, Long live Noble Jole.

※※

Chapter 11 ※ *Sublime poetical letter of Mr Attorney Spyplot, Grand Ceremony of the Capation.*

Trimmers and time Servers, being a Sort of people as Inconstant as the moon, . . . it is not the least matter of Surprize to find these Camelions, constantly changing Color and countenance, . . . but when men of a Constant and Invariable temper, who have always Steddily kept up to the same principles and professions, are seen of a Sudden to Change, or shift Sides, this naturally Inclines men to believe, that something of Importance is upon the Anvil, . . . this was the Case with the members of the ancient and honorable Tuesday Club at this present Juncture, when they perceived that Steady and Invariable assertor of Clubical liberty, Jealous Spyplot Esqr, all of a Sudden, turn a flatterer of his Lord presidentship, They rightly conjectured that this great man did not act this part so Inconsistent with the Character he had all along mantained in the Club for nothing, but that he had some deep designs in view to restore the Club to its lost liberty, by poisoning the Chair, and pampering up the presidential pride with extravagant doses of flattery, Remembering the Scriptural maxim, that *Pride will Surely have a fall.* . . .

At Sederunt 148, January 29, Jealous Spyplot Senr Esqr being high Steward, his Lordship delivered to the Secretary, a letter from the H:S: which, being read in Club, was ordered to be recorded as follows.

*To The Honorable Nasifer Jole Esqr, Ld Presidential
of the ancient and honorable Tuesday Club.*

My Lord Presidential,

Whatever Charm or virtue, the vulgar may Conceive to be
Inherent in high sounding titles and pompous names, yet, your
Lordship, and every man of your Lordship's consummate understanding and erudition, may well perceive and know, that
titles of honor, are only rewards and Guerdons of virtue, valor
and Integrity. . . .

The honorable titles, which your Lordship has had from
time to time accumulated upon you, in this here ancient and
honorable Club, are therefore, all of them expressive and des-
ignatory of that Inate worth, valor *Rightness* &c: &c: &c: so
plainly conspicuous in your Lordship's honor, for, as nothing
but good can come of Good, and nothing but evil of evil, so,
these high and lofty titles being good, or signifying what is
good and Excellent, . . . your Lordship's honor must have in
you, every thing that is Good, for, as the Saying is *κακον κο-
ρακος κακον ων,*[1] or, as the Garter express it *hony soit qui mal y
pense,*[2]—your Lordship's honor will forgive me for dealing so
much in foreign and dead languages, but, I must make this my
apology, that not any Language on earth, is capable to express,
the Great magnificence, Grandure, excellency, and Stupen-
dous Inconceivable redundancy of your Lordships honor's
most unparallelled perfections. . . . Come then! O come!
Thou bright Star of the North east![a] thou glittering and Celestial Luminary of the ancient and honorable Tuesday Club; and
shine upon us this evening, with that smooth Clemency &
Sweet benignity, that Exhilerating Serenity, which heretofore
used to clear away from our pericraniums, the heavy Clouds and
fogs of care, and exhilirate the Spirits, even more than potent

[1]This phrase was first used in a lawsuit by Tisias against his teacher Corax,
the first teacher of rhetoric at Syracuse; the case was thrown out by a judge
who called Tisias "a bad crow's bad egg" (*korax:* "crow"; see Aristotle's *Rhetoric* 2.24).
[2]"Evil be to those who think evil thoughts."
[a]Alluding to his Lordship's living in North east Street.

Bacchus, come, thou unparallell'd Celestial Influence, come, O come, and felicitate this evening, with your Lordship's honor's divine presence.

Janry 29th 1750/1   Your most obsequious
                       Most officious
                       Most dutiful H:S:
                       Jealous Spyplot Senr.

This Letter, is so different from the usual plain Stile, and blunt manner of Jealous Spyplot Senr Esqr, that it was believed by many of the members, not to be of his own proper inditing, but that Coney Pimp Frontinbrass Esqr, . . . had dictated it, and persuaded him to send it; others were of opinion, that the Secretary had a hand in it, but, be that as it will, it is certain, that Jealous Spyplot Senr Esqr, could never upon any account whatsoever have been guilty of writing or sending such a letter to his Lordship, if the native purity of his manners, had not already been in a great measure poisoned, by the many bad Examples of this Sort exhibited in the Club, . . . besides, it is apparent, that Mr Spyplot had a political design, in writing this letter, and was now Joined in a private or Secret Cabal with the Chancellor and Secretary to flatter and Cajole the president, in such a manner, as to make him lose himself, by loseing his understanding, and so, while his Lordship was mired in their puddle, and Entangled in their nets, they might easily regain the lost liberties of the Club, by pulling down the Tyrant.

✸✸

I am now to relate a transaction, the most Important of any within the whole compass of this Club history, a transaction, which for it's glory and Singularity, far surpasses all other Clubical transactions whatsoever, that have occurred, since the beginning of time, ever since Clubs were in being, and, if ever equalled, can never be excelled by any Club, that shall appear in future ages, upon the face of the Earth, This transaction is no less than the *Grand Ceremony of the Capation*, which I shall relate with that pomp and dignity, becoming so great and Important a Subject.

The *Cap of State* . . . had now fallen into disgrace, and was held in no esteem by his Lordship and the long standing members, being degraded, unto the mean office of being worn upon the head of a beef Salter, to keep the ears warm, This was brought about, by the Indefatigable Insinuations and advice, of his Lordship's privy Council of three, at the head of which, was Sir John, . . . the other two, were Laconic Comas Esqr, late a longstanding Member and Don John Charlotto, Gentleman of the Bedchamber to his Lordship. . . . Sir John's motive for acting in this manner, was no other, than to make himself appear a person of deep penetration and knowledge in the Secret caballs of the Secretary, and other designing members of the Club, and perhaps, he also had a mind, to put a Stop, to bestowing any more marks of favor and distinction on the Chair, by accumulating ensigns of State upon his Lordship. The motives of Laconic Comas Esqr, for entering into this private Cabal, or Council were two, first his love for lemon punch, of which he had many a Cool draught, when he paid his visits to his Lordship, . . . Secondly revenge against the Club, he having not as yet forgot the affair of the Comasian Conundrum; and this affords an Instance, how far the Spirit of Revenge, will carry men of a calm and Cool temper, and plain undesigning behavior, which was the Just character of Mr Comas in most transactions of life, . . . as for the motives of Don John Charlotto, they were no other, than an honest desire that his Lordship should not be Imposed upon, and In reality, he was the most Sincere and unbyassed member of the privy Council.

By the Constant application and assiduity of this Council of three, who were frequently shut up with his Lordship, the Secret History of the cap of State, as they Imagined, at last came to light, tho' they never could Clearly prove their asseverations; which was, that the Secretary, and one Gasperus Pickeringtonus, had laid and Contrived the whole Scheme (they should, to come nigher the truth, have mentioned Laconic Comas Esqr, as one Concerned in this Cap Cabal, and that the Scheme was hatched in his Chamber, but political reasons, prevented the Discovering of this material Circumstance) and, that they had Concerted and Contrived, under Color of doing honor to his Lordship's Noddle, to adorn him with a fools Cap, and make him a Common bye word and Joke, . . . thus, the whole Secret History of the Cap of State was discovered, and, with some difficulty his Ldship at last believed it. . . .

During these transactions of the privy Council of three, and political enquiries into the Secret History of the Cap of State, Coney Pimp Frontinbrass Esqr arrived from a Southeren clubical Expedition to Virginia, where, at a place Called Hiccory hill, as agent of the Ancient and honorable Tuesday Club, he had erected a Club by the name of the Thursday Club of Hiccory hill, under the Jurisdiction of the Right honorable the Lord President Jole, and appointed, Collonel Comico Buttman President thereof, the agent brought with him, letters from Mr President Butman, the purport of which were, to know, if he should own the Superiority of Sir Hugh Maccarty Esqr of New York, as the principal Presidential cap'd head of America, . . . he also had a letter, in an abusive hectoring Stile, from Sir Hugh Maccarty Esqr, directed to himself, in which that president upbraided him, and taxed him with disloyalty for paying so much deference to one Jole, of whom he spoke very Contemptuously, . . . These letters were the Cause of a grand Council of the Tuesday Club being Summoned, to meet in Annapolis, upon Tuesday the 18th of february 1750/1, in order not only to satisfy the Request of the President of Hiccory Hill, but to proceed in such a manner, as to humble the pride of that ambitious and aspiring President, Sir Hugh Maccarty Esqr, and let him know that the honorable Lord President Jole, was his Superior, in every respect; it was resolved then, that his lordship, should, at this grand council, undergo the Grand ceremony of the Capation, and he having Issued Summons to the several members, to convene in the evening at a tavern in the city, Prepared himself, a cap for that purpose, which was made of black velvet, in the plain & Simple form of a horseman's cap, or what is commonly called a Jockey Cap. . . . The Council then met at the time appointed, and the Grand Ceremony was performed by Coney Pimp Frontinbrass Esqr, in the manner below related.

※※

Grand Ceremony of the Capation

A Great table, being placed in the middle of the Room, a chair of State was placed upon it.

His Lordship, the master of Ceremonies and the agent, retired into the next room, and the door was shut.

Sir John the Champion with his broad Sword shouldered, stood upon one Side of the door, in the Inside, the Secretary with the great book of Records stood on the other, The long-standing members in a ring round the great table.

The master of Ceremonies without, and the agent Escorting his Lordship, knock at the door.

Secret: Who's there?

Mr of Cer: One whom you will know as soon as he enters.

The door opens, his Lordship Enters, the Company bow Low, and his Lordship returns a gracious nod, the Longstanding members march four times round the great table, Sir John shouldering the broad Sword of State, and walking before his Lordship, the master of Ceremonies behind, with the tongs shouldered, a blade on each Shoulder, The procession stops.

Con: P: Front: Ye Longstanding members, of this here ancient and honorable Club, I ask you, if you own this here Illustrious Gentleman for your Lord president?

L: St: memb: We do, we do, we do.

Con: P: Front: Are you willing his head should be Cap'd?

L: St: mem: We are, [here they bowed low, and his Lordship returned another gracious nod.]

Con: P: Front: Please your Lordsp to ascend the table [his Lordship ascended the table, and sat down on a Chair of State, and the orator pronounced the following short oration.]

Orat: Ye Longstanding members of this here ancient and honorable Club, look up with admiring, yea with astonished eye balls; behold your great patron and protector, the darling and delight of your hearts, whom you can never Sufficiently exalt and honor, behold, I say, exalted upon that table, and seated in that lofty Chair of State, the honorable Nasifer Jole Esqr, . . . the paragon of Presidents, and the very masterpiece of art, and wonder of nature, a person endued with authority, dignity, wisdom, perspicuity, Prudence, discretion, Sagacity, Integrity, Justice, Clemency, Circumspection, Sobriety, magnanimity, generosity, eloquence, urbanity, and In short, such a number of first rate qualities, that I neither have ability to ennumerate them, nor you time or patience to hear them all recited, . . . behold I say, behold him! but your eyes will never be satisfied with beholding,—admire, I say, admire him!—but oh, you never can admire Enough, *Dixi.*

Then Coney Pimp Frontinbrass Esqr, stepping with one foot upon the Table, desired his Lordship to kneel upon one knee, which his Lordship did, and the agent put the Cap upon his Lordships head, giving it three flaps, with the flat of his hand, while he pronounced the following words.

"I here, in the name of, and by the permission of the Longstanding members of this here ancient and honorable Club, Constitute and declare your Lordship, *a head of heads* (flap) *a Cap'd head of Cap'd heads* (flap) *Chief Cap and Cap'd head, of all the Caps and Cap'd heads* (flap) of his majesties dominions in America, in defiance of Sir Hugh Maccarty Esqr, and all other ambitious and assuming Presidents, in token of which, I ornament your Lordship's honorable head, with this here Cap of State."

Grand Ceremony of the Capation

L: St: memb: Huzza! Huzza! Huzza!

Then his Lordship arose, and sat down again upon the Chair of State, with the Cap of State on his head, while the orator pronounced the following short oration.

"Ye Longstanding members of this here ancient and honorable Club, I singly dowbly, and Trebly Congratulate you, upon the wise and prudent choice you have made of the right honorable the Lord Jole, not only for your Lord president, but for your Cap'd Lord president, a choice, which will display your profound wisdom and Sagacity, to all the discerning, all the admiring, all the gazing, all the gaping world; a Choice for which you shall henceforth rejoice and be glad; a Choice, on which only stands your happiness, as a Society, and your duration as an ancient Club; a Choice—I say—a Choice, which never had, nor ever shall have a parallel—hum—hum—and so I have done."

His Lordship then Descended from the table, the long Standing members gave another *Huzza,* and a low bow to his Lordship, who returns to them a gracious Nod, now a Cap'd Nod.

BOOK IX

*From the grand ceremony of
the Capation, to the Death
of Sir Hugh Maccarty Esqr,
and the mutilation of the
Frontinbrassian Articles.*

Chapter 4 ❧ *Speech of the orator Congratulating his Lordship's escape from an Imminent danger.*

※※

[At Sederunt 160, July 23d, 1751, the Secretary,] rising up, addressed his honor in the following Speech.

※※

"I hoped my Lord, that I should never have had any occasion to harangue your Lordship and this here ancient and honorable Club, upon any other Subject, but such as afforded Gladness, Joy and merry Glee, but alas! such is the unsteady, and fluctuating State of human affairs, that even the greatest and the wisest men, such, as your Lordship, and these here Longstanding members, must often submit to unavoidable cares, trowbles and accidents, . . . whilst fools, madmen, Scoundrels, and mean Low fellows, will unaccountably, and as it were, by the Capriciousness of their Stars, not only Escape and elude, the vindictive hand of Justice, but wallow in the favors of fortune, and Enjoy a full Swing of earthly prosperity and felicity, without so much as the Shadow of one single virtue to deserve them.

A person of your Lordship's profound discernment and penetration must by this time Clearly perceive, that the Lamen-

214

table Subject I am now to Harangue upon, is the Late happy, and unhappy nocturnal Incident, which befell your Lordship in bed,[1] unhappy, in the tragical Circumstances that attended it, and happy, O thrice happy! in it's agreeable, Surprizing and unexpected catastrophe, which catastrophe was in a great measure owing to your Lordships calmness, composure, and Steadiness of temper during the Hideous transaction, . . . Tho' great, very great was the provocation given your Lordship, tho' unmatched the audaciousness and Impudence of the hardened Villain, yet, your Lordship not in the least ennervated or unmanned with pusilanimous fear, but, with that placid Calmness and moderation, that masterly presence of mind, and perfect command of the passions, which become a virtuous and wise Philosopher, so checked and bridled, the Struggling effervescent *pathemata*,[2] within your Lordship's noble and heroic breast that, Instead of bursting and thundering out upon him, with that Just fury and Indignation, his Insolence and Impudence deserved, your Lordship addressed him, in Civil words, and Smoothing Speeches, so as to soften the flinty heart of the rugged barbarian, and turn his rough and Savage behaviour, in appearance, to the mildness and mollified carriage, the Gentle and Courtly address of a Civil and polite Gentleman.

※※

Methinks, I now see, your Lordship Supine upon your nocturnal pacific couch recumbent, composing yourself to partake of that Sweet repose, the meed and portion of the virtuous & upright, When lo! all of a Sudden, open flys your Lordship's Chamber door, and enters a most horrid, horrible, Grizly figure, armed with a pistol and dark Lanthorn, . . . barbarously

[1]Hamilton presents the robbery of Charles Cole in a humorous light, but in reality the people of Annapolis were less than amused. The two thieves were eventually captured, and the one who threatened Cole was publicly hanged (see *Maryland Gazette*, nos. 323–325, 329, 341 [July 3, 10, 17, Aug. 14, Nov. 6, 1751]).

[2]Violent emotions.

threatning your Lordship, in Infernal accents, with death and distruction, unless your Lordship's honor would deliver your Lordship's money. This Impudence, this audaciousness, this unmatched villainy, can scarce be parallelled in history, or meet with its equal in the annals of time, nay, not even the famous villain Guy Fox, that Infernal Tool of the Gunpowder Treason[3] with his dark Lanthorn, can match the barbarity of this att[acker.] But ah! can I say it without tears! this vile, execrable, detestable miscreant, bound your Lordships honorable hands, these munificent, these beneficent, these benevolent, these Innocent hands, here, I may exclaim with Hamlet's Ghost in the Tragedy

O horrible, O horrible! most horrible![4]

Now, your Lordship, tho in the utmost peril, and upon the point of being destroyed by that Lamentable assasin, still preserved that Steadiness of mind and Calmness of temper, so natural to your Lordship in the most trying Circumstances— where then, O where then was Sir John, your Lordships valiant and Intrepid Champion, where I say, was that Illustrious Chieftan, that heroe of antiquity [here Sir John plumed up, and sat with his arms akimbo] the defender of your Lordship, and this here ancient and honorable Club, alas! Sir John was not there, [at this Sir John exclaimed, what then Sir, behold me here] but sunk in soft repose, and surrounded with the Hypnotic poppies of the drowsy deity Morpheus . . . —but behold, in place of Sir John, there appeared another John,—a John, I may say, the Jewel and pearl of all Johns, who, for his brave behavior in this critical Juncture deserves to be knighted, this John, My Lord, no less a person than Don John Charlotto, your Lordship's faithful Gentleman usher, or principal valet de Chambre, by

[3]Guy Fawkes (1570–1606) was an English conspirator in the Gunpowder Plot to blow up the Houses of Parliament in revenge for penal laws against Catholics; he was subsequently executed.

[4]*Hamlet*, act 1, sc. 5, line 80.

Seasonably firing a gun, Charged with blank powder, and boldly exposing his brave Nob to the fire of the Enimy, saved and extricated your Lordship's honor, from this Imminent periclitation of your Lordship's honor's life and fortune. . . .

But it may perhaps be remarked by some Sophisters, that this noble and heroic deed, did not fall into proper hands, and that it's being executed by your Lordship's valet de Chambre, throws a tarnish over and sullies as it were the glory of the action, but my Lord, allow me to say, *Procul O Procul esto Prophani*,[5] the meanness and Lowness of the Instrument, I dare to say, in your Lordship's opinion, and, In the opinion of all other Sage Philosophers, abates nothing from the dignity and worth of a great action. . . .

Was not the City and State of Naples saved from a dangerous and desperate conspiracy by an old woman's oversetting an earthen Pitcher that stood in a window, as she hastily ran to look out, upon hearing an outcry in the Street, by the fall of which the brains of the Chief conspirator were knocked out, . . . would to heaven, your Lordship's valiant Don John, had knocked out the brains of that Lamentable villain, & sent his Soul a packing to the devil, tho it had been with a brown earthen piss-pot, and not a pitcher.

❋❖

Did not a number of old women, relieve the tottering and forlorn State of Sparta, by showing their nudities in an antic posture, to the timorous youth flying full speed from the enimy, which made them for very Shame, renew the battle and come off victorious.[6] It were to be wished, that the valiant Don John, had only shown that merciless Scoundrell his Nockandroe, or posteriors, thro' the port hole, and instead of firing a blunderbus, not loaded with bullets or Shot, have Saluted him with a

[5]"Keep back, keep back, you uninitiated ones!"—the utterance of the Sibyl to the companions of Aeneas (*Aeneid* 6.258).
[6]Hamilton is probably thinking of Plutarch's life of Lycurgus, where this role of women is described elaborately, though not the specific instance here.

volley of bum-gun-Shot, which would have made the paltry poltron fly as fast, from his villainy, as these Spartan youths ran to their duty.

※※

Finally, let these Instances suffise to show, that Great matters are often effected by mean and low Instruments, and allow me to conclude with wishing, that this here ancient and honorable Club, may never again Incurr the like danger of losing your Lordship's precious person, for, as we Surely stand or fall by your Lordship, so it is our duty and Interest to wish and pray for your Lordship's Safety and preservation."

The orator having made this oration sat down, and observing that most of the Longstanding members wore night caps, he made a short Speech upon Caps, but that being now a trite and wore out Subject . . . , it was so little regarded by the Club, as to be thought not worthy of the Record, neither was his Lordsp altogether pleased with his other oration, because it Insists too much on the praise of Don Jon Charlotto, for his Lordship was one of those Sorts of people, who like much to be praised and extolled themselves, but are disgusted with pangyrics bestowed on other persons, a foible, in which his lordship was not Singular, it being a mental disorder very frequent and Epidemical in human Societies, where envy never fails, more or less to spread her Influence.

Chapter 5 ※ *A heroic poem by the Laureat, on his Lordship's miraculous Escape.*

※※

At Sederunt 162, Philo dogmaticus Esqr, being H:S: The poet Laureat produced in Club, a heroic poem upon his Lordships late wonderful escape, from the hands of a merciless ruffian, which, after reading, did not meet with that Countenance, and favor from his Lordship, which the Laureat expected, for the same reason, (as it is thought,) that he did not approve of the Secretarie's late oration upon that Subject, . . . but, as it would be a great loss to posterity, to be deprived of this masterly performance, I have with some difficulty procured a Genuine Copy of it, and Inserted it into this history, which I should esteem Incompleat without it.

A Heroic Poem

On the late Tragical Scene acted in the bed chamber, of the Right Honorable Nasifer, Lord president of the ancient and Honorable Tuesday Club. Humbly presented to the Consideration of his Lordship, and his Longstanding members by

Their most humble Servant
The Club's Poet Laureat.

Dictate some Gloomy muse, my verse,
While I the Tragic Scene Rehearse,
The Tragic Scene that had almost,
Transform'd his Lordship to a Ghost,
Till brave Don John from Sleep uprising,
With Courage bold and Enterprizing,
Discharged the tremendous Gun,
That made the Villain fire and run.
   Night's Sable Chariot had well nigh,
Climbd to the Summit of the Sky,
And round, their Reign'd a Silence deep,
The rich awake, the poor asleep,
. . . .

Twas then his Lordship, snug and warm,
Lay on his bed, and thought no harm,
. . . .

His cogitations, peradventure,
On th'ancient Tuesday Club did Center,
How he with wisdom might Govern
And steer like pilot skilld at Stern,
How 'gainst Sir John to make resistance,
Till that proud Champion knew his distance,
How the [Sl]y Chanc'lor to withstand,
And keep him still, at his left hand,
· · · · · · · · · · ·

How to bring over to his fancy,
The members, so that none dares Gainsay
His Sage behests. In fine, how, wisely,
Strictly Solemnly and precisely,
To rule his Club in every matter,
That they might wiser prove and better;
· · · · · · · · · · · · ·

When lo! in the next Room, a noise,
Made all give way to quick Surprize,
"Ho! John! (his lordship Cries) g[o]! run!
In that there Corner stands a gun!
Quick! fire it off, some rogue I fear,
By force and arms has enter'd here,"
His Lordship spoke, but devil a gun
Was in the Room, nor valiant John,
Who, with a glass of rum well dos'd,
Himself in kitchen loft reposd,
And by his Side (as one may say)
His gun with powder loaded lay.
    Alas! his Lordship could no more,
Or say, or do, ope' bursts the door,
And, O most dread terrific Sight,
Shows a dark Lanthorn's gloomy light,
Which to his Lordship strait advances,
Next in his Eyes, a pistol Glances,
And, by the throat, a brawny fist,
His Lordship seiz'd with cruel twist,
And, while he struggled, well nigh Choakd,

Clapt to his breast the pistol Cock'd,
With "Dam your blood, you old Curmudgeon,
Tis not for nought, I've scald your Lodging,
Where is your money? quickly tell,
Or, 'S blood, I'll blow your Soul to hell,
Your Hoard of Cash,—declare old Chuff,
Or dam you, I shall use you rough."

❀❀

At last the Thief in Cruel Bands
Began to tie his Lordship's hands,
"Dam' your old blood (says he) beware,
For, if to call or stirr you dare,
I'll blow your brains out"—From Surprize,
His Lordship rousing, turn'd his Eyes,
To view the Rogue who talk'd so big,
And star'd upon him, like stuck pig,
Yet not with dastard fear oppress'd,
His Lordship Judg'd it might be best,
The Rugged knave to sooth and flatter,
Hoping to compromise the matter,
His Lordships Eloquence forth broke,
And thus in honey'd words he spoke.
"O Dearest, kindest friend, I pray,
Dont murder me, while here I Lay,
In bed thus bound, and unprepar'd,
For that would Cruel be and hard,
Cash I have none, but had I any,⎫
You should be welcome to each penny,⎬
Your Carriage is so Gentlemanny,"⎭
. . . .

His Lordship spoke—The Rogue replies,
"Sweet honey, dear,—and dam' my eyes,
One hair o' your head, I will not offer
To hurt, but must ransack your Coffer,
Tis but your money, I demand,"
Then strait he seiz'd with Cruel hand,
His Lordship's throat, as if he'd strangle him,

Who, while the thief did thus Entangle him,
Gave many a Lamentable Groan,
That would have pierc'd a heart of Stone.
 When Brave Don John, who, as we said,
Lay high in kitchen loft a bed,
Heard in his Lordships room a noise,
Which made him quick from Couch to rise,
. . . .

He spied a rogue below, expecting,
Th'event of what within was acting,
Who seeing John's Courageous face,
In such an unsuspected place,
Swore "Dam' ye, speak, or make a noise,
I'll blow your brains out in a trice."
"Oho! quoth John, and is it so,
Then faith 'tis time for me to go."
Then stepping back, he seizd the gun,
And quickly to the port hole run,
Where, taking neither aim nor mark,
He boldly fir'd her in the dark.
. . . .

 Thus brave Don John, discharg'd his gun,
And made the Rugged Ruffian run,
But e'er he run he fir'd a pistol,
Round John's Brave nob, the Slugs did whistle
And luckily stuck in the wall,
So John Receiv'd no harm at all.
 The Rogue within, who heard the Rattle,
Believ'd there was a furious battle
Abroad, and without more delay,
Thro dormant window made his way,
. . . .

And with his fellow rogue did fly,
The devil go with them both, say I.

❀❀

Oh! valiant John, thy fame & Glory,
Shall Cut a ——— dash in future Story,

. . . .
Bards yet unborn, shall sing thy praise
And with thy name adorn their Lays,
. . . .

For Sure like Hercules thou art,
And has't a very Sampson's heart,
Long life to thee may heaven afford,
Still to protect and guard my Lord,
And may his Lordship ne'er forget,
How vastly he is in thy debt,
Who has't as 'twere renew'd his breath
And snatchd him from the Jaws of death;
And since I chuse no more to sing,
God save my Lord, the Club and King.

❦❦

Chapter 6 ❧ *The Genearchy of the Club.*

Genearchy is a form of Government, which I have not seen in all my reading, treated of in that full and ample manner, which the nature and dignity of the Subject deserves; and it were to be wished, that some able pen would undertake the Subject, and unfold the mysteries of it in all its parts; I must not be thought to mean here, the government of States and Empires, which have frequently been in the hands of women famous for heroism and policy; and, by nature, seemingly, as well adapted to Govern as the Male, tho' custom has settled it otherwise, . . . we read of Zenobia the Empress, who supported her State long against the Strength of the Romans, after her husband's death, 'till Aurelianus vanquished her, and led her in triumph thro' the Streets of Rome, . . . we are told also of Semiramis, who became mistress of the whole assyrian Empire, and enlarged its bounds more than any of her predecessors;[1] . . . But these were the She tyrants of antiquity, and, tho their fame is sounded forth by historians at an Extravagant Rate, yet not all of them together can be Compared with our Illustrious Elizabeth of England, either for true Courage, wisdom, or policy, that renowned lady, being of more value and Significancy, than the whole Group of these ancient heroines. . . .

Neither am I to be supposed to mean here, that Sort of universal genearchy which the fair Sex, have mantained ever since the beginning of the world, procured and supported by bright Eyes, Jetty locks, arched Eybrows, Ruby lips, Snowy bosoms &ct: &ct: which we find minutely and Circumstantially described in our moderen Love Songs, odes, Cantatas, Bellets doux, Romances and novels, for really, that Subject, has already been so Largely discanted upon, by poets Enthusiastic Lovers, and soft Historians, That I should look upon it to be a work of Supererogation, to write or say any more Concerning it, . . . and therefore, that I may not be guilty of a waste of time, paper and Ink, I shall offer nothing on the Subject.

Nor do I mean that Sort of Genearchy, which takes place in private families, mantained by fainting fits, pearly tears, Sighs and soft complaints, and sometimes by the rougher method of eternal talking, bawling, flouncing, Scolding, nay, by the discipline of the fist and broom Stick, This being Sufficiently displayed, in many of our moderen Comedys, and opera farces, and is touched in a very Elegant and natural manner, In the Ingenious Mr Ward's *Matrimonial dialogues.*[2]

But that Sort of Genearchy which I speak of, is, that which Takes place in Clubs, where the members must be ordered and regulated, by the Caprice and humor of their wives, whether

---

[1] Zenobia ruled over Palmyra, in Syria, in the third century A.D., and sought power over the Roman East. She was defeated by Aurelian and exhibited at the head of his conquered captives. Semiramis, legendary queen of Assyria, built many cities and conquered many countries.
[2] See above, VII, 1, n. 3.

Present or absent; I say, it is a pity some able pen has not treated Largely on this novel Subject, as it would afford abundance of matter to be learned and witty upon, this Subject, (tho I had a capacity adequate to it) yet, is too extensive for me, at present to meddle with, having the weight of this Important History on my Shoulders, which I must discuss in as Succinct a manner as I can, for fear of Incurring that Common fault of being too voluminous, and Committing a *great Sin* by giving birth to a *great book*, so, having given this hint to the wits of our age, . . . I shall proceed to relate a remarkable Instance of Genearchy or petticoat Government, which at this period happened in the Ancient and honorable Tuesday Club.

At Sederunt 165, on the 8 of October, 1751, there appears this Entry on the Record.

"The Club met at the house of Huffman Snap Esqr, pursuant to an order of last meeting, Tho it should have met at the said house last Tuesday instead of this day, but, by reason of the necessary attendance of several of the members of this Club, at a Rehearsal of music for a Charitable Concert, . . . it was by some rebellious members, without the Consent or privity of the honorable President adjourned and put off"—

* * * * *

There is here a most horrible Gap or hiatus in the Records of this ancient and honorable Club, which posterity may be at a loss for, tho it is questioned by some, whether they will suffer any loss thereby, It cannot therefore be positively conjectured, what Individual members were present at this Sederunt, but . . . it is pritty certain, that the Honorable Nasifer Jole Esqr, the Lord president, was not present, which we have from a well vouched tradition or report, that the Club sent for his Lordship about eight o clock in the evening, no Commission for a deputy appearing, and his Lordship not Intimating to the Club at meeting, that he either could, or could not attend, as usual; This messenger was no less a person than Quirpum Comic Esqr, who . . . waited on his Lordship in his bed Chamber, being ushered

by Don John Charlotto, and found his Lordship, Just stepping
into bed, having his breeches in his hand; he delivered his message in a Succinct manner, Informing his Lordship, that the
Club requested his attendance, to which his Lordship made reply That he could by no means attend that night,—Then the
Emissary demanded a Commission for a deputy, which his
Lordship would not grant, so Quirpum Comic Esqr, returned,
and made his report to the Club, taking notice of the Circumstance of the breeches. . . .

The Club upon hearing Quirpum Comic's report or answer,
from his Lordship, resolved, that since the honorable breeches
were laid aside, that the honorable petticoat should supply their
place, and govern the Club for this Sederunt, accordingly, three
Great female officers were appointed, vizt: a lady Lord president, a Lady Sir John, and a Lady Chancellor, Philo Dogmaticus Esqr, having the Complaisance to surrender his office
for one night. But who these Ladies were, cannot now be
known, the Record being Irrecoverably lost,[3] so that the memorable transactions of this Sederunt, to our great grief and
Shame, must be buried in perpetual oblivion.

❀❀

Chapter 7 ❧ Arguments in Club, against the Genearchy, Club Search warrants Issued, Speech of the Orator.

❀❀

At Sederunt 167, several arguments were started In club, Concerning the Genearchy, which was Established on Sederunt
165, . . . and after much ratiocination, the Club could not well

---

[3]Hamilton does not identify these ladies in the "Record," but he mentions
there that women did serve as officers at this memorable sederunt.

tell how to proceed in this puzzling and knotty affair, till Jealous Spyplot Senr Esqr, who seemed to have been asleep all the time that the point was argued, took the Club book, and very gravely arming his nose with his Spectacles, tossed the leaves, backwards and forewards for a Considerable time, Then rising up, addressd the Chair, saying That he found on Sederunt 165, that this here Club was Governed by certain women, . . . and as he reckoned such Innovations to be dangerous to the constitution of this here Club, he humbly moved that his Lordship would issue his warrant, *de ventre Inspiciendo,*[1] for searching and Inspecting these females, in order to discover, whether or not they were Effectual, and true Longstanding members.

The Club much approved of this motion of Mr Attorney Spyplots, and the Secretary back'd him Strenuously in a pithy Speech, the Substance of which is now lost, some ungracious, malevolent and profane hands, having lacerated and mutilated the Club Records, in this place, for which we wish them, (whoever they are) no worse punishment, than that they may never have a Scrap of paper to wipe a Certain part, (which modesty forbids me to name) in Case of necessity, however we shall Endeavor to sum up the Substance of this Speech here.

The Secretary brought instances from ancient and moderen History, of the danger of admitting females to be Concerned in government affairs; . . . he mentioned Messalene of Rome, who was a fury, a composition of lust and a Devil Incarnate, . . . he also brought the example of Pope Joan,[2] who . . . obliged the venerable and Reverend Cardinals, ever since, to use a groping Chair, to examine and Scrutinize his holiness by,

[1] A warrant "to inspect the womb" (permission given by a judge to midwives to determine the fact of pregnancy).
[2] Messalina (first century A.D.), the wife of Claudius, was famous for her profligacy and political influence; she was executed for conspiring against him. Pope Joan was an apocryphal female pope of the ninth century who died in childbirth.

. . . and lastly, he mentioned, the Renowned Sue Lilliston, of this place, and of our own times, who, in the disguise of a merchant, transacted affairs on the 'Change at London, forged bills upon an honest Planter, and had it not been for Capitano Giovanni Carpentiro, who, it [is] supposed, discovered her by groping, would have eff[ect]ed her wicked purpose.

When the Secretary had done, the chancellor rose gravely from his Seat, and without any particular address, to either his Lordship or the Club, spoke as follows.

"For my part, I approve very much of Mr Attorney Spyplot's motion, and urge, that the Search shall be begun Immediatly, and since his Lordship has given no proofs of his virility as yet, I move, that it may be Scrutinized, whether we have not now, a Pope Joan, in the Chair."

If the Longstanding members might take upon themselves to Physiognomize, they could not but presume to think, that this Speech of the Chancellor's, might . . . have been as well let alone, for his lordship's countenance Changed much, during the delivery of it, and showed a mixture of Scorn and Indignation. . . .

At the 168th Sederunt, held upon the 26th of November, 1751, The honorable Lord President Jole being H:S: an Enquiry was made concerning the great Seal, which did not appear upon the table as usual, . . . Solo Neverout Esqr declared, that he had delivered it to the Secretary, . . . this the Secretary did not deny, but asserted, it had been stole from him, and (as he suspected) by Protomusicus himself, which the other put him to prove, but the Secretary could produce no legal evidence. . . .

The Chancellor's Indignation was very much stirred up at these proceedings, and he began to meditate revenge against his Lordship, Protomusicus and the Secretary, whom he looked upon, as all equally guilty in Secreting and concealing the Badge of his office, and, really, . . . we cannot be much Surprized at his Indignation, especially, when we consider, that, that State officer was of a warm & Impetuous Temper.

❀❀

Chapter 8 ❧ *Death of Sir Hugh Maccarty Esqr, and the mutilation of the Frontinbrassian Articles.*

Knowledge, next to power, wealth and beauty, seems to be most desired or coveted by men; all are fond of being thought knowing and wise, tho few are put in the proper way to become so, and still fewer are born with a genius adapted to receive and contain this eminent ornament of the mind. . . .

From this violent desire of knowledge, Implanted in mankind, proceeds that Strong Inclination, that all men have to be Informed of novelties or points, which they were before Ignorant of, and every man who entertains a notion that his neighbour is more knowing than himself, Imbibes his dictates with great greediness, and, thinking himself on the fair road to Improvement, stores up his maxims as so many truths and oracles. By a mutual Intercourse or Conversation then, particularly in Clubs, it is, that men Improve one another, . . . but, it is absolutely necessary, before conversation can be rendered in any degree Improving, that it should be highly Seasoned with Truth, and Sincerity, for, when falshood and dissimulation accompany the Conversation or Intercourse between man and man, the best Issue that can come from them is a Sullen Mysanthropy, accompanied by Ignorance & absurdity. . . .

It will be no matter of Surprize then to our Readers, when they find, the honorable Lord Jole, in the Sequel of this History putting no manner of Confidence or trust in any of the Longstanding members, and, looking upon every proposal in Club with a Suspicious Eye, as if some trick lurked under it, since that old Gentleman, had lately had several notorious falshoods palmed upon him for Truths, by the ill timed and mischievous Industry of Coney-pimp Frontinbrass Esqr, and the Secretary, relating to the Cap of state and the History of Sir Hugh Maccarty Esqr, of New York, which Clubical heroe, his Lordship had now discovered, to be only a creature of the Imagination, and the Cap of State, to be nothing but a Fool's cap. . . .

About this time Mr Humbug Fibber, an Inhabitant of Annapolis, and an Intimate acquaintance of all the Longstanding members, having returned from a Journey to New York, Brought an account, that Sir Hugh Maccarty Esqr, of New York was dead, and that he had seen him there decently buried, at this many were Surprized, hearing that a man should die and be buried, who, they were Sure had never lived, but his Lordship showed neither concern nor Surprize at the tidings, for with him, for some time passed, the said Sir Hugh Maccarty Esqr, was dead and Damnd, tho' not buried. . . .

A few days after Mr Fibber had brought this Lying news, was held the 168 Sederunt, of the ancient and honorable Tuesday Club, when . . . an odd occurrence happened, which seemed in some measure to confirm Mr Fibber's Supposed lie, concerning Sir Hugh, which was this. A certain tall, Gygantic negroe fellow, bringing into the Club room, the Bass viol, on which the Secretary that night performed Solo, elevated on his head, in a great deal board Case, pritty much in the Shape of a Coffin, encountered his Lordship full but, at the door, and not stepping back, with that respect and deference, which he ought to have showed to so Illustrious a personage, hit his Lordship, a terrible Thump with it on the forehead, Just over one of his Eyebrows, which made his Lordship stagger back, and Rub his face with his hands, but the blow was so violent, that it soon raised a frightful bump upon the place, the Club were very much alarmed, at this accident, and thinking some assasin In-

His Lordship encounters Sir Hugh macaulys Coffin

tended to destroy their President, started up in great Surprize
and stood in a posture of defence, and, it was said, that Sir
John, the Champion, drew forth from the Scabbard his tremendous blade, but finding, that the thing was only accidental,
they again composed themselves, and his Lordship asking what
that fellow had brought into the room, some person made answer, that it was the Coffin of Sir Hugh Maccarty Esqr of New
York, who had lately departed this life, and there the affair
rested.

At this Sederunt also, came upon the Carpet, the Frontinbrassian articles, which his Lordship had some material objections to, the first was, to the Salvo, or Saving Clause at the Conclusion, concerning the natural and political rights of the State
officers, and Longstanding members, his Lordship observed,
that neither the Longstanding members nor officers, had any
rights that they could lay Claim to, but those derived from the
favor and Grace of the Chair, and, that it was still in his power
to bestow these rights and to take them away. The Chancellor
made some Clamor and Stirr against this malicious and villan-
ous maxim, as he called it, but was soon overpowered by the
majority of the Club, and the Stentorian Vociferation of Mr
Protomusicus, who, now had gained much favor with the chair,
by his opposition to this State officer, the Club at last, were so
far Infatuated, as to cut off this article, and very quietly suffered
his Lordship to talk in this Dictatorial Strain, a glaring Instance
of the Despicable Slavery and Subjection, they had, by their
foolish Concessions brought themselves under.

His Lordship then objected to two Articles in the Lump,
vizt: to the 6th and 7th, concerning the privilege, granted the
Longstanding members, to kiss his Lordship's hand on Anniversary days, and the first Club Night after new Years day, and
the right given to members at admission, and to Strangers Invited to the Club, to do the same, professing, that he chose to
keep his hand for other uses, . . . the Club had some dispute

as to this point, and with some difficulty at last gave up this un-
doubted privilege, as it is called.

※※

Thus were the famous Frontinbrassian Articles, of which his
Lordship was once so fond, reduced from the Number eleven
to Six, a remarkable Instance, of the Instability of all Sublunary
things, and this act of the Club, was Called the mutilation of
the Frontinbrassian Articles.

BOOK X

From the Death of Sir Hugh Maccarty Esqr,
and the mutilation of the Frontinbrassian Articles,
to the end of the Chancellor's Rebellion,
and Civil wars concerning the Great Seal.

Chapter 2 ❧ *Beginning of the Chancellors Rebellion, and the great Commotions and uproars in the Club.*

Civil and domestic wars, as well as foreign, are distempers of the body politic, proceeding from Sloth Luxury and repletion, In the same manner as disorders in the natural body take their rise from the same Causes. The humors being thus Increased in quantity and Corrupted in quality, must have an evacuation, and as soon as that happens, the State returns to its former tranquillity and ease. . . . At this present Juncture, [the ancient and honorable Tuesday Club was] now ripe for such a Calamity, and the Cause of it was, that of ambition, pride and revenge, and not the thrist of Gold, tho Indeed Silver had some Concern in the affair, for the true or pretended cause of this uproar and rebellion, was the great Seal, which was made of Silver, of this memorable Transaction, at its first breaking out, I shall give a particular account in this Chapter.

❦❧

[At Sederunt 169, December 10th 1751,] Solo Neverout Esqr, being afraid of the Chancellors displeasure, . . . took the Secretary aside into a corner of the Room, and acquainted him, that he had the great Seal, that everlasting bone of contention in his

234

pocket, and that he had a mind to deliver it out of his hands in such a manner, as that he should not be suspected for Secreting it, but the whole blame should Light upon another, which would afford some diversion or *Fun,* as he called it, in Club; by this Subtle trap he Insnared the Secretary, who was a person whose volatile Genius or natural levity, led him very much to promote fun or diversion, and was loath to lose a Joke at any time, whatever the Consequences might be; Mr Protomusicus then, privately putting the Seal into the Secretarie's hands, told him, that, if he could by any means slip it into his Lordship's pocket, while he sat at Supper with his Longstanding members, he himself, would make a motion after Supper, that there should be a general Search for the Seal, and, that its being found upon his Ldshp, would afford abundance of mirth & Jocularity in Club; The Secretary objected to this, saying, that it would not be altogether safe, to pass the Joke upon his Ldshp, who might be revenged upon the Club, by retaining the great Seal for ever in his own hands, . . . and therefore he thought it would be much better, to put the Joke upon some one or other of the Longstanding members of the Commoners. Accordingly Jealous Spyplot Senr Esqr was pitched upon, as the most proper person to bear the burden of the Joke, and the Secretary agreed to slip the great Seal, into the pocket of that Gentleman, while he sat at Supper, which he did in such a dexterous manner that it was not perceived.

Supper being over, the Longstanding members for some time sauntered about the room as was usual, before they re-placed themselves round the Great table, . . . during this Idle Sauntering Interval, Mr Crinkum Crankum playd some In-terludes on the organ, and while this musician was exercising his art with a book of pricked music before him, Jealous Spyplot Senr Esqr, tho' he understood nothing at all of musical Or-thography, took it in his head to look over the notes, and for that purpose began to rummage in his pockets for his Specta-cles, but Instead of the Spectacles, to his great Surprize, laid

his hand upon the Seal, which Lugging out, he exclaimed with
a loud voice—Hey day!—what have I got here!—how came I
by this!—why 'tis the great Seal says one—It is so, says another,—Be it so or not, says Mr Spyplot, I know no more than
the pope of Rome, how the Devil it came into my pocket,—no
matter for that Good Sir, says the Chancellor, we shall Enquire
into that matter Presently, but I am Glad how ever, that I have
found the badge of my office—and taking the Seal out of Mr
Spyplots hands, he laid it upon the table before the presidents
Chair, . . . presently after this the members took their places,
and the Club was Just going to enquire how Mr Spyplot came
by the great Seal, when to the great astonishment of all present,
that Illustrious Symbol was a missing, and could no where be
seen, this put a Stop to the Intended Enquiry, and they Immediatly began to use the Strictest diligence to discover the person that had pirated it . . . ; at first his Lordship was not suspected for having seized upon it, till a general Search was
resolved upon, and all the members having undergone a Strict
Scrutiny, and turned their pockets outside in, when the Search-
ers came to his Ldshp he absolutely refused to undergo a Search,
and made a most violent resistance, putting on a very angry and
terrible Countenance, and Commanding the Longstanding
members to desist, on peril of his high displeasure; on this the
Chancellor, suddenly fell into a most violent rage, and rising
from his Seat all pale and Ghastly with anger, he told his Ldshp,
That he was a Tyrant, an old fool, an assuming Coxcomb, and
a hundred other such abusive epithets, and peremptorily In-
sisted upon his being searchd, saying That the members of the
Club would not only be despicable Slaves, but Insufferable asses
and blockheads if they allowed themselves to be so Imposed
upon,—what, says he do we come here to be hectored and dom-
ineerd over by an old absurd obstinate ass, who will not harken
to reason— . . . you may look somewhere Else Sir for your
Seal, said the President, you shall not search me for it I assure

you—I have had no peace in this Club since you came Into it, and I wish to God I had never seen your face, tis a Lamentable Thing, that I must be perpetually put into these flusters and blusters for nothing at all, . . . when you give [your Seal] up into every bodys hands, how can it otherwise be than lost? and when lost why do you blame me for it?—I'd have you to know Sir, that I scorn you and your Seal both, and so find it where you can, dont blame me for it.—The president being out of breath with this Long Speech, fell back on his Chair, and the Chancellor with a Ghastly and Enraged countenance, got up and harangued the Club to this effect.

"Gentlemen, must we then submit to this Insolence, this un-parallelled tyranny and oppression—must we be such dupes, such Simpletons, such asses—you have here set an old fool in that there Chair to rule over you, who will not submit himself to the rules of reason and equity, but attempts to carry every thing with a high hand, as he sees fit,—if you have a mind to be Slaves, despicable Slaves, vile contemptible drudges, sub-mit, I say submit to his caprice and humors,—for my part, I declare, I will not— . . . will you see me abused—trod upon, Insulted, contrould and brow beaten by that old Coxcomb in the Chair, will you suffer your faithful Chancellor . . . to be made a Cypher, a person of no Influence or Significancy in this here Club, by an arrogant Prig, who owes his exaltation to you, . . . for Shame! rouse up your heroic Spirits, dont suffer your selves to be piss'd upon—pull him down I say!—pull him down! if he knows not how to command, let him be taught to obey, evacuate the chair of such a load of absurdity—dispossess the tyrant and put some other in his place, that will be more Just, more humane, more grateful—I request and beseech you, for your own Sakes to take my part, and support me against the threats of this Tyrant in grain—suffer me not to be trod under foot, but in supporting me, support the honor, the dignity, the Liberties and privileges of this here Club, but, if this will not prevail, if you are deaf to my Just complaints—I must fly from you, I must leave you, to sink under that mean and despicable Slavery, with which you are at present Threatned."

This Speech of the Chancellor, was delivered with so Strong an Emphasis, accompanied with so much of the Pathos, with such violent agitations of body, with such a furious & pallid Countenance, that it struck many of the members with a pannic, enraged the majority, and quite silenced his Ldshp, and Immediatly, such a terrible Hurly burly and Tumult arose, that it is Impossible to give a description of it, at the Close of a Chapter in this History, and therefore I must refer you to the following Chapter for a full detail of it.

Chapter 3 ❧ Effects of the Commotions and uproars in the Club, and the Decathedration of his Lordship.

❀❀

The Chancellor, as has been related in the foregoing Chapter, was Enraged to such a degree, that most of the members kept aloof from him, esteeming it a very dangerous attempt to come within his reach; for he was in such agitation, as that he resembled an Infernal fury, more than a human Creature, his Long Crane like neck was streched out to its utmost extent, his mouth, as he uttered his words, gaped horrendous, and seemed to spue forth fire, . . . his countenance was pale & wan, and his eyes staring and flaring like two burning Candles, while his fists were Clenched h[ard], which he balanced and poised on both Sides, ready to give the decisive blow, . . . The high Steward, Prim Timorous Esqr, was in the utmost consternation and terror, & forgetting his office of Serj: at arms, and throwing aside his white Rod of authority, he betook himself for protection, behind his Lordship's Chair of State, and would now and then

Slyly peep at the Chancellor, from one Side of the Canopy now, and then from the other, according as the Chancellor changed his place or Situation, . . . for, that furious Incendiary, while he delivered his Seditious Speech, did not stand stock still, but walked about, like a peripatetic.

During this furious extacy of the Chancellor, and Consternation of the Longstanding members, his honor the president was fixed like a monument of marble in his Chair; he moved neither to one Side, nor to the other, but like one in a Catalepsy, seemed to have nothing left about him but the faculty of breathing, all the other parts of his Corporeal frame, vizt: muscles, Eyes, hands, being fixed and Immoveable, as one thunderstruck or under some Strange diabolical fascination or Incantation.

While affairs were in this alarming Situation, and the fire of [Rebell]ion, like an Impetuous flame Confined within a Close Chamber, was ready to burst forth every moment, and Carry the whole Edifice before it, Huffman Snap and the Secretary endeavored to mitigate the rage of the Chancellor, and persuade his Lordship to deliver up the Seal, but it was too late, the first thro' the violence of Rage was deaf to all Intreaties, the other, thro' astonishment, was rendered Incapable of Listening to any overtures or proposals.

Upon this, the majority of the Club, were absolutely determined, since the Seal could not by fair means be made forth coming, to use force, to recover that valuable badge of office, Huffman Snap swore, Dam him, if it was not an Impudent Imposition on the Club, to rob them of their great Seal, and that such an Insult ought not to be suffered.—Why do you suffer it then, replied the Inflamm'd Chancellor, why dont you Immediatly seize upon this Tyrant of your own setting up, and pull him down again since he knows not how to rule with moderation—Come on—I will lead the way—I will give the word, and let every Stanch member here use his utmost endeavors, by main force to detect the thief. . . . The Chancellor and his

forces had now advanced towards the Center of dominion, or
the Seat of Empire, to wit, his lordship's great Chair of State,
and made a formal atack upon it, besetting it on all Sides, . . .
vizt. Huffman Snap Esqr, took the dexter quarter of his lordship, and Solo Neverout Esqr, seized upon the Sinister quarter,
they began the attack first by seizing on, and securing his Lordship's arms, which, with one fist on each Side they pinned down
fast to the arms of the Chair, and each with his other hand, attacked the dexter and Sinister pockets of his Lordship, to search
and rummage for the great Seal, his Lordship recovering, from
his astonishment, threw a tremendous look, first on one Side,
and then on the other, and asked the two Champions in a pre-
cipitate manner, and with a Surprized tone of voice if they Intended to rob him, but they made no answer, continuing still
their Search, while the chancellor spurred them on with In-
flammatory Speeches, commanding them to fight like Lions for
their liberty and property. His Lordship then began to struggle
most violently and to lay about him to the right and to the left,
as lustily as he was able, and had like to have knocked down and
discomfited his left hand Antagonist, in this Scuffle his Ldshp,
had his ruffles tore in a most Lamentable manner, and the posture of his wig was altered much for the worse, having the tail
turned foremost, however his Lordship still kept his Seat, and
would not suffer himself to be moved one Inch to one Side or
other; upon this the general attack was renewed with greater
fury; there was a General Cry among the Longstanding members, and nothing was heard but Burn the Chair!—Burn the
Canopy!—Burn the book!—on which, the Secretary was advancing towards the fire to throw the book in the midst of devouring flames, and Commit to oblivion in one moment, all the
transactions of this ancient and honorable Club, when the wisdom and discretion of Jealous Spyplot Senr Esqr, prevented this
dreadful Calamity, for, he perceiving the Secretaries design,
pulled him back, and seizing the book out of his hands, took it
into his own care and protection, Then Quirpum Comic Esqr,

having beat Prim Timorous Esqr from his station, behind the
Chair, took off the Canopy of State and was approaching towards the fire to Committ it to the flames, when he was stoped,
by Jonathan Grog Esqr, who with heroic Intrepidity rescued
that Ensign of State from the distroyer, and disposed of it in a
private corner out of the way of danger. Prim Timorous Esqr,
Serjeant at arms and H:S: was thrown into such a terrible pannic
that he swore several times over *God—bless the king,* and run
and hid himself in some private Corner, so that he was not seen
again on the field till the battle was over. . . .

His Lordship still keeping his Seat with unshaken Intrepidity, the Chancellor fearing that the destinies would turn the
Scale against him, gave orders for a fresh attack, calling out to
the Longstanding members to take Courage, and not lose Spirits, on which the uproar and hurly burly, encreased to a great
degree. Quirpum Comic Esqr, one of the principal heroes in
the opposition, seeing that it was but labor in vain, to move his
Lordship from his Seat by tugging and pulling, went behind
the Chair, and with his brawny fist fetched several violent hard
blows under the Bottom of it, which . . . gave such a Strong
concussion and repercussion, to his Lordship's buttocks, that he
rebounded at least half a foot from his Seat at each blow, and
was obliged to quit his Chair of State, rushing precipitatly from
the Step, and falling upon one knee, but soon again recovering
himself, notwithstanding the uninterrupted thumps and blows
of the enimy, he run with precipitation to the fire, and to the
great astonishment and Surprize, of every person present, who
Imagined that his Lordsp in the height of his frenzy and des-
peration, was going to sacrifise his own carcase to the devouring
flames, he threw the great Seal into the middle of the fire, and
rammd it down, into the hottest part with his foot, while Quirpum Comic Esqr, threw the Chair of State over his Ldsp's head,
which pitched into the fire at the same Instant with the great
Seal. There was Immediatly a most furious Scramble, to save
these two precious Ensigns of the Club from Immediate de-

struction, and Huffman Snap Esqr, dexterously snatched the
great Seal from the danger it was in, . . . and with a Low bow
put it into the Chancellor's hands, who received it with a lowd
hollow of *Victory*, and Tunbelly Bowzer Esqr, at the same Instant, rescued the Chair of State from the fatal Combustion with
which it was threatned; his lordship stood now in the middle of
the floor, very much astonished, and seemed to be quite disabled
and out of breath, and Loud peals of *Victory* from the Chancellor's party rung thro' the Room; and Indeed the Chancellor
had no great Reason to boast of his Superiority, Considering
that he had by much the advantage of his Lordship in numbers,
for, upon his party, were the following Intrepid Champions,
vizt: Huffman Snap Esqr, Solo Neverout Esqr, Tunbelly
Bowzer Esqr, Quirpum Comic Esqr, Jealous Spyplot Senr
Esqr and the Secretary. On his Lordship's Side were only, Prim
Timorous Esqr, who had not Courage to stand the brunt of the
battle, . . . Slyboots Pleasant Esqr, Jonathan Grog Esqr, and
Mr Josua Flutter, an honorary member, who did but little Service, . . . [what] contributed much to his Lordship's defeat in
this battle, was the absence of Sir John his Champion, who, had
he been present, would, either by the terror of his Countenance,
and the virtue of his broadsword, have altogether prevented the
fray, or discomfited the Chancellor and his partizans. . . .

Chapter 4 ❧ *Clubical Interregnum, Carmen Seculare.*

❦❦

The honorable Lord Jole, tho his passion had been stirred up
to a great Pitch, by the Rude usage he met with and the Scurvey
Language that was bestowed upon him by the Chancellor, in
the Late Clubical Tumult, yet was his heart so swoln, within his
magnanimous breast, that his passion during that Scuffle, could

not find a proper vent to discharge itself; he therefore, against his will, retained it, till the battle was over, and then, having had some time to breath, as he stood staring round him, in the middle of the floor, he found the vent holes of his Indignant bosom begin to enlarge, and his anger, threatned to rush forth with great violence and fury, which he perceiving, and fearing lest he should be guilty of some Inconsiderate action, beneath his Station and dignity, Immediatly took his hat, Cloak and Cane, and having Gravely put on the two first, and taken the Latter in his hand, he, with Great State and Solemnity, walked out of doors, and left the Longstanding members, staring after him with great astonishment, being wrapt in admiration at his Lordship's heroic Command of his passions.

※※

Thus was this furious battle fought in Club, and decided in favor of the Chancellor, who bristled and plumed very much on his victory, and was Just going to ascend the Chair of State, in the shatter'd condition it was in, when he was pulled back, by some of the Longstanding members, and desired to take his proper place in Club, and thus, notwithstanding, his being flushed with Success, was he disappointed, in his designs to seize upon that honorable Seat, . . . but we shall presently see, this ambitious Grandee, mounted on that Seat of honor, dealing his commands about him in an Arbitrary manner, which made it plainly appear, that the Quarrel betwixt my Lord Jole and he, with regard to the Club, was the same, as of old, the Quarrel between Cæsar and Pompey, with regard to Rome, that is, the thing aimed at, was power and dominion, and not Liberty, as was pretended.

And thus was decathedrated, in a most Lamentable manner, The Illustrious Nasifer Jole Esqr, Lord president of the ancient and honorable Tuesday Club, whose personal worth and merit, had recommended him at first to be exalted to that Great Dignity, and, who had now possessed that Chair of State, for upwards of Six years; a woeful example to all, who suffer themselves to be misguided by flattery, and Immerged in the soft allurements of Luxury, which mislead them into ambitious and aspiring designs, and projects, which at last terminate in their utter Ruin, . . . and this ancient and honorable Club, which from this very time, was perpetualy upon the declining hand, ought to be a warning to other Clubs, how they follow these dangerous paths of Luxury, vain pomp and excess, and practise the arts of adulation, which, as they proved the bane of this Club, so they will Surely prove the bane of every other Club that Indulges them.

᠁

[At Sederunt 171, January the 7th, 1752,] the Club understanding by Certain Intelligence, tho' not from his Lordship himself, that his Lordship was very much Indisposed with the Gout; which, (had he been otherwise well disposed,) would have prevented the Club from Enjoying his gracious presence, the members, according to ancient Custom, . . . agreed, that there should be a Condolatory address wrote by the Club, and directed & sent to his Lordship upon this Lamentable & mournful occasion, which was accordingly done, and after some Consideration, on the matter, it was agreed, that it should be Entituled *Carmen Seculare*, . . .[1] the Tenor of this address follows.

Carmen Seculare

Being a most mournful Condolance, of the ancient and honorable Tuesday Club, addressed to the honorable Nasifer Jole Esqr, Lord President of the said Club.

Ah wretched Club! must thou again,
Resume the Lamentable Strain,
By Cruel fates doom'd once a year,
To sigh, and shed, the doleful tear.

[1]Literally, "secular song or verses," borrowed from Horace's *Carmen Saeculare*, composed for the Secular Games in Rome.

Christ'mass in vain his dainties pours,
Alas! these dainties are not ours,
What dainties can to us give pleasure
While press'd down by my Lord's displeasure,
Yet, not my Lord's displeasure only,
Makes us so dull, so moap'd and lonely,
But that the Cruel gout once more,
Has made my Lord both Sick and Sore.
    O Gout, of all our ails the worst,
Brother of Nemesis the Curs'd,
Who to us mortals does dispense
Blue plagues and Ghastly pestilence,
Whoe'er you with your torments grieve,
His Lordship's precious members leave,
. . . .

For whilst his Lordship you molest,
You Rob his ancient Club of Rest,
His ancient Club, which cannot stand
Without his Strong Supporting hand.
    In vain the huge and pond'rous pye
At Supper strives t'attract the Eye,
. . . .

Nor pye, nor Turkey, nor the punch,
Can screw our mirth up half an Inch,
Nought will avail to raise our glee,
'Till we his Lordships face shall see.
His gracious face, in every wight,
Would rouse up mirth and make hearts light,
Whilst all would sing with Joyful Strain,
May he no more feel gouty pain,
And, may this ancient Club no more
Fall under his displeasure Sore,
Thus, freed from Gout and discord's rage,
We'll see again, the Golden Age.

If one Considers well the frame and tenor of this Poem, he will be Surprized not alittle at the Caprice and humor of this ancient and honorable Club, who, but two Sederunts before this, in a most outragious manner, decathedrated their Lord president, and now pretend to write mournful verses, Condoling his Indisposition, absence and displeasure.

※※

Chapter 6 ※ *Special Embassy of pacification of the Longstanding members to his Lordship, and the Conference that happened thereupon.*

※※

We find the ancient and honorable Tuesday Club at Sederunt 173, had appointed Plenipotentiaries to treat with his Lordship, and demand of him a Categorical answer, concerning his resolution, with regard to the Club, vizt: whether he ever Intended to return to it again, and if so, in what Quality, whether as president or a private member? One would think, that this was a plain Question, and easily resolved; but, his Lordship, tho pressed much to it, by the Plenipo's, did not think fit to return a positive or Categorical answer to the question, as we shall presently see, nor Indeed, would the deputies of the Club, have got access to his Lordship to propose any such question, had not some deep drawn Club Politicians industriously spread about a report, that the Longstanding members Intended to place Philo Dogmaticus Esqr in the chair, which alarmed his Lordship, so much that he readily Granted admission to the Emissaries of the Club, tho he had before determined obstinately to deny them access.

These three Clubical Commissioners then, vizt: Jonathan Grog Esqr, Slyboots Pleasant Esqr, and Mr Secretary Scribble, one afternoon, took their progress towards his Lordships house in north East Street, and marching along Incog, without pomp or Ceremony, to avoid Suspicion, came to his Lordshp's outer gate, where, giving a Signal, they were admitted into the Court yard by Signior Don John Charlotto, . . . after having politely answered some questions put to him by his Lordship Concerning the business of these Gentlemen, as well as he could, he returned, and acquainted the Emissaries, that his Lordship was ready to receive them. Whereupon, they were Immediatly Conducted by the said usher, into his Lordships privy Chamber, who received them sitting, bolt upright upon his bed, being still under the agonizing pains of the Gout, his body was wrapd about with blankets, and his head covered with many Caps, one over the other, so that his lordship looked very like a Great Chinese Mandarin in his Grand Chamber or Saloon of public audience.

The Deputies at their departure, entertained no favorable opinion of the Success of this negotiation, but however, it turned out better than they expected, they, accordingly at Sederunt 173 made report to the Club, that they . . . [had] Presented to his Lordship, the *Carmen Seculare* Composed at Sederunt 171, and that his Lordship was pleased Graciously to receive the same, and Read it, sitting in his bed, and that then they proceeded, according to the express orders of the Club, to demand a Categorical answer to the following question, vizt: whether his Lordship ever Intended to return to the Club again, if yea, in what quality, as president, or private member, to which his Lordshp after a short fit of musing, made answer, that he would desire further time to think of it, and would give in his final answer against next Sederunt of the Club.

At this Report, Philo Dogmaticus the Chancellor, and H:S: was angry, and said It was an Insult upon the Club, and the members would be very great Simpletons, if they would rest satisfied with any such prevarication and Juggling, Then taking hold of the great Chair, while Mr Comic the deputy was out of it, having step'd to the Door to make water, he vaulted into it, and knocking upon the Table with his fist, he told the Long-standing members, That once he had the honor to possess that Seat, he would teach them to behave themselves like men. . . . Some were Intimidated by this bold behavior of the Chancellors, and others minded it not much, and, it was thought, had the Champion been present at this Sederunt, the Chancellor durst not have assumed these airs, he however kept his Seat, during the Remainder of this Sederunt, In Spite of the united force of the Club, yet, was much out in his politics, in taking upon him this authority, as it proved a Bar to the Success of his ambitious Schemes in the Club.

※※

Chapter 8 ❧ *Happy Conclusion of the great Rebellion, his Lordship's happy Restoration.*

It is said that one Injury produces another, . . . but should any one thence Infer this maxim, that one Injury calls for another, I will not be so rude as to call him a lying Doctor, but Sure with propriety, I may denominate him a bad Christian, as to return Injury for Injury is a practise expressly Contrary, to the excellent rules prescribed us by Christianity, besides, if Injury called for Injury, this would turn out a very ridiculous Sort of a world, for there would be nothing but quarelling to be seen; Socrates was of opinion that Injuries were to be overlooked, for he thought none but fools or madmen would offer them. . . . The notion of this Philosopher differs in that particular vastly from that of our moderen Smarts, who think the best method of putting up an Injury is, to run the fool who offered it thro the Guts, or blow out his brains, and, that they may not seem to do this out of anger or Spite, they will frequently shake hands with the Silly Coxcomb, Just before they dispatch him to the other world, . . . but these times we live in, differ from the age, in which the aforesaid Philosopher Lived, and these heroic feats are done for the Support of a Certain Moderen Phantome, which has assumed the name of *honor,* and with this particular kind of *Gothic* or *Moderen Honor,* Socrates & his bretheren ancients were quite unacquainted. . . .

Whether the honorable Lord Jole, president of the ancient and honorable Tuesday Club, regulated his Conduct with regard to the Chancellor and the Club, who had lately put upon him such great Injuries, by the example of Socrates or any other ancient Sage, . . . I shall not be so bold as to declare, being quite In the dark, as to the real motives, that actuated that Great man, but Sure I am, that, in the mildness, and Gentleness of his behaviour, Towards the said Chancellor and the Club, he showd a degree of heroic patience, forbearance and forgiveness, that whatever his motives were, he deserved at least in the Charitable Judgement of the world, the character and name of a Good christian, and tho' he was spurred on to wrangle and brangle with the Club and the Chancellor, particularly by his Champion Sir John, . . . he chose a much more prudent method, to be reconciled to his rebellious Chancellor and Club, as we are now going to relate.

At Sederunt 175, march 24th 1752, The Club Convened at the house of the worshipful Sir John, H:S: and soon after the members were met, the worshipful the H:S: acquainted them, that the honorable the Lord President, was in the next room, upon which the members went into Serious Consultation, concerning the manner In which they were to behave to his Lordship at this Juncture, and, finding, that his Lordship, had made as great a Step towards a reconciliation as was Consistent with the honor and dignity of his place, they Concluded, that a Select number of the Longstanding members, . . . should wait upon his Lordship in the next room, and request his Lordship to come into the Club room and take the Chair. Pursuant to this Resolution, the worshipful Sir John, H:S: & Champion, The respectful Prim Timorous Serjeant at arms, Huffman Snap, Tunbelly Bowzer, and Slyboots Pleasant Esqrs went, and Solemnly waited on his Lordship in the adjoining Chamber, and making a very low and profound bow, Prim Timorous Esqr, Spokesman for the Deputies, delivered himself in this manner.

"My Lord, we are sent by the ancient and honorable Tuesday Club, Convened in the next Room, to request your Lordship to come and resume your Lordship's Chair of State in the Club, and to take again the reins of Government into your Lordship's hands, that good order and peace may be reinstated in our at present Confused Society." His Lordship answered this Speech with a nod of the head, which being understood as a Signal of assent, the Deputies made a lane, by ranking themselves, on each Side of the Door way for his Lordship to pass thro', and his Lordship accordingly, walked in State thro' that lane, with much the same air and Countenance as other Great men assume on the like occasions, and coming into the Club Room, the first person his Lordshp encountered was the Chancellor, who took his Lordship by the hand, led him to the Great Chair, and placed him in it, while this Solemn Ceremony was a performing, these two great men, vizt: the President and Chancellor, smiled very pleasantly upon one another, but this Reciprocal Smile was Judged to be only from the teeth outwards, like all Complaisant Smiles, which now a days appear on the faces of our thorro'pac'd Statesmen and Courtiers.

꧁꧂

Thus was restored again, to his dignity honor, and authority in this ancient and honorable Club, the honorable Nasifer Jole Esqr, their Lord president, after an Interregnum of 15 weeks, during which Space, the Government of the Club, was very Confused, and Irregular, and withal arbitrary, The Chancellor taking upon him to order and manage every thing with a high and Imperious hand.

꧁꧂

BOOK XI

From the end of the
Chancellor's Rebellion,
and Civil wars Concerning
the Great Seal,
To the Convention of the
Grand Committee.

Chapter 2 ❧ *Celebration of the Seventh anniversary, with the anniversary Speech, libel on his honor the President and Club, in the New York Gazette.*

Far the greatest part of mankind, give themselves no manner of trowble about forming a true Judgement of things, they Judge altogether from outward appearances and the ear and eye are the Chief guides. Hence we see, that a fellow in a rich and Splendid dress, with a pompous equipage, gains Immediate esteem among the Multitude, . . . while a ragged and Shabby mortal is utterly disregarded, and spoke to with a kind of reluctance, as if the Sordidness of his Character, was of a piece with that of his dress, . . . This is a very absurd association of Ideas, and yet, it generally prevails; it was doubtless from the Consideration of this weakness in Human nature, that the honorable Mr President Jole, condescended at first, contrary to his natural modesty and Good Sense, to ornament his person with several gaudy trappings, as Caps of State, mallets of State, Canopies of State, and presidential Stars and badges of State, knowing, that the Longstanding members, as men, being liable to the Common foibles of humanity, would, from these gaudy ornaments sooner conceive that high opinion of him, which it was necessary they should entertain of their president, but, that once obtained and confirmed, by his wisdom and Conduct, that Great and wise president, thought it now high time to throw aside these bawbles and vanities. . . . He had also laid aside the Title of *Lord President,* as vain and assuming, but one piece of Grandure, he still retained in his own hands, as thinking it of some Solidity and Signification, vizt: the privilege of celebrating at his own house, with the usual pomp and grandure, the anniversary of the Club, a relation of which Solemnity, Celebrated now for the Seventh time, I proceed to deliver.

❀❀

At Sederunt 179, May 12th 1752, being the Seventh Anniversary of the ancient and honorable Tuesday Club, the Longstanding members met in their badges, at the house of the honorable Mr President Jole. . . .

His honor the President as h:s: entertained the Club very magnificently, as usual, upon this Grand and Solemn occasion, the entertainment consisting of a Genteel Supper, where boiled, roast, and baked made a gorgeous appearance, in Splendid dishes, and were washed down with variety of good liquors.

❀❀

The orator after Supper was Called upon to deliver the anniversary Speech, and his honor being seated in the Chair of State, he stood up, and making a Low obeisance, first to his honor, then to the members, he spoke as follows.

Anniversary Speech

Honorable Sir,

It has been observed by some learned historians, (I forget who, nor would it be much to the purpose, if I should name them) that had it not been for that whore Hellen, and the Sacking of Troy, the world would have been deprived of Homer's most excellent poem, *The Iliad;* and, on the other hand, had it not been for the poet Homer, that memorable Transaction of

History would long agoe have been buried in the ruines of Time.

If it be not too bold and assuming in me, to draw a parallel between the Trojans and their City, and this here ancient and honorable Club, (for Sure we are all Trojans true as ever pissd[a] and in that chiefly consists our antiquity,) and between that most Excellent Poet Homer and myself, I will presume to affirm, that posterity, some Centuries hence, (supposing this here Club to be obselete and out of date, as is now the City of Troy) will have Just cause to make the same observation, upon your honor, your ancient Club, and your orator, They will bless and hug themselves, that such a president and such a Club ever existed, . . . and, at the same time, they will observe with Justice, that, had it not been for the tongue and pen of your extraordinary orator, your honor, The worshiful Sir John, the Chancellor, Poet Laureat, Protomusicus, Serjeant at arms, and other Illustrious personages, Longstanding members of this here ancient & Honorable Club, must all have been lost and swallowed up in oblivion together with the very name of your ancient Club itself; Just as old Priam, his Sons, his nobles and his City itself would have been, had it not been for the Song of Homer, that Immortal bard.

And now, most honorable Sir, as both your honor and your ancient and honorable Club, are themes never to be exhausted, themes Replete with such multitudinous and multifarious matter and copious inexhaustible Subject, . . . So I, who profess myself, but of a midling so, so, Capacity for a Club orator, far, O far Inferior to the bright Geniuses, who have been my predecessors in that office, vizt: The Learned Mr Quaint, and the Ingenious Mr Comas, the first of whom was distinguished for his Incomparable tropes, metaphors and figures, the Latter, for his Significant and moving gestures, being a man of but few words, and these pritty pithy, . . . I, I say, who am but of a

---

[a]Cottons *Virgil Travestie* lib 1. [Ed.: Charles Cotton (1630–1687) was an English poet remembered chiefly for *Scarronides; or, Virgile Travestie* (1664). Hamilton is recalling the opening lines from *Scarronides*, "I sing the man (read it who list, / A Trojan true as ever p————."]

mean Capacity for a Club Orator [Pres: Psha! theres too much of this!] —to avoid as much as possible, being caught in a Labyrinth of Intricacies, . . . shall take your honor, and your principal longstanding members upon this anniversary occasion, *Singulatim* and *Separatim*, one by one Slyly, each after another in a String [here the President shifted about in his Chair, & Sir John Yawned hideously]

And first for your Self, most honorable, most excelsified, most profound, most oblong, most oblate, most dilated, most unparallelled, most excentric, and most unexemplified Sir, I must profess myself amazed and astonished every time I behold and contemplate you, the head, the director, the first mover, the *Sine qua non*, and *Archæus Faber*[a] of this here ancient and honorable Club, when I consider the depth of your understanding, the height of your Genius, and Conceptions, the breadth of your Clemency and Sapience, the Length of your memory, authority, and . . . monostatical Protuberances, . . .[1] the best way for any Club Orator to express them to purpose, is, (after the elegant manner of my Immediate predecessor in this office, with true Comasian Eloquence) to hold his peace, and say nothing, except it be only some aspiratory, Interjectionary and admiratory, hums, hahs! and huts! . . .

Your honor and Valor, most unexemplified Sir, shines forth, conspicuous, in the person of Sir John (heretofore Oldcastle) your most unparallelled knight, the bruitt of whose arms and heroic atchievements have already reached, Lord knows how

[a]A Term of van Helmont's the Physician, by which he meant a Certain head director or overseer, of the operations of the animal œconomy, who had his Seat somewhere about the Pylorus, or mouth of the Stomach. [Ed.: Jean Baptiste van Helmont (1577–1644) was a learned Flemish mathematician, physician, and alchemist, whose works include *The Magnetical Cure of Wounds* (1650) and numerous other medical treatises. In chap. 5 of his *Oriatrike; or, Physick Refined* (London, 1662), van Helmont defines the Archaeus Faber as the "chief Workman, containing the fruitfulness of generations and Seeds, as it were the internal efficient cause" (*Van Helmont's Works* [London, 1664], 35).]

[1]*Monostatical* is Hamilton's invention, perhaps echoing *monostach*, a botanical term for plants bearing a single spike.

many Leagues around us, . . . under the protection of whose terrific arms the Longstanding members of this here ancient Club, Cling and cuddle together, in as great Security from foreign assaults and dangers, as a parcel of small Chickens, are defended from the bloody talons of the hawk, under the Spreading wings of the hen Mother, by whose terrific looks, and martial Countenances your honor sits secure in that there Chair of State, in Spite of all the machinations and Contrivances of ambitious and rebellious members, who wickedly would subvert our Constitution, and usurp the Cathedral dignity [here Sir John looked upon the Chancellor, with a Terrific Countenance]

❋❋

The Harmony of your honor's conduct and actions, the melodious Sound of your honors Sweet voice, are represented by your most expert and alert Proto-musicus, whose heavenly notes, like the warblings of the Sirens, enchant all that hear them, and many more besides; than which no thing can be Sweeter, unless it be your honor's dulcisonorous pipe, which (as it moves the members as well as the Stones) must be owned by all, to excell the modulations of Orpheus himself, who is said to have Charmed the Stones, trees, Cattle, and even the Infernal Imps with his melody, but your honor Charms the Longstanding members of this here ancient and honorable Club, which is all in all.

❋❋

Lastly, your honors oratory and Eloquence shines forth in the person of your Orator; an orator of all orators the most Garrulous and verbose, who can expatiate and hold forth, as much, and as long upon nothing, [Sr Jno: That's the truest thing you have said to night] as any orator that ever opened his mouth or mounted the Rostrum; but this Subject, I leave, for your honor and your Longstanding members to expatiate upon, being Sensible, that it is not only Improper, but unbecoming for a man to talk too much of himself, be it good or evil. . . .

As for the Residue of your honor's L:St: members, take them either Separately or Conjointly, they are altogether unparallelled, by any members whatsoever that have appeared, in ancient or moderen times, or in ancient or moderen Clubs; They

are *Long*, and they are *Standing*, which, I shall explain as Suc-
cinctly as I can, They are Long in their Deliberations, argu-
mentations, or, (to speak Clubically,) arguefications . . . , they
are long in their heads, that is, wise and Sagacious, they are long
in their Sight, that is foreseeing and foretelling, and discerning
at a distance, some of them are long in coming to Club, others
are long in going away, lastly they are long in their members,
such as their noses and so forth, and finally some are long in
their Speeches, as Mr Protomusicus & your humble Servant,
[Sr Jno: Thats true faith]

Now, as for their Standing, they are Standing as they yet
Stand and exist, They are Standing, as they Stand Cordially
together, They are Standing as they prop up your honor's Chair,
and are mutual buttresses to each other, . . . they are Standing,
as they are people of good understanding, they are Standing as
they live in mutual good understanding one with another, and
lastly, they are Standing, being the Cause (as it is said) of many
a Standing Joke. . . .

Now, to take Long and Standing both together, they are of
Longstanding, as they are the members of an Ancient Club,
they are long of Standing, as they never proceed in a hurry, but
by deliberate and gradual methods, and Sedate deliberations,
and, when they address your honor, it is a long time, before they
can be made to Stand up, and when up, many of them Stand
long, nay longer than your honor desires, as I do now at present
[Pres: I think indeed 'tis high time you were sat down] . . .
lastly, they are literally Long and Standing, which are two very
good qualities, Singularly useful and advantagious in some
mysterious Games, which, for brevitie's Sake, I shall here leave
unexplained, this Subject requiring a discourse by itself, and
belonging Solely, *Veneri et Priapo.*[2]

※※

Gentlemen, the Subject is so great, and the time so short, that
no orator whatsoever, can Sufficiently expatiate upon it so as to
make it Clear and Intelligible to the most understanding, and
therefore, I hope you'll excuse the abruptness and Imperfection

2"To Venus and Priapus."

of this discourse, and, without farther Ceremony, regale, and entertain yourselves, on this Solemn occasion, . . . let us all Join in one free and unreserved mirth, and with Jovial disposition, let us eat, let us drink, let us sing, let us dance, let us fiddle, let us pipe together like friends, let us meet and part like friends, and Join in one cordial wish, *long live his honor, and long live, the Ancient and honorable Tuesday Club—Dixi.*

The orator having pronounced this Speech, the Club gave the plaudite by Clapping their hands, the Chancellor leading the way.

Much about this time, appeared in one of the New York weekly Gazettes, a most Infamous and Scandalous Libel upon his honor the president and the Club, to this effect, "That on such a day arrived in this City (vizt: New York) from England, the honorable Coney Pimp Frontinbrass Esqr, Chancellor to the most high and Honorable Hugh Maccarty Esqr, President of the most ancient and Right honorable Monday Club of New York, upon whose arrival, the Honorable Sir Hugh Maccarty Esqr, Summoned a Special meeting, of the said Right honorable Club, and the said Honorable Coney Pimp Frontinbrass Esqr, was called before them, and tried at the bar, an Indictment being found against him, for treason and Conspiracy, against his Lawful lord & President, Sir Hugh Maccarty Esqr, in his Corresponding with a Certain pretended or Sham Club at Annapolis, called the ancient and honorable Tuesday Club, and with a Certain Nasifer Jole Esqr, Ridiculously stiled Lord Jole, their Pretended Lord President, a person of a mean aspect and awkward address, and, In his Clapping a Cap of State, upon the Lousy pericranium, of the said pretended Lord Jole, and betraying unto him, and his pitiful Club, the Secrets of the said Sir Hugh Maccarty Esqr, and his most ancient & right Honorable monday Club, upon which Indictment the said Honorable Coney Pimp Frontinbrass Esqr, being Tried and Cast, he was Expelled the Club, for ever and a day."

This Scandalous Libel, gave very great offence to his honor the president, and some of the Longstanding members, particularly the Chancellor, who resolved Immediatly to pen an answer to it, and it was the principal Cause, of the Great battle of Farce alia, that was afterwards fought in his honors back yard, as shall be related in its proper place. Most, if not all of the members, as well as his honor, firmly believed, that Coney Pimp Frontinbrass Esqr, was himself the author of this libell, for, as to Sir Hugh Maccarty Esqr and his Club . . . his honor and the Club believed them now, to be only mere Chimerical Nonentities, and the wild Creation of a maggoty brain.

Chapter 4 🐎 *The Great Clubical Battle of Farce alia, fought between Coneïus Pimpeïus Frontinbrass the Great on one Side, and Mr Secretary Scribble, Mr Solo Neverout, & Laconic Comas Esqr on the other, with the event of that dreadful Battle.*

If we look over history, we shall find several persons distinguished by the Epithet of *the Great*, There are Cyrus the Great, Alexander the Great, Pompey the Great, Mahomet the Great, . . . and in this present wicked Generation Jonathan Wild the Great, as the Ingenious Mr Fielding very deservedly stiles him. . . . What real merit these Great men had, to Entitle them to this pompous Epithet, let the discerning world enquire and Judge, It is none of my business, being but a puny Club historian, to determin and pass Judgement in these weighty and momentous matters, for, whatever my decision be, the world will still think & Judge as they please; however, I shall be bold to say, that, after the Strictest Enquiry, into the lives and actions of these heroes, (as they are called,) I find, that far the greatest number of them, were neither better nor worse than professed butchers, who spread desolation & Slaughter over the face of the earth wherever they came. . . . It will not then I hope seem Strange, that an honorary member, and agent for the ancient & honorable Tuesday Club, should be distinguished with this high title, since we find, several persons in history as little deserving of it as he honored with the Epithet, the person I mean, is Coney Pimp Frontinbrass Esqr, . . . who had, during his late absence from the Club, upon what account I know not, unless it was for his having encountered Sir Hugh Maccarty Esqr, or, for his having Caped the august head of the honorable Lord Jole, got the title of *the Great* annexed to his name, and was now Commonly stiled *Coneïus Pimpeïus Frontinbrass the Great,* tho' some are of opinion, he had not this Sonorous title at the time of his return to Annapolis, but obtained it by the Signal victory he obtained at the Great Battle of Farce alia. . . .

Coneïus Pimpeïus Frontinbrass the Great then, for so he must now be called, upon his Arival from his Northeren Journey, . . . could not procure admission to the Club, which he took so much to heart, that it utterly deprived him of his rest, nor could he in any manner Compose his perturbed Spirits, till he had procured an Interview with his honor the president, which at last he obtained, tho he was obliged to try several methods before he could succeed. . . .

After having been refused admittance to the Club, he wrote a letter to his honor the President, and superscribed it in a pompous manner, giving him the title of *Right honorable Lord Jole.* . . . This letter he dispatched with his own Servant, who delivered it to his honor, . . . [who] by the Superscription, knew Immediatly, from what Quarter the letter had come, and, putting it again into the Messengers hands, ordered him to redeliver it to his master, and withal acquaint him, that he received no such foolish letters, . . . at which Frontinbrass was much Surprized and dissappointed; he however, dispatched the letter to his honor again, and with another Superscription, and in another hand, . . . his honor, Immediatly suspecting the Trick, hurled the letter after [the messenger] with such force, that it got the Start of the negroe in his flight, and fell down in the Street before him, . . . being resolved to palm this Letter upon his honor at any rate, [Frontinbrass] sent it a third time, and gave the messenger positive Instructions not to deliver it into his honors hands, but to watch an opportunity, when he was not there, and throw it over the hatch door, or in at the window, or even down the Chimney, . . . expecting, that when his honor found the letter, his Curiosity would prompt him to open and read it, and by the humbleness of it's Contents, he should again get into his honors favor and good graces, but he was herein much mistaken, . . . for his honor, as he was stepping up Stairs to bed, passed thro the Store Room, and by the light of the Candle, perceiving a letter to lye on the floor, he picked it up; and finding that it was much of the same Shape and Size with the Letter Frontinbrass had sent to him twice, . . . he put it bye unopened and went to bed; but did nothing but toss and tumble and fret the whole night long, being so ruffled with Indignation and wrath, that he could not shut his eyes to sleep; so that at the break of day, he arose, and hurrying on his Cloths as fast as he could, he went directly to the Lodging of Laconic Comas Esqr, who happened to lodge at the same house, where Frontinbrass had taken up his quarters, and, getting admittance to Mr Comas's Room, he stood at the beds foot, bolt upright, all Ghastly and pale with Indignation and want of his natural Rest, and looked exactly like Margarets Ghost, in the old Song,[1] vizt:

[1]Hamilton is recalling the opening stanza from the popular ballad "William and Margaret" (see Allan Ramsay's *Tea-table Miscellany* [1724–1732], I, 143–145).

'Twas at the Dark and dreary hour,
When all were fast asleep,
In Glided Margarets Grimly Ghost,
And stood at William's feet—

So, his honor Glided in, and looked Grimly and wistfully upon Laconic Comas Esqr, as he lay fast asleep, and thinking of no harm, but at last, calling him by name, Mr Comas opened his Eyes, and was very much startled to find such a figure, standing at his beds feet, . . . doubting at first whether it might not be his honor's Ghost—What do you want?—In Gods name! Cryd Mr Comas, starting upright on his bum in bed.—I have been most Scurvily used by that Rascal Frontinbrass, replied his honor—Hut! dam him! what's that to me?—I come not to blame you Mr Comas, I only desire alittle of your asistance in the affair—No by God!—not I—I wont meddle with your damnd Club nonsense,—Nay!—nay Good friend, I want you only to deliver into his hands this Rascally Letter,—Rascally Letter!—by God not I—damme if I have any thing to do with rascally letters betwixt you and him—no, no—damn him I say—Pray Mr Comas have patience, this is a letter of his own writing and Inditing, which he has the Impudence to direct to me, and force upon me in Spite of my Teeth, so, I would desire the favor of you, as a friend, since I would not see, nor speak with the good for nothing fellow, to give him his letter again, and tell him from me, not to Trowble himself any farther, for I am resolved, neither to receive any of his letters, nor see him again while I live . . . on this his honor delivered the letter to Laconic Comas Esqr, being all in a tremble with Indignation and vexation, Mr Comas Promised to deliver it to Frontinbrass, and so his honor took his Leave and Returned home.

Mr Comas, as soon as Frontinbrass made his appearance at breakfast, according to his promise deliverd him the letter, at which Frontinbrass seemed very much Surprized, wondering how he came by it, but Mr Comas soon removed his Surprize, by acquainting him with the whole matter, as Just now related.

This made Frontinbrass still more uneasy, and he could not resolve how next to proceed, but was not long without a device, for he was fully determined, before he left the place, to have an Interview with his honor, . . . and to effect this, he thought of Picking a quarrel with the Secretary, which was to be so Contrived, as to begin at his honors back gate . . . and [run] Into his honors back yard. . . . The world Judged differently of these machinations between Frontinbrass and the Secretary. Some thought, that it was a political Contrivance between them, to procure a forceable admittance as it were, to Frontinbrass, into his honor's presence, . . . others believed that the Secretary knew nothing of any such plot, but was attacked by Frontinbrass of a Sudden, . . . that he might thereby get admittance into his honor's presence, under Color of pursuing his foe, others again thought that both Frontinbrass and the Secretary, were really in earnest, and that no Sham on either Side was Intended, Such are the various opinions Concerning the motives of great politicians, the depth of whose designs is hid from vulgar Eyes—but however this be, I shall here give a particular account of this great battle, and describe every Circumstance of it, exactly as it happened.

It came to pass then, upon friday the 19th of June, 1752, about 4 o'clock in the afternoon, That this Great Clubical battle of farce alia was fought in the manner following.

Solo Neverout Esqr, Protomusicus, and the Secretary, were upon their way to visit his honor the president, and talk of some Important matters, relative to the Club; The Secretary was unarmed, as suspecting no harm, but Mr Protomusicus was provided in a Good Hiccory Stick, which was Calculated by the maker both to give and ward off good hard dry blows . . . ; Just as these two heroes arrived at his honor's back Gate, and were about to enter, they were allarmed with the Rattling noise of Chariot wheels, and looking down Northeast Street, they

perceived the Enimy advancing, full Speed, vizt: Coneïus
Pimpeïus Frontinbrass the Great, mounted on a lofty Chariot,
. . . drawn by two fiery Steeds who Champed the bit, foamed
at their mouths and smoaked at the nosetrills, upon one of which
rode a bold youth as postillion, with Leather Cap and buckskin
breeches; Coneïus Pimpeïus Frontinbrass the Great was thus
armed, he had on his head a huge broad brimd helmet of beaver,
not plumed, a round bob wig scarce covering his ears, in his
right hand a whip of an Enormous Size with a long lash, which
he smacked as he drove along. . . . At Sight of this formidable
heroe the Secretary and Mr Protomusicus were much abashed,
and, it is said, showed some Signs of fear in their Countenance,
but soon recovering themselves, they halted at his honors back
Gate, and drew up their Phalanx of Infantry in the best order,
resolved to stand the Charge of the Enimy, Frontinbrass the
Great upon his coming up, stooped his fiery Steeds, not chusing
to take a dishonorable advantage of the enemy by oversetting
their Infantry, with the force of his Cavalry, . . . and Calling
out with a loud and enraged voice *You Scribble!*—addressing
himself to the Secretary—stood bolt upright in his Chariot and
Clubbd his whip, The Secretary, being unarmed, did not stay
to make him any answer, but ran precipitately into his honor's
back alley and Immediatly betook himself to flight, to save his
bacon; on this, Frontinbrass Jumped from his chariot on the
Ground, and his pence rattled in his pocket.[a] The brave protomusicus upon seeing this, was resolved to oppose him with
all his might, but Frontinbrass being Strongly armed, made
him at last yield Ground and he retired thro' the alley in a Ret-
rograde motion, . . . while thus the fury of the battle, was passing by the Gavel End of his honors wooden Tenement, several

[a]Fieldings Joseph Andrews,—his halfpence, rattled in his pocket. [Ed.:
Hamilton is perhaps recalling the scene in *Joseph Andrews* (1742) where
Fielding mentions that Joseph has "sixpence" in his pocket, but while turning out his pockets to demonstrate his poverty to the innkeeper Tow-wouse,
he unwittingly reveals a "little piece of gold" (bk. 2, chap. 2).]

hard and desperate thumps and blows fell upon the boards, which shook the house to its very foundations, but did no further dammage, for, the Strong arm and Cudgel of Protomusicus, warded them off so effectually, that neither he nor the Secretary received any hurt, and many Indeed, thought that there was no hurt Intended on either Side, tho' that is at best but conjecture, for the Combatants fought Seemingly as if the Devil in hell had possessed them, . . . at last they came into the back yard, where was the fury and heat of the battle, and so earnestly were they engaged, and the Clamor and vociferation was so loud and terrible, that they did not perceive in the said back yard, his honor The President, Laconic Comas Esqr, Smoothum Sly Esqr, Drawlum Quaint Esqr, who were partaking a Bowl of punch and a pipe of Tobacco with his honor, . . . and, by them also, stood in waiting Don John Charlotto, his honor's Gentleman usher, I say, the furious Combatants did not perceive these Gentlemen in the back yard, but kept dealing their blows about, and warding them off, in such a furious manner, as to overset and turn upside down every thing in their way. His honor the President Looked pale as ashes, being struck with a sudden Terror, and exclaimed with a Loud voice,—Go, run!—go run!—fetch the Constable!—I say run!—go! go! run!—To which Don John Charlotto answered,—yes Sir!—yes Sir!—presently!—Laconic Comas Esqr was taken with a fit of trembling, and could not hold still one Joint of his body,—he attempted to speak, but passion and rage Choaked up the passages of his voice, Drawlum Quaint, and Smoothum Sly Esqrs, were in such a Situation, as that they seemed to laugh and Cry at one and the same time, the muscles of their faces being in such a violent act of Gelasticity, as that the tears gushed plentifully out at their eyes, The battle in the mean time turned more furious—Let me have a fair Stroke at him Cried Frontinbrass,—damme if you shall, replied the heroe Neverout,— knock him down!—knock him down!—dam ye!—why dont you knock him down!—exclaim'd Laconic Comas,—then the thumps and blows fell ten times thicker than before, and the air whistled again with the violent vibrations of the whip and Cudgel,—his honor retired to a Corner of the yard, and stood Collected within himself, a pallid hue overspreading his Lamentable Countenance, and a pannic fear damping his animal Spirits, and as the blows Lighted nigh him he ducked and dodged his head to one Side & to the other; . . . the hurly burly and noise was such, as that it was Inconceivable, and drew many Spectators, who viewed the furious conflict, with great amazement and astonishment; mingling voices were heard to rend the air—damn you!—down with him!—let me have but one fair blow—ad rat you!—Stand fair you Scoundrell!—I'll break every bone in his body by God!— . . . Zounds, knock him down!—down with him!—trip up his heels—while this mad work was going on, The brave Laconic Comas recovering from his Surprise and vehement passion, began to wave his Cane, and dealt some blows with such a heavy hand, as soon made Frontinbrass the Great perceive that he was in earnest, for, at two thwacks he made the dust fly out at the Skirts of his Coat, and aimed a blow at his head, which Glanced along the left Side of his wig, . . . upon which Drawlum Quaint and Smoothum Sly Interposed, and Slyboots Pleasant and the Chancellor, coming into the yard providentially in the nick of time, the Latter being armed with a good hiccory Wattle, marched their fresh troops between the adverse parties, and a parley was sounded, and an end at last put to this most furious battle. . . .

Thus Ended this Great Battle, and the Company planted themselves round the table, and, handing about the punch bowl, the adverse parties, at the Request of his honor the president shook hands, his honor then began to enquire into the cause of the Squabble, and several letters were produced by Coneïus Pimpeïus Frontinbrass the great, wrote in a very abusive Stile, which he said, he had received from the Secretary. These letters were perused by his honor and the Company, and the Secretary was much blamed for his Incivility, upon which, the

Secretary Grew warm, and some high words passed which threatned the Renewal of the battle, but, by the Interposition of his honor and Mr Smoothum Sly, matters did not grow to such a pitch.

〄〄

Chapter 8 🐌 *Maxims of the ancient and honorable Tuesday Club, & other trivial matters.*

Proximus ipse mihi, That is to say, the Shirt is nighest the Skin;[1] is a maxim, which Self love (that necessary law of nature) has Inspired, and has been used by politic men to the prejudice of Friendship and truth, the famous Machiavel, who has delivered to the public, certain useful political maxims, . . . seems to have founded his reasoning on this principle, when he says, among other Glaring political truths of the like nature, that a Certain quantum of deceit and Craft, is Commendable in Princes and great men, but despicable in people of low Rank. . . .[2] Whatever approbation, the politic and discerning world may bestow on the maxims of the aforesaid Celebrated author, I cannot think, that that approbation (neither do I believe Socrates would have thought so) takes its rise from their being altogether built upon Justice and truth; and therefore, since the Machiavelian Maxims have been much applauded, I am in hopes, that the maxims of the ancient and honorable Tuesday Club, will meet with their due portion of applause, since it is evident, they do not deviate more from truth, nature & equity than the maxims of that noted Politician.

At Sederunt 189, the honorable Nasifer Jole Esqr being H:S: the members were very Elegantly entertained according

---

[1] Literally, "I am closest to myself" (paraphrases Terence, *Andria* 4.1.12).
[2] See *The Prince*, chap. 18.

to custom, by his honor, and after Supper a Strange occurrence happened in Club, which occasioned great Surprize and Consternation, not only in the Longstanding members, but in his honor the president, . . . the occurrence was this.

Crinkum Crankum Esqr, and Capt: Dio Ramble Entered the room armed with two muskets, apparently in a hostile manner, having Carried before them, in an Elbow Chair, a little Swarthy fellow, with a great Black patch, or rather plaister over one eye, dressed *a la mode du France*, whom they deposited upon the floor, at the foot of the Club table, and, making a low bow to his honor the president, told him, that this odd personage was Sir Hugh Maccarty Esqr of New York, whom they had taken prisoner and had brought to his honor, . . . to this his honor made no reply, but put on a very angry look—The Supposed Sir Hugh Maccarty Esqr, without moving from his Chair, Immediatly began to address his honor in a Sort of doggrel French, as follows. *Monsieur Jole* (says he) *Je suis Sire, le Servitur tres humble, et tres obeisant, de votre Seigneurie, et, Je vien ici, promptement determine, de vous payer cette hommage et, obedience, que a votre haute range & Grandure est due . . . ,*[3] his honor gave him no answer at first, for he really did not understand his language, and the longstanding members appeared full of astonishment, nay, the Epouvantable Sir John, the Champion, was so amazed, that he had not power to lay his hand upon his Sword, but kept mumbling and tumbling his Chaw from one Corner of his mouth to the other, at last his honor taking a Serious and Earnest Survey of the poppet in the elbow Chair discovered that it was a female in the dress of a Cavalier and said "So mon Moll', are you after these tricks? prithee lay aside this foolish disguise and assume your proper dress, which is more adapted to your Sex,—go into the kitchen, the fittest place for such as you to be in, and probably I may

---

[3]"Mr. Jole, I am, Sir, your very humble servant, and very obedient to your Highness, and I promptly come here resolved to pay you this homage and obedience due to someone of your stature."

order you some Cold vittles and Small beer, as a reward for playing the fool." At these words, the pretended Sir Hugh Maccarty Esqr, flew precipitatly from his Elbow Chair together with his guards, and were not seen again that night, . . . his honor the president could never forgive Crinkum Crankum Esqr, for this trick, as he Called it, and stuck in his Skirts for it a long time after, obstinately refusing to Confirm him a Longstanding member of the Club, after his Election.

❀❀

On the following Sederunt, which was on the 19th of December, 1752, Slyboots Pleasant Esqr being H:S: the Secretary presented to the president and Club some maxims, Entituled the maxims of the Ancient and honorable Tuesday Club, which were twice read, and ordered to lie upon the table for further Consideration; But, tho' these maxims were never afterwards read, or Entered in the Club book, yet, as they Contain, as it were, a Compendium of the Constitution and Genius of the Club, I give a Copy of them here, vizt:

Maxims of the Ancient and Honorable Tuesday Club of Annapolis

Drawn up December 19th 1752

1. This being a humorous Club, to take offence at any piece of humor That passes between one Longstanding member and another, is reckoned unclubical.

2. Tho Politics be Excluded the Conversation of this Club, [vid: Gelastic Law] yet distant Jokes, puns, or Conundrums on wrong headed politicians are not debarrd (opinion of Jon: Grog Esqr)

3. The privileges of his honor the president, as entered in the Club Records, are uncontravertable, and beyond dispute, and, to mutilate them would endanger the Clubical Constitution.

4. The Chancellor and Great Seal, are terms, titles and Ensigns, without any Signification or meaning in this here Club, being, according to his honor's opinion, of no manner of use or Service.

5. Bawdy in Club Conversation is not debard, providing it be cleanly wrapt up.

✿✿

11. That his honor the President must not be thwarted or contradicted, in any Scheme or project whatsoever, proposed by him to the Club, or directed by the Club in any matters, his Station raising him above all arguefication, or reasoning, within the narrow Capacity or understanding, of the Longstanding members.

12. That his honor the president's powers are Conveyd to him by a Supernatural power, and his authority is *jure divino*, and that he has in himself, an absolute Indefeasible right, to rule and domineer as he pleases in the Club.

13. That nonresistance and Passive obedience are absolutely necessary, in the Longstanding members towards the President, for the preservation of our Clubical Constitution.

14. That the president has more Sense and Judgement than all the members taken together, and therefore, his council and advice alone, is to regulate the affairs of the Club.

✿✿

28. That the Terms *whig* and *Tory*, are expelled this Club, being only Synonomous terms, signifying the same thing, for, the aim of both these parties is one and the same, being to procure to themselves Influence and power, tho' by different means, which Influence and power, must end at last in the same thing, vizt: oppression.

29. That all Tragical Subjects and Incidents, are absolutely Contradictory & Inconsistent with, the Constitution of this here Club.

✿✿

35. That it is a very dangerous thing to Incurr the displeasure of an old woman, as it sets a whole neighbourhood by the ears.

36. That these wicked excrescencies of wit, Conundrums

and puns, are often the Causes of violent dissentions & discord in Society, because the wit of all men is not measured by the same Gage, and because a wit will rather use his friend Ill, than lose his Joke (The opinion of Lac: Comas Esqr)

37. It is not Convenient, or agreable to the Constitution of this here Club, to be of the same Sentiment or opinion, for two minutes together.

38. This Club is of opinion, and Invariably so, which is an exception to the above maxim, that a man may Grope out his way to heaven without any of the external Ceremonies, of what our priests call religion, and another man may go headlong to the devil, with the whole load of the said Trumpery on his back.

※※

42. That it is Ill Judged and unclubical, to put a finishing Stroke to any points or matters disputed in this here Club.

as wll this v. finishd book

These Clubical maxims, or rather articles, in the opinion of many, are as Consistent and harmonious among themselves, as the 39 Articles of the Church of England *By Law established*, and as nicely Calculated for swearing to, without the Least danger of perjury, in the moderen acceptation of the word, or for laying a firm foundation for eternal wrangles and disputes, In fine, they equal them in every respect, and excell them in one material point, vizt: in number, there being three more of them, and the number three is granted by many Subtile doctors to be a mystical and mysterious number.

Chapter 9 🐉 *Examination of Negroe Jeoffry, Memorial of the Grand Committee.*

Trick is discovered by trick, and deceit by deceit. All agree, that the best way to catch a rogue, is to set another rogue in pursuit of him; a Set of very Learned and honest Gentlemen, for whom

I have a profound esteem, vizt: the professors of the Law, who perorate at our moderen bars, seem to be Sensible of these above mentioned truths, therefore, in treating of any Rogueish affair, it is always Customary with them, to put Cross questions to the Evidences and Culprit, by which they Catch the knaves in their own traps, . . . They follow here the method of Socrates, tho' they differ from that Celebrated Philosopher in this material Circumstance, that the Socratic Questions, were always urged for the discovery of truth, which is not the Case with the Enquirys of many of our Gentlemen of the Gown, . . . an Instance of this Sort of dexterity of both kinds, we shall, in this very Chapter display, in the Examination of Negroe Jeoffry, Taken by the Longstanding members of the Ancient and honorable Tuesday Club.

[At Sederunt 194,] a Report was made in Club, by the Secretary that a Grand Committee had met at Sir John the Champion's house upon friday the 12th Instant, and had presented a memorial to the said Champion, . . . who assured the Grand Committee, that it should be put to a proper use, and, after this doubtful, and ambiguous Expression, sprinkled it all over with Claret wine, and said, that it would thence appear to his honor, that there had been some bloodshed at the drawing of it up. . . .

After making this Report, a Certain John Jeoffry, a tall Negroe man, of a very personable appearance, entered the Club Room, and declared, that he was a Special ambassador from the worshipful Sir John to the Club, and Producing a Letter, the Secretary read it as follows.

*To The honorable The Tuesday Club
now sitting at Squire Neverout's.*

Gentlemen,
    You have got your Ends, that is to set Mr President and myself at variance, which you have now done compleatly, for, we

have had the devil to do about, as 'tis called, your damn'd rebellious Libellous memorial.

I wish you merry, but pray, not at the Expence of Grate men's characters, I mean those that live in high Stations of life, as your most honorable president and also one of the nine worthies.

Tuesday evening   *Sir John.*

Vengeance is the word, & Slaughter must Ensue,
So take care of yourselves, for you know tis your due.

❋❋

After Reading the above Letter, some members moved, that, before an answer should be given thereto, the ambassador Jeoffry should be examined by the Club, and accordingly, the said ambassador was sworn on the Club book, in manner and form following.

John Jeoffry's Oath
You John Jeoffry do swear and protest, by this great book, and all it's contents, be they true or false, Just or unjust, right or wrong, Sense or nonsense, that all & every answer you shall give to the Interrogatories put to you, by the Longstanding members of this here ancient and honorable Club, shall be the truth, the whole truth, and nothing but the truth.

This Solemn way of swearing on a book, according to the Custom of a wise and politic people, being over, Jeoffry tossed off a huge Glass of Rum, and the Club proceeded to examin him as follows. ❋❋

In: Do you know the President of this here Club?
An: Yes Sir.
Int: When was he last at your house?
An: On Sunday last.

Int: At what time?

An: In the afternoon.

A Long St: memb: That there Question is very material, pray Sir ask it again.

Int: When was he last at your house & at what time?

An: On Sunday last, & in the afternoon.

Int: What door came he in at?

Ans: At the back door.

※※

Int: Had he a cane, Sword or pistol?

Ans: A cane Sir.

Int: Are you Sure he had no Sword or pistol?

Ans: I can't tell Sir, unless he had them in his pocket.

Int: Was it usual for him to carry a Sword in his pocket?

Ans: I dont know Sir.

※※

Int: Did he piss before he went in?

Ans: I did not observe Sir.

Int: What was his business?

Ans: I cannot tell Sir.

Int: What did he talk about?

Ans: I dont know.

Int: What said he when he came to the door?

Ans: He asked if Sir John was at home.

Int: Had Sir John & he any dispute?

Ans: None that I know of Sir.

※※

Int: Did Sir John & the president part in peace?

Ans: I believe they did Sir.

Int: You heard no high words between them?

Ans: No Sir, as I know of.

Int: Did he not talk with a Girl with a high nose?

Ans: I cant tell Sir.

Int: Nor with any of the black wenches?

Ans: I can't affirm Sir.

※※

Qu: Com: This is a devlish Sly fellow, there's no trapping of him.

Int: Did you see Don John Charlotto at the house?

Ans: No Sir.

Int: Did you hear the president swear any oaths?

Ans: Not I Sir.

Int: Did you see any hatchet faced man in his Company?

Ans: No Sir.

Int: Do you know what a hatchet face is?

Ans: Not I Sir, how should I? I'm no Scholar.

❀❀

From the purport and tenor of the above Examination, the Club Concluded that the valiant Sir John had not faithfully & punctually executed the commission given him by the Grand Committee of the 12th Instant. ❀❀

It was ordered, that the memorial of the grand Committee should be Entered in the Club book, which was done as follows, vizt:

Memorial of the ancient and honorable Tuesday Club, in Grand Committee Convened, at the house of the Worshipful Sir John. . . .

. . . *Whereas,* it has evidently appeared of late, that his honor the President, not having the regard of the Club before his eyes, but moved and seduced, by the Instigation of evil Councellors, has behaved to this here ancient and honorable Club, with great Coolness, Indifference, frigidity, lukewarmness and Contempt, . . . without declaring the reason why or wherefore, it is requested, that the worshipful and valiant Sir John, who, in this doleful affair, they, *The Grand Committee,* have appointed their moderator and mediator, do enquire of his honor the Cause of this Coolness, Lukewarmness, frigidity, indifference and Contempt. ❀❀

This *grand Committee* therefore, humbly request & Intreat, and moreover absolutely Impower, the worshipful and valiant Sir John, knight and Champion of this here anct: and honorable Club, to take his honor the president into his warlike hands, and to mollify malax, soften, Intreat and request him in a mild and gentle manner, to rectify these Gross abuses, and to remove from his honorable person, his evil councellors, and advisers whosoever they be, and deliver them up to Prim Timorous Esqr, Serjeant at arms, that they may be duely punished for their treasons, . . . and, that his honor would again Condescend, to govern his longstanding members, in meekness, gentleness, mercy and peace, and throw aside all austerity Severity and Irregularity in his Government; and, if the said worshipful Sir John, cannot persuade his honor by gentle and fair means, he is hereby authorised to proceed to force and arms, and, if his honor should not submit to either of these methods, the said Sir John, is requested and authorised, . . . to Summons another grand Committee at his own house, to consider of ways and means, how he, the said Sir John, as next heir apparent to the Chair, shall take the government of this here Club into his hands.

All which is humbly submitted to the Consideration of the right worshipful and valiant Sir John.

	Loquacious Scribble
[Great Seal]	præs: deput: Elect:
	Philo Dogmatico Cancellario
	Solo Neverout Protomusicus
	Jonathan Grog M:C: & P:L:
Signd p: order	Prim Timorous Serj: at arms
Crink: Crankum Clk: Com:	Ελιουτος πλιςαντος[1]
	Quirpum Comic
	Tunbelly Bowzer.

This memorial shows to what a pitch the Club was now come in their republican principles; and Indeed, as they had had

[1]This line is nonsense.

nothing but Rhapsodies concerning Liberty and property sounded in their ears for these 4 years past, and violent altercations and loud protests against Slavery and Arbitrary power, promulgated by that Cunning and haughty officer, the Chancellor, it was no wonder, that they had now become mere Enthusiasts on these points. ※※

BOOK XII

*From the Convention
of the Grand Committee,
to the Trial of Quirpum
Comic Esqr.*

Chapter 3 ✥ *The humdrum Sederunt.*

Wit and humor is like the ebbing and flowing of the Sea, sometimes it runs high in Conversation, and at other times subsides,
or sinks very Low, and as the Ebbing and flowing of the Sea,
and the brains of madmen are Governed by the moon, so I am
apt to think that wit, particularly Clubical wit, and the brains
of wits, particularly the brains of Clubical wits, are Intirely
governed by that Inconstant, nocturnal planet, Clubs being
nocturnal assemblies, and often of an Inconstant and variable
Nature. . . . This is further evidenced, by the disposition of
the ancient and honorable Tuesday Club, who at some Sederunts
were extremely Smart and witty, and at others, extremely
Phlegmatic and dull, this was probably owing, to the particular
times of the moon, in which that Club held their Sederunts,
and, I'll venture to lay an equal wager, with any person that will
take me up, that, if they Consult old almanacks, as they read
this History, they will find what I say to be true, and that the
moon was arrived, at either her first or third quarter, or in her
quadratures, at Sederunt 200, on the 17th of April 1753.

At this Sederunt it was, Philo Dogmaticus Esqr being H:S:
and Slyboots Pleasant Esqr, deputy President, that the time
passed away, without so much as one Clubical matter being handled or discoursed upon, so that we cannot help observing here,

that this Sederunt, was of all Sederunts the most unclubical, since the first Institution of this here ancient and honorable Club, which some Critics perhaps, in after times, will attribute to the absence of that most Ingenious and bright wit Jonathan Grog Esqr, Poet Laureat of this here Club, and on this account, I cannot help stiling this Sederunt *The Humdrum Sederunt*.

In fine, this Sederunt would have proved altogether flat and Insipid, had not the Secretary, who spared no pains to furbish up and enliven the Club at these times, produced, Just before their breaking up, a Copy of a Newgate Song, sung by Squeak Grumbleton Esqr, a Stranger, Invited to the Club at Sederunt 194, which is as follows.

Newgate Bird Song, sung by Squeak Grumbleton Esqr[1]

As I derrik'd along, to dorse on my kin,
Young Polly the froeful I trouted,
She nailed a Cull of his tilter and Nob,
But in foiling his tatler was routed.
As I haiked along she Grappled my Shell,
She tipt me young boeman, I knew her full well,
The harman spikd after, but dam' him to hell,
I plumpt him, and savd her from Limbo.

❈❈

Whilst snug in the kin, we sat, sluicing our Gobs,
She tipd me the Gum very Cleanly,
I swear it will never be out of my Nob,
The Brimston, she wheedled so beenly.
Round Scrag, her dear duddles, she loving did fold,
I tipt her the velvet, her daylights she rolld,
I love you, said she, for your quiddish and bold
And will dorse with my Jamie till Jamin.

❈❈

[1]This song is titled "A Cant Song" in John Sadler, *The Muses Delight* (Liverpool, 1754), 178. Noting every slang term in this poem would destroy the fun—and the intended bewilderment—that comes with reading it.

This odd Song seemed to excite alittle Spirit of Gelasticism in the members, tho' they understood nothing at all of the Language or dialect in which it was wrote, but the Secretary produced it alittle too late, vizt: at eleven o'Clock at night, when all the Longstanding members were in a yawning disposition.

※※

Chapter 6 ※ Misbehaviour of the Chancellor, The Chancellor's trial.

Zoilus the Critic, who wrote against Plato & Homer, and who, perhaps, (more *criticorum*) thought himself the wisest man of that age in which he lived, was remarkable for nothing so much, as the extraordinary length of his Beard, and so Curious was he, of this Signature of wisdom, . . . that he kept his head always Close Shaved, that none of that nutritive Juice might go to supply the hairs of his Cranium, which he chose rather should be bestowed upon the Inferior part of his face, in order to add to the voluminousness of that *Sapientific brush,* which was a Sign hung out, by that vain glorious Critic, to show all passengers, what a rare Stock of wit was in the Inner Chambers, as the bush at a Taveren door, shows what fine liquors are kept, by the Jolly landlord within.

But, whatever might be the opinion of the ancients, with regard to the beard's being the Symbol, or Signature of wisdom, we find that beards have been in such disrepute with the moderens for some Centuries past, that they kept gradually Lessening, till they arrived in the days of our K: Charles I. to only a pair of small whiskers, a diminutive peak on the Chin, shaped according to the humor and fancy of the wearer, till at last they were quite disused, and now every moderen, who would appear in the least degree like a gentleman, shaves as close as the back of my hand, and nothing is reckoned a greater mark of Slovenliness, Stupidity and Clownishness, than an overgrown, dirty, Squalid beard.

It appears from thence, that the moderens have no notion of the beard being a type of wisdom, and therefore reject the use of it altogether, but, as we cannot esteem these moderens such Sots and Idiots (however far, in other matters they may be besotted or sunk Into idiotism) as to pay no regard at all to wisdom, . . . we must therefore, to set matters right, find out what Signature the moderens use, to Symbolize or represent wisdom; I must own, I have Employed my thoughts for some time upon this Important Subject, and after Intense thinking and Indefatigable Scrutiny, can find no type or Symbol among the moderens, so apt and Significant for this purpose as a large *full bottomed wig*, as this is a Signature, often used, by our wise Judges, and wiser Senators. . . .

In consequence of this theory, the Longstanding members of the ancient and honorable Tuesday Club, who in every respect were moderens, and ruled themselves by moderen modes, tho' members of an ancient Club, Thought it adviseable, to adorn the head of their new Created attorney General [Solo Neverout Esqr] with a full bottom'd wig, as most expressive and Significant of the wisdom and Sagacity of that Learned and Ingenious Gentleman, who, as they thought had little of the Substance within his Cranium, and therefore stood more in need of a large quantity of the Symbol or Shadow without, and that Sapientific wig, they Chose should be made of tow, to signify the fleeting, light and Combustable nature of human wisdom, in General, and of this Gentleman's in particular. We shall therefore, have occasion more than once, in the Sequel of this history, to see this gentleman Introduced upon the Clubical Stage, ornamented with this voluminous flaxen head attire.

At Sederunt 206 July the 10th 1753, Jonathan Grog Esqr . . . being H:S: Philo Dogmaticus Esqr, the Chancellor, pleading a law of the Club, as usual, mounted the Chair, and affirmed, with a Confident face, that he would mantain his place, till he saw, a Superior authority to make him leave it, the Club seemed some what Surprized at this Rodomontade, tho' it was not the first time, that this Gentleman had behaved himself in this Imperious manner; but, the Secretary producing a letter, wrote upon a Scurvy piece of paper, directed to himself, and without either proper address or Subscription, as is usual in letters from well bred persons, appointing the worshipful Sir John, deputy for the night, the Chancellor Immediatly left the Chair, and the worshipful Sir John taking that Eminent Seat of honor, the proceedings of last meeting were read as usual.

※※

The Chancellor objected to this letter, that it was Wrote in a rude unmannerly Stile, without either Civil address, or mannerly Conclusion, and moved that it should be burnt by the hands of the hangman, but, on the Objection's being made, that there was no such officer in the Club, he offered, rather than it should not be done, to perform the office himself.

※※

At Sederunt 208, august 7th, 1753, Mr Secretary Scribble being H:S: Mr Attorney General Neverout appeared in Club, in his proper dress of office, having a large broad hat, or *Chapeau pointu*, as the French Call it, a full bottomed wig, curiously wrought of tow, a band, and a black gown, and makeing a profound bow to the chair, he deposited his great hat, and delivered some papers to the Secretary, then with a grave Solemn face, telling his honor, that he had matters of the utmost Importance, to lay before him and the Club, vizt: criminal matters, charged against the Chancellor of this here Club. . . .

Then he Rectified his wig and band, and took a pinch of Snuff, The Chancellor, alittle flustered, told him, that he was not Surprized to see him behave so much like a pert fellow and a buffoon—but that he did not care a whistle for him,—Tho he talked till his guts came out. To which the attorney General Re-

plied with great gravity and Stayedness of Countenance—
Sir—I assure you Sir,—upon my word and honor Sir,—I shall
talk a great while before my guts come out.—Then the Secretary Read the Indictment. ⁂

Indictment

Tuesday Club Ss:

You Philo Dogmaticus, stand Indicted, by the name of Philo
Dogmaticus Esqr, Late Chancellor of the ancient and honorable
Tuesday Club, . . . for that you, as a false traitor, against the
most Illustrious and Serene President Carlo, due reverence to
the said President in your heart not having, nor weighing your
duty towards his august Chair, but, being moved and seduced,
by your own wicked Instigation, . . . and endeavoring and Intending, with all your might, the peace and Common tranquillity, of this here ancient and honorable Club to disturb, and
the Laws of the same Established to overthrow, to pull down
and bring into contempt, the said Serene President Carlo, and
his Chair, and, the said honorable Chair, wickedly, devilishly
and maliciously to usurp, you, the said Philo-Dogmaticus Esqr,
upon the third day of July, in the eight year of the dominion,
of the said Serene President Carlo, in a Street Called Charles
Street, in the City of Annapolis, in the hall of Jonathan Grog
Esqr, . . . with force and arms, of malice aforethought, then
and there, wickedly, an assault did make, upon the person and
Chair, of our said Serene President Carlo, . . . and with a loud
Stentorian voice, pronounced the following execrable, detestable, abominable, horrible, dreadful, malicious and rebellious
words, vizt: *That a Certain letter, wrote by our said Serene pres-*
ident to our Secretary, was a Scandalous Scrowl, unmannerly, rude,
Impertinent, opprobrious and Clownish, or such like abusive
words, and, that *the said Letter ought to be burnt by the hands of*
the Common hangman, against your alegiance, due to our said
Serene President Carlo, and setting a bad and pernicious ex-

ample, to all your fellow longstanding members, to be Guilty of the same, against the peace of our said Serene President Carlo, his Chair and Dignity.

❋❋

[Then] the attorney General rose up, and made the following Speech to the Chair.

"May it please your honor,

The case which I am now to open before your honor and this here ancient and honorable Club, is a Case—a case may it please your honor—I say Sir,—a Case of plots and plottings, full of high Crimes and Misdemeanors,—of high Crimes, may it please your honor, Charged against no less a person, than the venerable Chancellor of this here ancient and honorable Club,—I say Sir the venerable Chancellor of this here ancient and honorable Club, and keeper, may it please your honor, of the great Seal of the said Club, and also keeper, may it please your honor, of your honor's political Conscience.

It is with the utmost reluctance, honorable Sir, that I take in hand, this here prosecution—I say Sir, this here prosecution, and I Sincerely wish it had fallen into other hands, for this here Chancellor, may it please your honor, is a person,—I say Sir a person, for whom I must have some degree of respect, as being by his office,—I say Sir his office, nighly related to your honor's honorable Chair, but, in Cases of this Sort, may it please your honor, all respect of persons must be set aside,—I say Sir, all respect of persons must be set aside, and the office I bear in this here Club—I say Sir, the office I bear in this here club, as your honor's attorney General, lays me under a Strict obligation to take Cognizance of all trespasses, plots, misdemeanors and Crimes without favor or affection, to any person or persons, be their quality or degree what it will in this here Club,—I say Sir, be their quality or degree what it will in this here Club.

❋❋

I must own, may it please your honor, that it grieves me—I say Sir, it grieves me, to think, that our Chancellor, a person, who, on account of his eminent degree,—I say Sir, his eminent degree in this here Club, ought to have behaved himself in a manner more agreeable, to his Supposed wisdom and dignified Station,—I say Sir, his Supposed wisdom and dignified Station— I grieve much, may it please your honor, I say, to think that this here Chancellor,—I say Sir this here Chancellor, should have so deviated from his duty, especially against your honor—I say Sir against your honor, a person Remarkable for mildness and Clemency, whose government of this here Club, is so gentle and easy, that the most turbulent Spirits, cannot otherwise but be quiet under it, so, that may it please your honor, it may be said of your honor, as a Certain old author said of a Certain good man, *oinom Duonorum pleorumei virom illom optimom esse consentiont,*[1] or, as the Celebrated Gil Blas says, in his Greek annotations, *Tois, nois*—hoh!—hoh!—[here an Interruption]

Jon: Grog: He, he, hi, hi, hi, hih.

Attor: Gen: *Nois, Presidentois,*—chi, chi, chuck!

Quirp: Com: Ha, ha, he, hi, hi.

Att: Gen: *Is te Cox-Comboy*—pugh—Pho—

Jon: Grog: Comeboy! aha, aha, ahi, ahi. The attorney Calls the horses, aha, aha, ha, hi.

Att: Gen: *Kay Clodepateon, nidjotton, hoi fooleroi asinos-s-s-soi,* hoh,—hoh. [here the attorney seemed to hesitate much]

Sir Jno: Hoh, hoh, hoi, hoh, ho, hoi, hoh, ho, hoi, lancets! lancets!—hoh,—I must be Immediatly blooded, hoh,—else I shall die—hoh, hoh,—the laughing at this Stuff—hoh—has given me a damn'd Stich in my Side—hoh, hoh—o.

Omnes: Aha, aha, aha, ahe, he, hoh.—

---

[1] "Of the good men, a great many agree that he was the best man." The "Certain old author" could refer to almost anyone, since the passage Hamilton provides is a variant of the frequently quoted inscription in early Latin on the tomb of the Scipios.

Att: Gen: And therefore, I conclude, as that Ingenious author does,—*Cheateron ton Biteon, Smoke o' the Gullum.*[2]

Quir: Com: Ay, ay, right Sir, right, there you have hit the nail o' the head.

Attor: Gen: And therefore, may it please your honor, whatever the Station or degree of that there Chancellor may be, in this here Club, yet, his Station and degree will not protect him from the penalties Inflicted by our Clubical laws, in such Cases, for which I shall quote several Learned authors.

Jodocus Colloverius says, *libro Quarto, Capite nescio quo, omnes plotatores Capitaliter Condempnare debent,* and, Joannes Treverius Gwellengerius *libro primo, de Institutionibus diabolicis,* roundly affirms *Quod plotator, est omnium aliorium animalium turpissimus, maliciosissimus, horrendissimus,* and a Gentleman Called Ovid, says of a Sirnia, or dissembler, *Sirnia Quam similis, turpissima bestia nobis. . . .*[3] But I shall endeavor, to make the facts evident and clear, against this here Chancellor, and, for that purpose, I shall proceed to examine my evidences."

The Chancellor, here desired the Attorney General to proceed no farther, since, notwithstanding all his evidence, it was evident, he was not the person accused, the words in the Indictment, being *late Chancellor,* whereas he was now actually Chancellor of the Club.

[2]This pseudo-Greek appears neither in Alain René Le Sage's romance, *Gil Blas of Santillane* (1715–1735), nor in Edward Moore's comedy, *Gil Blas* (1751); rather, it appears in Beaumont and Fletcher's *Wit at Several Weapons* (1647), act 1, sc. 1.

[3]Collover and Gwellenger are fictitious. The passages read: "All plotters should be capitally condemned [from] book 4, I know not what chapter"; "A plotter is the dirtiest, most malicious, most horrendous of all other animals [from] book 1, on diabolical institutions." The passage from Ovid as it occurs in Ennius reads: "How like us is the ape [or dissembler], the basest of beasts."

The attorney upon this acquiesced, and owned that the Indictment was quashed, by this very objection.

※※

Chapter 9 ※ *The Champions departure from the Club, Trial of Quirpum Comic Esqr.*

※※

[At Sederunt 216,] the Club tried again to exercise their poetical Genius . . . upon the lamentable occasion of the honorable the president's Indisposition, and absence from the Club, . . . but the muses would not answer their Call, the Longstanding members, being Remarkably dull and low Spirited, which some looked upon, to be an ominous presage, of the *Great Sir John, the Champions leaving the Club.*

※※

This being the last time, that the Great Sir John appeared in Club, we cannot take our leave of this heroe, without bestowing a few words on him. It cannot be Certainly ascertained, wherefore he left the Club, or Indeed, whether he had reasons or no reasons for doing so, tho' some Imagined, . . . that he found his Interest with the President so much lessened, since the affair of the Grand Committee, and was so picqued, at the Influence and power of the Attorney General, that he could not brook, or bear the thoughts of being under that haughty officer, as he had always looked upon himself to be the Second man in the Club, and the Right hand prop of the Chair, . . . by the Great part the Champion has had in this History, it would seem that the Club would suffer much by his departure, but it happened otherwise, his honor the President did not seem to take it at all to heart, and, the Chancellor's leaving the Club soon after, restored such peace and tranquillity in the Clubical Constitution, that there was no occasion for a Champion, and Indeed the honorable the President, expressly declared several times, *ex Cathedra*, that for the future, he himself should be Champion for the Club. . . .

At Sederunt 217, Mr Secretary Scribble being H:S: and Crinkum Crankum Esqr, Deputatus Electus, the attorney General Rising up, Called upon Quirpum Comic Esqr to answer unto a Trespass on the Case, in as much, as he, the said Quirpum Comic Esqr, had offered the Presidential Chair, with all it's appurtenances to public Sale, wherupon Quirpum Comic Esqr, rising up, denied the said Charge.

❈❈

Then Dr Nolens Volens,[1] a Stranger Invited to the Club, was Examined.

Att: Gen: Doctor Nolens Volens, declare to his honor the deputy and this here Club, what you know of this here affair.

Dr N: V: Who?—I Sir—

Q: Com: Pray Sir, in what Ship did you come to this here country?

Dep: Pres: You have no right to ask that Question Sir.

Q: Com: Pray upon what terms did you come here Sir?

Dep: Pres: Psha! let us hear what he has to say. The gentleman seems confounded, ask him the Question again Mr Attorney.

Att: Gen: Dr Nolens Volens, Sir I call upon you to declare what you know of this here affair Sir.

Dr N: V: It was offered to Sale in divers parcells, The footstool, Canopy and Seat were exposed separately, but the Seat would not sell, because some body said it smelt of a fox.

Dep: Pres: How! of a fox Sir?

Att: Gen: Pray Sir, give his honor and the Club a particular account of it, according to the Best of your knowledge.

❈❈

---

[1] This Latin pseudonym is roughly equivalent to *willy-nilly*.

Dr N: V: The person buying this Chair Sir, was to hire it out to the Club for the future when they wanted it, and the whole might have been sold, had it not been for that same perfume as I said.

Q: Com: If that be proved, I shall Surely be hanged.

Att: Gen: How then Sir. Pray proceed.

Q: Com: Take care what you say, you are a young man Sir, consider the oath you have taken.

Dr N: V: Sir, tho' I be a young man, yet we all know that *Philosophum non barba facit.*[2]

Q: Com: Sir, I dont understand greek or Hebrew.

D: Pres: Greek and hebrew! eh, eh, eh, Greek and hebrew! eh, eh, eh.

Q: Com: Pray Sir, did you take notice of the Seat and foot-stool?—I may ask the evidence some questions may I not Sir?

Chanc: Yea Sir, but you have no right to ask that there Question—what do you say to those matters that the evidence has already delivered, have you any thing to plead in your own defence, before Sentence is passed upon you?

Q: Com: Sir,—I say—that he says that I said it,—and I say—that he said it—I know not what else to say faith—not I.

Att: Gen: I find we have got a Cunning fellow to deal with,— we do nothing here but prevaricate & quibble.—ho! Silence there—why, you Pitiful delinquent, I have Good evidence of your saying so, your very Identical Self.

Q: Com: Whose evidence, pray Mr Attorney?

Att: Gen: Why you Incorrigible Brute, your own Brother told me so.

※※

Chan: What say you to that Culprit?

Q: Com: Gentlemen, you wont permit me to ask the evidence any questions—avast there I say,—no dragoon Law.

Chanc: Yea Sir—but Club law—Club law.

---

[2]An old commonplace, meaning "The beard does not make the philosopher."

Dr N: Vol: Is that what is called *argumentum Baculare?*[3]

Secr: As this trial, Gentlemen, seems not in a way to be soon determined, I would move That as this Gentleman is to leave the Club soon, he may, from a Longstanding, be transmogrified into an honorary member, as others before him have been.

Q: Com: Sir, I humbly second that motion.

Jon: Grog: Why Mr Secretary, you would not have us to dock the Gentleman, I suppose the member, however he may stand now at this Juncture, is as long as ever.

Dep: Pres: Ha, ha, ha, the longstanding members methinks are waggish.

Mr Electro Vitrifrice [a Stranger Invited to the Club] Longstanding members, I think Gentlemen, with Submission, are not so properly waggish, because if they stand they cannot wag.

Chanc: Yea, but with your leave Sir,—I say these members must stand before they can wag.

Thus did this learned trial proceed, and was not determined any how, the delinquent privately slipping or wagging out of the Club room, for fear of some Severe Sentence being passed against him.

❖❖

[3]"Argument of the rod."

BOOK XIII

*From the Trial of
Quirpum Comic Esqr,
to the Chancellor's
Farewell to the Club.*

Chapter 3 🦎 *Altercation of the President and Chancellor.*

Discretion and Goodness in Rulers, and obedience in Those that are ruled, are the two principal Ingredients In the happiness of a State, Community or Club; without these there can be no tranquillity or peace, nor can there be any harmony or order in their proceedings. What made Scipio, the Roman General, so Successful a Conqueror, was his own discretion and wisdom in directing, and the readiness of his Soldiery in obeying his orders, which made him say, at a review of his troops, that there was not one man among them all, but would, should he Command him to do it, throw himself from a precipice into the Sea; The Great Inconvenience of Stubborness that Consul knew, when, meeting with an obstinate fellow, he sold him and all his effects, declaring that he had no use for that Citizen that would not be obedient.

Whether the want of obedience, in most of the Long Standing members of the ancient and honorable Tuesday Club, particularly in the Chancellor, towards his honor the president, . . . was owing to any Indiscretion or misconduct, in the said honorable President, I shall not be so bold as to declare, . . . but this I may with Confidence affirm, that not one of the Longstanding members of the ancient and honorable Tuesday Club, would have, at his honor's command, Jumped from a precipice into the Sea, nay, not even from a Table upon the floor, and, as for the Chancellor, his honor thought him so obstinate, and so refractory a member, that, had it been in his power, he would have done with him as Scipio did with the ungovernable Citizen, That is, sold him, and all his Clubical Effects, vizt: his bag and great Seal, both of which, he now from his heart, hated and dispised.

※※

[At Sederunt 220,] a most violent dispute, arose between his honor the president, and the Chancellor, the occasion of which was this. Crinkum Crankum Esqr, again urging his confirmation, and moving that his petition might be again read and maturely considered, by his honor and the Club, his honor told him, that . . . it signified nothing, his giving himself any further trowble about the matter, for, that by that means, he should still be farther from his desired end. This answer affected the Gentleman much, and he sat down with a very Sorowful Countenance, but, getting up again, he used an argument with his honor, which he thought would prevail, . . . knowing his enthusiastical fondness for old England and every thing pertaining to that happy Country; he begg'd his honor, to favor him at least for Country's Sake, that he was his Countryman, and, the only old Englishman now In the Club, besides his honor, and his honor's attorney General. . . . To this his honor made reply, that he set no value upon that, and that he always Judged of a man by his behaviour, and not by his Country. This was an excellent Sentiment & came from his honor unawares, he not being given to think so Philosophicall or Justly, when old England was Introduced into the Conversation, which evinces that even resentment at times, may make a man utter Philosophical truths. . . .

The Club, after this kept Silence for some time, and the Chancellor swell'd and puff'd with Inward rage, scarce being able to contain himself, and had frequent recourse to his Snuff box, dawbing the breasts of his Coat all over with that Sophisticated powder, so that it might be said in a literal Sense, that the Chancellor took Snuff at this, at last, a member moved, that the law passed at Sederunt 114 might be read, and alledged that that law gave Crinkum Crankum Esqr, as full and ample privileges, as any longstanding member of the Club, . . . which being done, the President declared *ex Cathedra*, with the Haughtiness and peremptoriness of a pope, That this was an unwarranted Insolent proceeding, altogether Illegal and rebellious, and that if that law stood, he'd never set foot in Club again, upon this the dispute between his honor & the Chancellor began, which was Carried on by dialogue as follows.

Chanc: And who Cares a fart, whether you do or not, we should be much better without such a Tyrant, what! must the Club be kept under by such humors and whims? has not the Club a power of making laws for their own regulation?

Pres: No, they have not, so long as they have made me their governor and Ruler.

Chan: That's a damn'd lye, they did not give up all their rights and privileges, when they made you their President, they only committed a trust into your hands, which trust, they never Intended should be used to Inslave them.

Pres: Prithee moderate your voice, you quite deafen me.

Chan: I will speak to be heard, and must be heard, this Tyranny is most unsufferable, and the Club will never be so Simple as to bear with it.

Pres: For God's Sake, if you speak to be heard, speak to be understood, speak English, & then I'll understand you.

Chan: Speak english! what do you mean Sir? dont I speak English?

Pres: You may speak English words for aught I know, but I would desire you Sir to mend your pronounciation, for you utter your words so broad, that I cannot understand you.

Chanc: That's a damn'd piece of foppery, Sir, I can speak as good english as you can.

Pres: Nay, for that, I appeal to the Club, the Secretary is your Country-man, yet, tho' his dialect be broad, he speaks more properly than you, and I can understand him better [here the Secretary bowed low to the President]

Chanc: Sir, I'd have you to know, I can speak better English than you.

Pres: You may speak more grammatically than I perhaps, because the Study of Grammar has been your business, but to say you speak English with a better accent than I, who am an Englishman born, and you a Scots man is absurd.

Chanc: Of all the old fellows I ever met with you have the most abusive tongue, and there is no bearing with your Scurrility, I wish you'd learn to mend your manners.

Pres: I am not to come to Learn of you, you have no Right to advise me.

Chan: I'll let you know Sir, I have a right to advise you in this here Club.

Pres: As how pray?

Chan: By my office of Chancellor.

Pres: Your office of Chancellor! what right does that give you to advise me? I dispise your office and every thing belonging to it.

Chan: Sir, I'd have you to know, that that office, gives me an authority over you.

Pres: As how?—what! must I be hectored over in this manner, and none take any notice [looks about him] as how?—I say.

Chanc: As keeper of your Conscience Sir.

Pres: You keeper of my Conscience, pray who made you keeper of my Conscience?

Chanc: The Club.

Pres: The Club!—The Club make you keeper of my Conscience?

L: St: memb: Ha, ha, ha, ha.

Pres: No Sir, I'll have it under no such Sorry keeping.

Chan: 'Tis lucky for you that it is under such keeping, the Conscience of a fool is apt to go astray unless under good Custody.

Pres: Can any one bear this usage?

Chan: If your Conscience be tender, it must be alittle roughly handled to harden it.

Pres: Prithee let my Conscience alone, I cannot see what business you have with my Conscience.

Chan: More than you Imagine, I tell you again I am keeper of your Conscience.

Pres: Who the Devil made you my Conscience keeper?

L: St: memb: Ha, ha, ha, ha.

Chan: Who but the Club.

Pres: The Club make you my Conscience keeper!

L: St: memb: Ha, ha, ha, ha.

Chanc: Yea Sir, I am the Club's officer.

Pres: You are the Devils officer, I think, which does not become your Cloth.

Chanc: Augh! (yawns) there's no ending with you, you have an eternal tongue, and will have the last word, [here the president looked about him, and none in the Club taking notice, he abrubtly left the Chair and the Club broke up Confusedly]

꽃꽃

Chapter 4 ❧ *Celebration of the Ninth Anniversary, Anniversary Speech.*

Democritus the Philosopher has been much wondered at, and much blamed for his Laughing humor, by persons of a particular Solemn and Grave turn and, for this Reason, has had the

Character of a Coxcomb and Impertinent Buffoon; But if one Seriously Considers the humors of this Transitory world, in which we live, he will wonder, how any person can be so Stupid as to forbear laughing at almost every occurrence that happens around us, would it not provoke one to Laughter to observe, on what the Generality of men place their esteem, . . . to see the Incommensurable flow of idle Compliments, that are Current among people of fashion and grimace, . . . To see how dowble tongued flattery, with the Slipperiness of a Snake, creeps into favor and Esteem with the Great, till it Empoisons and Corrodes their Substance, . . . To see human wit and Cunning, eagerly employed in finding out the Arcana of Nature, with deep and curious Scrutiny, and at last discovering neither more nor less, than that a Straw is a Straw, and an atom an Atom; I say, who can see or observe this medley of absurdity without Laughing Immoderatly, either with Democritus, or any other Gelastic Philosopher; and who can blame the members of the ancient and honorable Tuesday Club, for Laughing at all the world, as well as at themselves, and furnishing a fund of Laughter to all those who have a turn for the Gelastic humor, . . . and, in fine, who can blame them, for Laughing Immoderately, at the Clubical altercations between the honorable the President and the venerable The Chancellor.

At Sederunt 222, was Celebrated the Ninth Anniversary of the ancient and Honorable Tuesday Club. . . .

After supper, the Secretary as orator of the Club stood up in his place, and delivered an anniversary Speech as follows.

Anniversary Speech, delivered by the Orator.

❋❋

Our Anniversary, honorable Sir, which has hitherto been an occasion of Rejoicing and mirth, a day of Singing, fiddling, dancing, Jesting, drinking, eating and laughing, a day of pomp, Show and magnificence, grandure and triumph, . . . is

now, (I am sorry to say it, and particularly on this occasion
when such complaints may seem Improperly urged) likely to
become a humdrum, dull, moaping day of dejection, a Spirit-
less, tasteless and tedious pastime to the longstanding members, who, cannot but perceive a great .decline and falling
away, of the wonted Glory and magnificence of this here Club,
evident and apparent by the late long adjournments it has
undergone, the very last Club preceeding this present Anniversary, having been held on the 26th of march last, and not
one single Sederunt Intervening, O Lamentable! that for the
Space of almost three months, the honor, Glory and dignity of
this our ancient and honorable Club, should be buried and Enveloped, in darkness and oblivion, whilst no body can tell for
what.

Did I say, honorable Sir, no body can tell for what, I grant
it, perhaps more out of Complaisance to your honor, and this
here ancient and honorable Club, than for any truth the assertion contains in it Self, because I would shun giving offence,
especially to great men and State officers, but Surely a man must
be very short Sighted, if he cannot at least conjecture for what,
permit me then to trespas alittle on your time and patience,
while I offer my conjectures.

May I not then be allowed to conjecture, for I dare not proceed to positive assertions, that Luxury has in a great measure
got footing in this here ancient and honorable Club, Luxury,
in the opinion of all wise men has been the bane and ruin of
States and nations, and therefore must at last be the ruin of
Clubs, where it has been admitted, are there not longstanding
members here present who have seen, the primitive times of this
here ancient and honorable Club, did they not in alittle time see
an end to that virtuous and heroic frugality, that prevailed in it,
at its first Institution, have they not seen Luxury, peeping from
behind the Scene, and preparing for her pompuous entry upon
this Clubical Stage, have they not seen this bold actress, take
one Great Stride at her first advance, and proceed afterwards,
with a *grand pas*, to expell Simplicity and plainness from the
Club, and Introduce pomp, Show, and extravagance, her Con-

stant pages and attendants, while another, her Companion and Coactor, with the like buskined pride, playd the part of a Momus or mimic, this was no less a person than Ceremony, as much a beau, as the other is a belle, whom you have seen also, showing his pragmatical front, on the most conspicuous part of the Scene, and Introducing Certain fantastical punctillios, forms and modes, by which, he has so disguised and Intoxicated the behaviour and manners, of the L:St: membrs: of this here anct: & honle: Club . . . that they now seem not to be the same persons that they were at their first Institution.

Happy, thrice happy, in those heroic times of Innocence & Simplicity, were the Longstanding members of this here anct: & honble: Club, for then, without molestation, could they sit with their legs accross, loll, upon a table or elbow Chair, smoke their pipes, . . . drink toasts, either loyal or amorous, Crack Jokes, frame *Puns* or *Conundrums,* and, should their Stomachs call for a whet, without Ceremony or trowble to themselves or fellow members, they might rise up, go to the Side board, & after having taken their Sliver of Gammon or Slice of Cheese standing, Return again to their Compotation, Jocosity or Clubical Conversation, how Charming, how regular, and how like the Simple frugality of the Golden age was this, and how different from the present Luxury, and profuseness that prevails in most Clubs.

And now, honorable Sir, and Gentlemen, I think, having discussed this point of Luxury, I have dispatched the burden of the Song, but, permit me, before I conclude this long Speech, to make a few more Conjectures, concerning the causes of the decline of this here Club.

May we not reasonably conjecture, that Certain bickerings and contentions of late, sprung up among us in a great measure contributed to eclipse the Glory of this here Club, so, that to use nigh the words of a late Celebrated poet, it has been with us, as with the Oliverian Saints.

Here Civil dudgeon has grown high,
And *we* fell out, *we* knew not why

While hard words, Jealousies & fears
Set *us* together by the ears.[1]

And how have we been set by the ears, may we not reasonably
Conjecture, by the ambition and pride of our Great men, striving for power and Influence; Lamentable was that day, in which
so many State officers were appointed in this here Club, woeful
was the accursed time, when a great Seal and bag were thrown
in among us as a bone of Contention, dreadful was the period,
when titles of honor and badges of State, were bestowed upon
some restless and aspiring Spirits who knew how to abuse them,
but not well how to use them.

※※

In fine, honorable Sir, and Gentlemen, I have presumed to lay
[these] matters before you, that you may have a Clear view of
the present deplorable State of this here ancient and honorable
Club, and the ruin that threatens it, if proper means are not used
to prevent it, therefore, you will Remain without excuse if you
do not use these means, which are, to reinstate the Club in its
ancient Simple constitution with regard to expences, to secure
to his honor the president his Just prerogative, to curb and restrain the growing power of your State officers, . . . to revise
and correct the body of Laws, to hold Committees for wholesome advice, and to put down that pestilent Custom of long adjournments lately crept in among us by enacting Severe penal
laws against those who presume to hold Sham Clubs or Illegal
Committees. If these expedients are not Speedily taken, this
here Club will soon be at an End, and, this, probably, may be
the last anniversary we shall see, whereas, if proper care be
taken, before it is too late, we may yet see many a Joyful Return
of this day of Rejoicing, may often with pleasure, behold our
noble president, exalted in his Chair, smiling upon his
Club. . . . Then may we often hear the poet Laureat repeating
his elegant odes, the chief musician warbling his dulcisonorous
notes, Signior Lardini drawing Charming Sounds from Cat

[1]Hamilton has personalized (by using the italicized words) the opening lines
from Samuel Butler's *Hudibras*.

guts with nimble fingers & Skillful bow, and your poor orator perorating his anniversary Speeches while nothing but peace, harmony, mirth and Jollity prevails among us, which, ought to be the wish of every longstanding member, of this here Club, as much as it is of

Your humble Servant
The Orator.

The orator having finished this oration, neither the president nor the Club seemed pleased with it, notwithstanding the fine flourish at the Close, which shows how little men care to be told of their faults, The orator was in none of the best of humors at the delivering of this oration, and was resolved, since he found he could not advance himself by flattery, and dissimulation, which he had tried for a great while, to speak the naked Truth for the future.

Chapter 5 🜺 *The Chancellors farewell oration.*

At the aforesaid Anniversary . . . Mr Chancellor Dogmaticus Rose from his Seat and arming his Nose with a pair of Spectacles, delivered to his honor and the Club, the following harangue.

"Honorable, worshipful & worthy Gentlemen,

The occasion of my present address to you, is truely mournful to me,—Tho', I hope, will prove no loss to you,—I am— alas!—how can I utter it,—I am now to take my leave of a Society, that I honor, esteem and love; in which I have Enjoyed much pleasure; a Society that has not only admitted me to a participation of their ordinary Joys, but even their highest honors;

let me Gratefully Commemorate each of these—I have been an associate in your ordinary pleasures—but why do I say ordinary, the smallest of them are extraordinary, if compared with what any other Society could ever produce,—It is this Club alone, that has Improved the Gelastic faculty which distinguishes men from brutes, to the most extensive and useful purposes, using it, not only as a natural expression of Inward pleasure, but to communicate pleasure to others, by the admiration and Imitation, of it's extravagance, and, which is more wonderful, made it a useful Instrument of punishment. . . . *This unparallelled Club, has found the Secret of Inlarging their pleasure by making Sense and Nonsense, equally the objects of it, so suiting all Capacities, between the wise and the foolish, the Learned and the Ignorant.* Can the pleasures of such a Club be with any propriety Called ordinary?

※※

Liberty and property, you know, have always been my darling objects, and, if in defence of them, and perhaps mistaking the meaning and design of our honorable and worthy president, the life and Soul of the Club, I have sometimes given him offence, I yet acted honestly, as things appeared to me, and now beg your honor to take my behaviour in this light. . . . Now Gentlemen, as equity, the Constitution and privileges of the whole & every member of this Club, in their different Stations, were my peculiar Care and trust, so, that relation I have so long bore to this honorable Society, obliges me, while it does subsist, & as my Last good office in it, to offer my friendly parting advice.

First, that your honor will be content with such power as is Consistent with, and Sufficient to enable you to promote, the peace, honor and happiness of *this here Club*, . . . that you will always acknowledge the fountain of your power, and be satisfied to owe it to those who alone could bestow it, and can take it away, firmly persuaded, that it is more honorable, and can yield more rational delight to rule & do good to a free people, than to exercise dominion, over Cringing Sycophants, and Submissive

Slaves, in fine, that you will be always Governed by that Glorious maxim, *Salus populi, Suprema lex.*[1]

And You worthy Gentlemen, my dear Compatriots of the Club, let me leave it upon you, that you be always persuaded of the duty and necessity of supporting your President, In those powers and privileges that you have Conferred upon him, for the General Good, and, always pay him, that honor and regard, that the toils of his beneficent Service Justly Claim, as the least reward due to him—absolute power, Gentlemen, is, no doubt, the best Instrument of Government, provided it be always in the hands of a very good man, and perhaps, you could not trust it more safely than with your present *Archon,* but, as you cannot promise yourselves such a one always, . . . I rather recommend to you, the General and Salutary Aphorism, of being always watchful and Jealous of your liberties, giving away no more power than is absolutely necessary and Checking Incroachments. . . . But, at the same time, remember human frailty, and never Contend obstinately about triffles, where the remedy may prove worse than the disease.

I am now come to the bitterest part of my present task, to say—Farewell—and resign my office of Chancellor of this Club, in which I was Invested, by delivering me this Seal, which I redeliver in the same manner as I received it, into the hands of our trusty Secretary, from whom I received it by the vote of the Club, . . . as I never used it, but by his honor's directions and Commands, so, it has never suffered any hurt in my Custody, but that once by a fatal convulsion, it fell into the fire, and singed the bag alittle, may it never have such a mishap again, nor the Club such a dismal Omen of it's final Catastrophe.

❉❊

To Conclude, there remains to me, I hope, the pleasure of another relation to this Noble Club, that of being one of its honorary members, which, tho' I could Claim, from the Consti-

[1] "The safety of the people is the highest law" (Cicero, *De legibus* 3.3.8).

tution and use, yet I'd rather owe it to your free and Chearful Suffrages, . . . in favor of one, who will always think himself bound in Duty of Gratitude, to wish well to, and promote the happiness of the *Ancient and honorable Tuesday Club—Long live Illustrious Jole.*"

※※

Thus finished this 9th Anniversary of the Ancient and honorable Tuesday Club, with less mirth and Jollity than usual, the bad humor of the Secretary, and the departure of the Chancellor, putting the Club in a humdrum humor.

※※

Chapter 6 ⚝ *The Chancellors poem on the Club, Mr Protomusicus's answer to it.*

Homer by many, was Called by way of eminence *The Poet,* and, I think the Stagyrite was the first that gave him that name,[1] and the appellation is highly distinguishing and honorable, signifying in the greek Language, *The maker;* Homer, the master poet, and those mighty Geniuses among the ancients, that were Cast in a simular mold to his, were esteemed *makers* or *Creators,* producing from their inexhaustible fancies, new Images or Creations, both Instructive and Entertaining. . . . In a like manner our poets now a days may be Called *makers,* as being *Makers of Rhimes,* and verses, and masters of a particular kind of fiction, which the ancients seem to be utterly unacquainted with, as not having nature for it's groundwork, but something else of a *Je ne sçai quoi,* which cannot be described, . . . the main Ingredient in the genius of an ancient poet, being a knowledge

[1]See Aristotle, *Poetics* 1.11.

in nature, and an ability to Copy after that perfect pattern, we
need not be Surprized that they attain'd so easily to the heights
of poetry, but now a days it is not so easy a matter to become a
poet, several things being absolutely necessary to be understood
to accomplish a moderen bard, the principal Rule is that which
you will find in the very beginning of Horaces art of poetry,
which is what belongs to that peculiar Sort of Grotesque painting used by our latter poets,[2] The next that comes in view, is
the Ingenious art of *Crambo*,[3] which is altogether Inseparable
from the Composition of a moderen poet. . . . There is also a
large magazine of poetical Ideas, to be stored up in the brain of
a moderen poet, such as quaint puns, dowble Entendres, trite
Similies and allusions, . . . and a vast number of Sentiments,
Concerning Groves, Grottos, . . . Suns, Constellations, &ct:
&ct:&ct: all Compared and assimulated to Certain things to
which they have not, never had, or ever will have any likeness
or analogy, This is a short Summary of the Qualities absolutely
necessary to frame a moderen poet, of a Genius adequate to that
of Jonathan Grog Esqr, and the other moderen poets or Bards
of the ancient and honorable Tuesday Club, of whose Incomparable Genius, we have already given several Specimens, in
this history, and shall have occasion to exhibit more before we
have done.

※※

At Sederunt 225th, Crinkum Crankum Esqr being H:S: and
Jonathan Grog Esqr, Deputy in the Chair, a poem was presented In Club, left with the Secretary by the late Chancellor,
. . . who said, at the time of his presenting it to the Secretary,
that he left this poem, as a peace offering to his honor and the
Club, to stand as a Salvo for his late Speech, that had given so

---

[2]In the opening of *Ars poetica* (1–13) Horace warns that yoking together
various kinds of verse is like coupling a human head with a horse's neck.
[3]In the game of *Crambo* one player composes a line of verse for which the
next player must provide a rhyme.

much offence, and added also, that he never once in his life time
had thought of being either a poet or an orator, till the Tuesday
Club had made him both, The Poem follows.

Carmen Sociale,

*In praise of the Ancient and honorable Tuesday Club in
Annapolis, wrote in the year 1751, by one of it's admirers.*

Sicilides Musæ, paulo majora Canamus. Virgil[4]

Invocation	Once more Thalia,[5] Tuneful maid,
	Let me Invoke thy needful aid,
	A nobler Theme ne'er tun'd the Lyre,
	Worthy the poet's brightest fire,
	The Grecian bard, or Mantuan Swain,
	Might hence Immortal honors gain,
	For not Achilles' frantic rage,
	Nor Ithaca's more Crafty Sage,
	Nor Bully Ajax' Stamps and frowns,
	Nor Thread bare tales of Ships and towns,
	. . . .
	Can such an ample field afford,
	A field with such description stord.
Proposition	I sing the *Club*, whose ancient name
	Stands high upon the Rolls of fame,
	"The Tuesday Club, Annap'lis Glory,
	While human things shall live in Story."

❀❀

Description	Full to the Sight, & next the Bowl
1st The President	Exalted shines Illustrious Jole,
	. . . .
	"With air mysterious, see him nod,
	In Imitation of the God
	Whose thunder keeps the world in awe

[4] "O Sicilian (pastoral) Muses, let's sing somewhat greater things" (Vergil, *Eclogues* 4.1).
[5] Muse of comedy and pastoral poetry.

And gives a Sanction to his Law,"
Not greater on his lofty throne,
Or more Superb sits Prester-John,[6]
Like him our Chief, vain and elate
With Satrapæ that on him wait,
Scarce deigns one Sidelong glance to throw,
On those that suppliant round him bow.

. . . .

2d The knight   In Sullen pride, upon his right,
   Champion   Sir John, Yclep'd the Champion knight,
Tremend'ous sits, with penthouse brows,
To whom none equal he allows,
Prepar'd his title to mantain,
Alike by dint of Sword or brain.

3d the Chancellor   His left, a priest, with look demure,
In Character of Chancellour,
"Guards—Ready with his Skill profound
All knotty Questions to expound,
Or puzzle what needs no Comment,
Litigious Disputes to foment,"
But stop my muse for reasons known,
'Twere better Let the Church alone.

4th the Secretary   Slow and majestic see arise
The Scribe—on him their eager eyes,
The whole Divan direct, while he,
In Clubic Stile, the Noble Three,
My Lord, the Chancellor and knight,
Harangues, and proves, that black's not white,
Explores the philosophic truth,
While lab'ring with eternal drouth,

5th the Poet   The Poet Laureat, honest Soul,
   Laureat   In Raptures views the Sparkling bowl,
Dear object of his fondest wish,
His darling Joy, and greatest bliss.

❀❀

[6]Legendary Christian priest and king who reigned both in Asia and Africa
in the 12th century.

6th The musician	"Next hear how Proto musicus With Croaking voice obstreporous, And front of Brass Claims Orpheus' praise, Just so Pan with Apollo vies, Yet to his merit no small praise is due, As every Ravishd hearer, must allow."
7th & 8 Two private members	Spyplot could the pow'r of verse But half thy oddities reherse, How much like Socrates thy face, The self same Lineaments they Trace, But ah, how near allied in mind Baffles the muses art to find,

. . . .

"Thy oddities however can divert
And much Gelastic Pleasure do Impart."
    Dear Slyboots Sure for friendship form'd,
No anxious thought yet e're alarm'd,
Thy peaceful breast, let others wear
Out life in dul Chimeric Care,

. . . .

Whilst thou at ease experience,
The Charms of Sacred Indolence,
"And others please with humors Sweet & free,
Averse to Jars, and friend to mirth & Glee."

Conclusion	Thus far the muse has plac'd in view, The happy Corps. Still would pursue The Pleasing theme, did not the task A Butler or a Fielding ask. *In magnis voluisse sat est, Valete.*[7]

The apostrophed lines in the preceding poem, are those,
which the Chancellor affirmed, were purely his own in the composition, as for the others, he had help in forming them, after
the reading of this poem The Secretary produced another, wrote
In answer to both the Chancellor's performances, to wit the

[7]"In great affairs, it is enough to have tried. Farewell" (Propertius 2.10.6).

Speech and the poem, by Mr Proto musicus Neverout, . . .
a Copy of which follows.

Poem

By the attorney General, against the late Chancellor.

Infernal muses, Guide the pen,
To sing the Crabbedest of men,
Who lets his Devlish Genius loose,
Men in high Stations to abuse,
. . . .

This Chancellor so Diabolic,
Whose Rhimes would give a man the Colic,
Whose Speeches at a single look,
Would make a man both ———— & puke,
With Billingsgate they so abound,
Each Gentle hearer they Confound,
Raise Indignation in each Soul,
Whilst they traduce Illustrious Jole,
Illustrious Jole! our pride & glory,
Unmatch'd in old, or moderen Story,
Whom none can equal or excell
In Spite of pride or th'devil in Hell.
    See him rising from his Chair
With look malicious, Grim, Severe,
His nose he pulls with handkerchef,
With Snuff well loaded, Snotty, Stiff,
. . . .

He Coughs, then spits, the bowl he takes,
Then to the Chair a Stiff bow makes,
And with unequal'd Impudence
Palms on us Sophistry for Sense,
Dwells on the liberty of Clubs,
Giving his honor Scurvy rubs,
He wipes the Sham tears from his Eyes,
Pretending kindly to advise,

And feigning Grief and deep contrition,
Would stirr up Strife and dire Sedition.

❀❀

Infernal muses next reherse
His talent Shreud at dogrell verse,
When vainly he Invokes the muse,
The Club & Pres'dent to abuse,
. . . .

Next on Sir John he vents his Jeers,
Sir John, the prime of Cavaliers,
. . . .

The orator and poet too
He sets for laughing Stocks in view,
The first, he says, like fool holds forth
From Sense as wide as South from north,
The Poet Guzzles punch and Grog,
And 'Musicus Croaks like a frog,
Of Spyplot makes a *Je ne sçay quoi*
And Slyboots Calls an Idle boy.

❀❀

The Chanc'lor thus, in Jingling measure
To teize the muses takes a pleasure,
By Introducing Jarring Sounds,
He all their harmony Confounds
. . . .

For of Sweet poesie's he's no master,
Nay, is not even a poetaster,
His dogrell works, or I'm a Rogue ho,
Are like a new born *Caco fogo*[a]
Which, tho it bears a human Shape,

---

[a]Caco fogo, a monstrous birth, said to be as Common among the east India women as Soutrekins are among the Dutch, being a figure in a human Shape apparently but scarce animated, that dies almost as soon as born—making a noise like an explosion of air. [Ed.: A *cacafuego* is a spitfire or braggart (from the Latin *cacare*, meaning "to void, as excrement," and the Spanish *fuego*, meaning "fire"). Hamilton's facetious note enhances the derogatory nature of the word.]

Has not the Judgement of an ape,
For soon as it has op'd its Eyes,
It eats, speaks, Grumbles, farts and dies,
And sooner than a man would Think,
The lump expires in Noise and Stink.
   So 'tis with all such Dogrell Scrub,
As touch our president and Club,
And so 'twill be in after times
With this vain Chanc'lor & his rhimes,
For these shall neither hear nor see,
Either his doggrel Rhimes or he.

Thus was this great officer, the Chancellor, who had been so Signally Serviceable to the Club, in Contending for its liberties and privileges, against the arbitrary proceedings and tyranny of the Chair, treated with burlesque poems and Satyrs, at the same time with his leaving of it, an Instance of the great depravity and degenerate State of the Club, at this time, and a Shoking example of the Corruption and Ingratitude of the times, when true Patriotism and worth, become the Subjects of Satyr and ridicule.

BOOK XIV

Chapter 3 ❧ *Speech of the orator.*

❋❋

[At Sederunt 235 Janry 21, 1755,] the Secretary Informed his honor, that he had prepared a Speech or oration, which he beg'd leave to deliver to his honor and the Club, In quality of their orator, which having been Granted him, he read a Set Speech from a written paper, using Spectacles, at the beginning of it, the writing being very small, on which his honor observed, that he did not at all become Spectacles, making at all times, but a very ordinary figure without, and a much worse with them. . . .

Speech of the Orator

Honorable Sir,

Tho your honor and these here Longstanding members, may be long ago Thorro'ly tired, with hearing of my Speeches, yet, I can never be tired of delivering them. The first probably arises from your love of your own Ease, the latter, I am Sure springs from my own vanity; I am thorrowly persuaded that it is always good to speak well, and in Season, tho' sometimes it may be quite safe to say nothing at all, little said indeed, is soon mended, but a flow of words may display follys, which we are not aware of, yet, a Settled Silence proceeds as often from moroseness and Stupidity, as from wisdom and prudence, which made a certain Philosopher observe, wisely enough, who did not think a man's face the true Index of his mind, upon seeing a promising fair countenance in a silent man, that he should desire to *hear* that person speak, that he might *see* him.—I therefore, remembering the maxim of this Philosopher, (who ever he was) propose now to speak to your honor, and these here L:St: members, that you may *see me*, and, tho' I make no question, that you know me Sufficiently, long agoe, from what I have already said in this here Club, yet, I must beg once more to Indulge my vanity at the expence of your Repose.

I think it proper, as the new year is now making it's entry, to welcom it with a Speech (which I dont remember I ever did in this here Club before) and, I shall be very cautious how I offend your honors ears, or those of your L:St: members, by using any Improper Stile (tho' quite Clubical,) such as, frequent repititions of *this here* and *that there*, of late so Justly condemned, by your honor's accurate and Ornate Judgement, and that of your honor's Learned Attorney General, I shall rather endeavor to make it Succinct and Concise, in the mercantile Stile, which is now Looked upon, by the best Judges, to be the most ornate manner of declaiming, as well as writing.

Have ransaked my brain, once and again, to find proper Subject to entertain, your honor and L:St: members, on this occasion of General mirth and Jollity, this frolicksom time when Gaiety and good humor abound, and all mankind thro the large Scene of Christendom seem Clubically inclined, but cannot find Invention capable of striking out any thing in itself, so novel and uncommon, as to be fit to amuse & entertain, your honor and Club—had like to have said *this here Club.*

Have the honor to be now, the only Remaining old Standing Member of this Club, and therefore, hope your honour, out of regard to Seniority will overlook, many Clubical Imperfections, which may appear in my Stile, phraze, Diction and demeanor, while pronouncing this Saturnalian oration, not because I think any more than your honor, that Seniority gives a man a privilege to play the fool or be Silly, but, in so far, as it

cannot otherwise be, than, that Have a more profound respect
for your honor, and this Club, than to cook up a dish of blunders
and absurdities, on purpose to entertain them, on the aforesaid
Saturnalian occasion, or Indeed on any occasion. . . .

Shall not presume, honorable Sir, to molest or Irritate your
auditory organs, with any Set Subject or dull method, that Sort
of declamation, being too much Confined, shakled and fettered,
and Improper for the freedom and vivacity of the Season, neither shall take upon me, to be licentious or blunt, . . . Briefly,
I shall neither be too lax nor too restricted, in my manner, but
following the footsteps of your honor's attorney General (who,
I now perceive is fast asleep) address your honor and this ancient
Club, in the easie, Genteel elegant, and purblind manner of that
extraordinary Genius, not discerning or minding my Subject,
till it comes within half an inch of my nose—but, as Subjects
are now very much dried, shrivelled and shrunk up, by too
much handling & tumbling, I shall leave them, to such as carry
about with them, the Lubricating unguents of Parnassus, that
they, by Gentle friction & embrocation, may bring them to
their proper plumpness and lubricity, . . . and knowing well,
upon what Side my bread is butter'd, shall meddle only with
such topics, as will sit as easy upon me as an old Shoe, and therefore shall not trowble you, with quotations from authors, but
pass off all for my own. . . .

Now, honorable Sir, (as they say) this is a merry time, and
set apart for Laughter, let every one expand his Jaws and dilate
the muscles of his face, to such a degree, as becometh the Hi-
larity of the occasion, for, as we are often told, in the margins
of old almanacks, that is, as often as there is room for Inserting
it, *Post est occasio Calva,* and ὁ χρονος ου χρονιζει,[1] we ought
to seize occasion by the forelock, and be always merrily dis-
pos'd, so often as we may, for, as the Philosophers wisely tell
us, if we let occasion slip to day, we may not find her to morrow,
and a bird in the hand is better than two in the bush. . . .

But, as some finical fellows distinguish mirth into two Sorts,

[1]Latin commonplace meaning "Opportunity hath a bald spot behind";
Greek commonplace meaning "Time does not tarry."

vizt: high mirth and low mirth, you, perhaps may expect, shall enter into a disquisition, upon this nice bipartition, but, have no mind to entertain you, with any such Idle Subject, . . . Some pragmatical fellows, Ind[eed] ma[y] say, and I believe have said, that the wit of the Club is Low, b[ut] leaving these formal Critics to stiffen in their own Starch, so as to become Incapable of bending either to humanity or good nature, without splitting their Rump box or *Os Sacrum*,[2] as anatomists term it, shall set our wit in opposition to theirs, and leave the world to Judge, but, as for our mirth, let it be purely natural, without constraint or affectation, and it will never fail to please and satisfy ourselves as well as others, in the exercise of this mirth, our risible faculties, ought to be Employed, upon proper Subjects, both within doors and without, that is, among ourselves, towards one another, and towards the whole body of mankind. By proper Subjects, mean Subjects fit to be Laughed at, which are so Infinite, that there is no end to Laughing, as often as a man has a mind to it, . . . but, as every one does not know how to laugh with propriety, that is to say, how to laugh, without giving offence, or being the Cause of Scandal, be pleased to observe this General Rule, let your Laughing or Gelastication, be accompanied with good humor, a pleasant open, and Candid Countenance quite strpt of Satyr, Sarcasm or Sneer, and a Cynical air of Superiority, for, by Laughing in this manner, we shall be always safe, and always in a pleasant vein, the other methods of Laughing, to say, the Cynical and Sarcastical methods, are sometimes, nay, many times, followed with weeping and wailing, and, if we do not at least, draw the laugh upon ourselves, by Laughing Sarcastically, we may perchance do *worser*, that is, pull an old house about our ears.

Question not, but all the L:St: mem[be]rs of this Club, who now hear me discourse upon this [si]gnificant Subject, know very well how to laugh, both in time and tune, and the antiquity of our Club is a plain Demonstration, that this noble art of Gelastication has been very well understood in it, and also very well timed, else, their Constitution would never have remained

[2]Literally, "holy bone," the lowest bone of the spine.

Intire so many years, nay may say, so many Centuries, but would before now have been shook to pieces, as has been the Case with many other Clubs, . . . let us then preserve that true taste of mirth, which we have hithertoo preserved, and we need neither fear envy, nor the Rage of time, we shall flourish while other Clubs fall, we shall be admired and Commended by the wise, and, probably misunderstood by the foolish, but whatever fools, or (whom I esteem no better) pretended wise men, may say, or think of us, let it not divert us from the direct and up-right course of Laughing with propriety, . . . Say it again, for tis worth remembering, that to laugh with propriety is of more Significancy and Importance, than many people think, and, some men of moderate parts and Capacity, have acquired the Character of Consummate Philosophers, from their under-standing only this single art, and have been admitted into the lofty presence of Emperors, kings, Popes, . . . archbishops, Cardinals, Bishops, and even Club Presidents, upon no other merit or recommendation.

But Least should Tire your patience with long winded dis-courses after the manner, of a Certain gentleman, learned in Clubical Law, whom I have now in my Eye (tho Indeed his eyes are shut upon me, and every one else, here present) I shall Con-clude all with drinking up this Bumper of Good liquor,

Wishing this ancient Club may always be,
Promoters of facetious mirth and Glee,
And, that our members all may be expert,
At the Great punning and Conundrum art,
And that our Laureat's muse may ever warble
Our fame to Last as Grav'd on Brass or Marble,
And while Gay Laughter furbishes each Soul,
Let each a bumper drink, to *Noble Jole.*

Appendix

Pseudonyms of Tuesday Club Members and Associates

This list provides brief identifications of the characters mentioned in this edition. For further information on these figures and others associated with the Tuesday Club, see Alexander Hamilton, *The History of the Ancient and Honorable Tuesday Club*, ed. Robert Micklus (Chapel Hill, N.C., 1990), "Biographical Sketches," I, lxxix–cv.

Bavius, Bard. Thomas Chase (1703–1779). Rector of St. Paul's, Baltimore County. Baltimore Bard.

Blunt, Bully (Sir John Oldcastle). John Bullen (d. 1764). Mayor of Annapolis, commissioner of the Paper Currency Office, and captain of the City Independent Company. Oldstanding Member and Club Champion.

Bowzer, Tunbelly. Richard Dorsey (1714–1760). Brother of Edward Dorsey (v. Drawlum Quaint); clerk of the Paper Currency Office. Longstanding Member.

Butman, Comico. William Fitzhugh (1722–1798). Colonel, planter, and close friend of George Washington. Honorary Member.

Carpentiro, Giovanni. John Carpenter (d. 1748). Ship captain and prosperous trader.

Charlotto, Don John. John Charlette. Servant to Charles Cole (v. Nasifer Jole). Clerk of the Kitchen.

Comas (Comus), Laconic. John Lomas (d. 1757). Merchant. Oldstanding Member and Orator.

Comic, Quirpum. John Beale Bordley (1726/1727–1804). Studied law under his half-brother, Stephen Bordley (v. Huffman Snap); judge, planter, and agronomist; elected to American Philosophical Society. Longstanding Member and Master of Ceremonies, then Honorary Member.

Coppernose, Comely. Anthony Bacon. Brother of Thomas Bacon (v. Signior Lardini); tobacco trader and eventually one of England's wealthiest tycoons. Honorary Member and Agent for the Club in London.

Crankum, Crinkum. William Lux (of Annapolis). Merchant. Longstanding Member.

Dogmaticus, Philo. Alexander Malcolm (d. 1763). Rector of St. Anne's, Annapolis, and St. Paul's, Queen Anne's County; mathematician, grammarian, and musician. Longstanding Member and Chancellor, then Honorary Member.

Fibber, Humbug. Samuel Chew (ca. 1734–1786). Stepson of Daniel Dulany; planter.

Fluter, Joshua. James Hollyday (1722–1786). Lawyer. Honorary Member.

Frontinbrass, Coney Pimp. Thomas Cumming (d. 1774). Quaker merchant. Honorary Member and Agent for the Club in America.

Grog, Jonathan. Jonas Green (1712–1767). Public printer of Maryland, poet, and publisher of the *Maryland Gazette*. Longstanding Member, P.P.P.P.P. (Purveyor, Punster, Punchmaker General, Printer, and Poet), then P.L.M.C. (Poet Laureate and Master of Ceremonies).

Grumbleton, Squeak. John Wollaston (f. 1736–1767). Painter of more than three hundred portraits from New York to Virginia.

Gundiguts, Dumpling. Mark Gibson. Liquor merchant.
Longstanding Member.

Hasty, Joggle. George Atkinson. Merchant. Honorary
Member.

Jole, Nasifer. Charles Cole (d. 1757). Merchant.
Longstanding Member and President.

Lardini, Signior. Thomas Bacon (1700–1768). Brother of
Anthony Bacon (v. Comely Coppernose); rector of St.
Peter's, Talbot County; accomplished musician and one of
colonial Maryland's most prolific authors. Honorary
Member and member of Eastern Shore Triumvirate.

Maccarty, Sir Hugh. ?

Makefun, Merry. Robert Morris (d. 1750). Merchant;
father of Robert Morris, the financier and statesman.
Honorary Member and member of Eastern Shore
Triumvirate.

Mevius, Bard. Thomas Cradock (1718–1770). Rector of St.
Thomas's, Baltimore; author of numerous sermons and
poems. Honorary Member and Baltimore Bard.

Motely, Prattle. Witham Marshe (d. 1765). Secretary to the
Maryland Commissioners at the treaty in 1744 with the
Six Indian Nations and later secretary for Indian affairs.
Oldstanding Member, Secretary, then Honorary Member.

Muddy, Roundhead. Andrew Lendrum (d. 1769). Rector of
St. Anne's, Annapolis, and of St. George's, Baltimore
County. Longstanding Member, then Honorary Member.

Neverout, Solo (Protomusicus). William Thornton (d.
1769). Brother of Thomas Thornton (v. Nolens Volens);
merchant and sheriff of Anne Arundel County.
Longstanding Member, Chief Musician, and Attorney
General.

Phraze, Courtly. Edward Lloyd (1711–1770). Colonel,
planter, and merchant. Honorary Member.

Pickeringtonus, Gasperus. Stephen Pickering (d. by 1765).
Merchant.

Pleasant, Slyboots. Walter Dulany (d. 1773). Son of Daniel Dulany and brother of Dennis Dulany (v. Dio Ramble); merchant, naval officer, and commissary general. Longstanding Member.

Polyhistor. Dr. John Hamilton (1697–1768). Brother of Alexander Hamilton; physician. Honorary Member.

Quaint, Drawlum. Edward Dorsey (1718–1760). Brother of Richard Dorsey (v. Tunbelly Bowzer); lawyer. Longstanding Member and Speaker.

Ramble, Dio. Dennis Dulany (1730–1779). Son of Daniel Dulany and brother of Walter Dulany (v. Slyboots Pleasant); naval officer. Honorary Member.

Round, Broadface. John Hamilton (d. 1773). Rector of St. Mary Anne's, Cecil County. Honorary Member and member of Eastern Shore Triumvirate.

Sly, Smoothum. John Gordon (1717–1790). Rector of St. Michael's, Talbot County. Oldstanding Member, Master of Ceremonies, then Honorary Member and member of Eastern Shore Triumvirate.

Smirker, Theophilus. James Dickinson (ca. 1726–1790). Merchant. Honorary Member and member of Eastern Shore Triumvirate.

Snap, Huffman. Stephen Bordley (ca. 1710–1764). Lawyer, naval officer, attorney general, and commissary general. Longstanding Member.

Social, Serious. Robert Gordon (ca. 1676–1753). Merchant, judge of the Provincial Court, and commissioner of the Loan Office. Oldstanding Member.

Spruce, Seemly. William Rogers (1699–1749). Chief clerk and register of the Prerogative Court. Oldstanding Member.

Spyplot, Jealous, Jr. William Cumming, Jr. (1724–1793). Planter and attorney. Longstanding Member, then Honorary Member.

Spyplot, Jealous, Sr. William Cumming, Sr. (ca. 1696–

1752). Jacobite rebel; sold as a servant; studied law while a servant and became a practicing lawyer. Oldstanding Member and Attorney General.

Surly, Huffbluff. Robert North (d. by 1751). Honorary Member.

Timorous, Prim. Thomas Jennings (d. 1759). Judge, chief clerk of the Land Office. Longstanding Member and Sergeant at Arms.

Vitrifrice, Electro. Benjamin Franklin. The *Maryland Gazette* for Jan. 17, 1754, states that Franklin had "arrived in Town, to regulate and settle the Affairs of the Post Offices."

Volens, Nolens. Thomas Thornton (d. 1791). Brother of William Thornton (v. Solo Neverout); curate to Thomas Bacon (v. Signior Lardini) at St. Peter's, Talbot County.

Composition

Four separate stages of composition went into the making of *The History of the Ancient and Honorable Tuesday Club*. As the club's secretary, Hamilton first kept its minutes from 1745 to 1756; during that time, he also prepared a fair copy of the minutes, the "Record of the Tuesday Club"; he then drafted the *History*, a fictionalized account of the club's proceedings; and finally he rewrote the *History* from first page to last, replacing the names of the club's members with pseudonyms and further embellishing the narrative. The following paragraphs summarize my conjectures about the probable dates of composition of these four stages. (Locations of the manuscript holdings are provided in parentheses.)

1. Minutes of the Tuesday Club, volumes I and II (John Work Garrett Collections, Milton S. Eisenhower Library, Johns Hopkins University, Baltimore, Md.; Peter Force Collection, Series 8D, Item 170, Library of Congress, Washington, D.C.). These are the actual minutes of the club (written in

several hands, but mainly Hamilton's), composed at or shortly after each meeting from May 14, 1745, to February 11, 1756. The first volume runs from May 14, 1745, to February 25, 1755; the second volume, from May 27, 1755, to February 11, 1756.

2. "Record of the Tuesday Club" (MS. 854, Maryland Historical Society, Baltimore, Md.). This is a careful revision of the minutes, covering the period from May 14, 1745, to April 22, 1755. It includes club drawings and music. It is uncertain when Hamilton began revising the minutes, but it was probably no later than 1750. Elaine G. Breslaw's edition, *Records of the Tuesday Club of Annapolis, 1745–56* (Urbana, Ill., 1988), includes the "Record" and the second volume of minutes.

3. Draft of the *History*, volumes I and II. (The only extant portion of the drafted text [containing pp. 465–700 of volume I and the index to that volume] appears at the end of volume III of the manuscript of the *History*. The table of contents has been mistakenly placed at the front of the "Record.") Hamilton began drafting the *History* in the fall of 1752; he probably stopped working on the draft around January 22, 1754, the date of the last event (Quirpum Comic's trial) listed in the table of contents.

4. *The History of the Tuesday Club*, volumes I–III (John Work Garrett Collections; pages 503–564 of volume III are in the Dulany Papers, MS. 1265, Box 3, Maryland Historical Society; sections of volume III are missing [pp. 301–332, 455–502, and the final pages]; a draft of the dedication and the first two pages of a draft of the preface have been mistakenly placed at the front of the "Record"; the remaining portion of Hamilton's draft of the preface is also in the Dulany Papers). Hamilton probably began writing the final version of the *History* around September 9, 1754, the date of the dedication. The title page to volume II states that that volume was written in 1755, and the eyewitness account of Dr. Upton Scott, Ham-

ilton's good friend and fellow Tuesday Club member, indicates that Hamilton continued writing the *History* up until his death in May 1756 (letter dated Aug. 28, 1809, Howard Family Papers, MS. 469, Maryland Historical Society).

Bibliographical Note

The most complete study of Hamilton and his works is Robert Micklus, *The Comic Genius of Dr. Alexander Hamilton* (Knoxville, Tenn., 1990). J. A. Leo Lemay provides an excellent chapter on Hamilton in *Men of Letters in Colonial Maryland* (Knoxville, Tenn., 1972), 213–256. For informative discussions of Hamilton's political satire and his intellectual milieu, see Elaine G. Breslaw, "Dr. Alexander Hamilton and the Enlightenment in Maryland" (Ph.D. diss., University of Maryland, 1973); "Wit, Whimsy, and Politics: The Uses of Satire by the Tuesday Club of Annapolis, 1744 to 1756," *William and Mary Quarterly* (hereafter, *WMQ*), 3d ser., XXXII (1975), 295–306; and "The Chronicle as Satire: Dr. Hamilton's 'History of the Tuesday Club,'" *Maryland Historical Magazine*, LXX (1975), 129–148. Breslaw has also edited the Tuesday Club's minutes: *Records of the Tuesday Club of Annapolis, 1745–56* (Urbana, Ill., 1988). Essays focusing more on the literary value of the Tuesday Club papers include Robert Micklus, "Dr. Alexander Hamilton's 'Modest Proposal,'" *Early American Literature* (hereafter, *Early Am. Lit.*), XVI (1981), 107–132; Micklus, "'The History of the Tuesday Club': A Mock-Jeremiad of the Colonial South," *WMQ*, 3d ser., XL (1983), 42–61; and David S. Shields, "The Tuesday Club Writings and the Literature of Sociability," *Early Am. Lit.*, XXVI (1991), 276–289.

The best study of the Tuesday Club's music (only a sample of the fifty-two pages of music included in *The History of the Ancient and Honorable Tuesday Club* has been reproduced in the present edition) is John Barry Talley, *Secular Music in Colonial*

Annapolis: The Tuesday Club, 1745–56 (Urbana, Ill., 1988). Talley reconstructs and evaluates all of the club's original music and also provides information on the borrowed songs and catches that were played in the Tuesday Club. Some of that music is performed on a compact disc, *Over the Hills and Far Away*, by David Hildebrand and Ginger Hildebrand (Albany H 103).

A good discussion of Hamilton's pen-and-ink drawings (forty-eight are included in *The History of the Ancient and Honorable Tuesday Club*, fourteen in the present edition) is Georgia Brady Barnhill, "Remarks on the Drawings," in *The History of the Ancient and Honorable Tuesday Club*, lxi–lxvii.

Index

Library of Congress Cataloging-in-Publication Data

Hamilton, Alexander, 1712–1756.
    The Tuesday Club : a shorter edition of The history of the ancient
and honorable Tuesday Club by Dr. Alexander Hamilton / edited by
Robert Micklus.
          p.   cm. — (Maryland paperback bookshelf)
    Includes index.
    ISBN 0-8018-4968-3 (alk. paper). — ISBN 0-8018-5008-8
(pbk. : alk. paper)
    1. Tuesday Club (Annapolis, Md.)—History—18th century—
Fiction.   2. Annapolis (Md.)—History—Colonial period, ca. 1600–
1775—Fiction.   3. Maryland—History—Colonial period, ca. 1600–
1775—Fiction.   I. Micklus, Robert.   II. Hamilton, Alexander,
1712–1756. History of the ancient and honorable Tuesday Club.
III. Institute of Early American History and Culture
(Williamsburg, Va.)   IV. Title.   V. Series.
PS763.H35H57   1994
813'.1—dc20   94-20542